Institutional Alternatives
and Governance of Agriculture

Published by Academic Foundation
in association with the

INSTITUTE OF RURAL MANAGEMENT
(IRMA), ANAND, GUJARAT, INDIA

IRMA
सा विद्या या विमुक्तये

Institutional Alternatives and Governance of Agriculture

Edited by
Vishwa Ballabh

ACADEMIC FOUNDATION
NEW DELHI

First published in 2007
by

ACADEMIC FOUNDATION
4772-73 / 23 Bharat Ram Road, (23 Ansari Road),
Darya Ganj, New Delhi - 110 002 (India).
Phones : 23245001 / 02 / 03 / 04.
Fax : +91-11-23245005.
E-mail : academic@vsnl.com
www. academicfoundation.com

in association with:

Institute of Rural Management, Anand (IRMA).

Cataloging in Publication Data--DK
Courtesy: D.K. Agencies (P) Ltd. <docinfo@dkagencies.com>

Institutional alternatives and governance of agriculture / editor, Vishwa Ballabh.
p. cm.
Contributed articles.
With reference to India.
Includes bibliographical references.
Includes index.
ISBN-13: 9788171886012
ISBN-10: 8171886019

1. Agriculture and state--India. 2. Agricultural subsidies--India. 3. Agricultural innovations--India. 4. Agricultural industries--India. I. Ballabh, Vishwa, 1957-

DDC 338.185 4 22

Typeset by Italics India, New Delhi.
Printed and bound in India.

CONTENTS

Part II

Prices and Subsidies

Part III

Research, Technology and Extension

Part IV

New Vistas: Vertical Coordination

List of Figures, Tables and Appendices

Tables

Figures

Appendices

Editor/Contributors

Editor:

Vishwa Ballabh is a Professor in Economics. Prior to joining XLRI, he was Reserve Bank of India Chair Professor at the Institute of Rural Management, Anand. Prof. Ballabh graduated in Agriculture from Pant Nagar and holds a Ph.D. in Agricultural Economics from Indian Agricultural Research Institute, New Delhi. He has been a Post-Doctoral Fellow at the International Crop Research Institute for the Semi Arid Tropics (ICRISAT) and was a Visiting Scholar at the Indiana University, USA and a Visiting Scientist at the International Rice Research Institute, Philippines. He has over 20 years of teaching and research experience. His major area of research interest has been institutions and natural resource management. He is a member of several national and international professional societies in agricultural, natural resource economics and development fields. He was Vice President of Indian Society of Agricultural Economics 1996-97. He has published widely and co-edited two books titled, *Farm Forestry in South Asia* and *Co-operative Management of Natural Resources.* He is presently editing books on *Governance of Water: Institutional Alternatives* and *Political Economy* and *Droughts and Integrated Water Resources Management in South Asia—Issues Alternatives and Futures* (with Jasveen Jairath). He has also co-authored a monograph titled *Organising for Rural Development.* Widely travelled, Prof. Ballabh has participated in several national and international conferences and has provided consultancy to several national and international development organisations such as the Ford Foundation, Royal Netherlands Embassy, UNICEF and International Water Management Institute.

Contributors:

S.S. Acharya, former Chairman, Commission for Agricultural Costs and Prices, Government of India, and former Director, Institute of Development Studies, Jaipur (IDSJ) is currently Honorary Professor at IDSJ. He has over 46 years of experience as teacher, researcher, extension worker, development administrator and policy advisor. He had been Professor of Agricultural Economics in Rajasthan Agricultural University and also held the ICAR Professional Chair of National Fellow. He has been and continues to be the Chairman/ Member of several national and international Committees/Task Forces/Panels. Dr. Acharya has presided over annual conference of the Indian Society of Agricultural Economics (1996), and Indian Society of Agricultural Marketing (1994), and is currently the President of Agricultural Economics Research Association of India. He is well known for his contributions in Agricultural Marketing, Agricultural Prices, Agricultural Development and Policy Analysis. He has to his credit 11 books and several research papers and articles in national and international journal of repute. He is the Chief Editor of Indian Journal of Agricultural Marketing.

B.C. Barah is presently Principal Scientist (Economics) at the National Centre for Agricultural Economics and Policy Research (NCAP), New Delhi. His research interest includes risk management in agriculture, sustainable agriculture particularly the sustainability of agriculture in fragile areas, technology and institutions for the risk prone areas and the patterns of growth and development. He has served various institutions including ICRISAT, Central University, Hyderabad, NABARD, Cornell and Duke Universities in USA, International Rice Research Institute, Philippines to name a few.

B.S. Baviskar was educated at Pilkhod, Chalisgaon, Satara, Pune and Delhi. He taught Sociology at the University of Delhi for over 30 years. Currently he is Senior Fellow at the Institute of Social Sciences, New Delhi. He has held visiting appointments at the Institute of Development Studies, Sussex; Institute of Social Studies, the Hague; McGill University, Montreal; and the American University in Cairo. He was President of the Indian Sociological Society during 2000-2001. His major publications include: *The Politics of Development: Sugar Co-operatives in Rural Maharashtra* (1980); *Who Shares? Co-operatives and Rural Development*, co-edited with D.W. Attwood (1988); *Finding the Middle Path: The Political Economy of Co-operation in Rural India*, co-authored with D.W. Attwood (1995); and *Social Structure and Change*, 5 volumes, co-edited with A.M. Shah and E.A. Ramaswamy (1996-98); Series Editor, *Themes in Indian Sociology*, 7 volumes (2003-05).

G.S. Bhalla is at present Professor Emeritus, Centre for the Study of Regional Development, Jawaharlal Nehru University, New Delhi. He is a former Member of the Planning Commission, and former Chairman, Commission for Agricultural Costs and Prices, Government of India. Professor Bhalla was a professor of economics at Jawaharlal Nehru University, New Delhi and Dean, School of Social Sciences, Professor at Punjab University Chandigarh, and an Associate Professor at Carleton University, Ottawa, Canada. Prof. Bhalla is a member of several committees of the Ministry of Agriculture, Ministry of Commerce and Industry, Ministry of Labour and of the Planning Commission. Prof. Bhalla has written, edited or co-authored a large number of books and articles. His recent books are *Globalisation and Indian Agriculture* (2005), *Agriculture and the World Trade Organisation: Indian and French Perspectives* (2002), *Indian Agriculture—Four Decades of Development* (2001), *Suicides in Rural Punjab* (1998), *The Impact of GATT on Punjab Agriculture* (1996), *Economic Liberalisation and Indian Agriculture* (1994), *World Economy in Transition: An Indian Perspective* (1994), *Patterns in Indian Agricultural Development: A District Level Study* (1989) and *Green Revolution and the Small Peasant: A Study of Income Distribution among the Punjab Cultivators* (1983).

Pratap S. Birthal is presently working as a Senior Scientist at the National Centre for Agricultural Economics and Policy Research (NCAP), New Delhi. He has published profusely on issues related to animal husbandry, agricultural diversification and vertical coordination. He has twice been awarded with D.K. Desai Prize by the Indian Society of Agricultural Economics for his quality contribution to agricultural economics research. He is also a recipient of the Young Scientist Award of the Indian Council of Agricultural Research (ICAR). Recently he has been awarded with National Fellowship by the ICAR to work on issues related to livestock and poverty. Dr. Birthal has a number of research articles and books to his credit.

Ramesh Chand is currently ICAR National Professor at National Centre for Agricultural Economics and Policy Research, (Indian Council of Agricultural Research), Pusa, New Delhi. He has worked in senior academic positions as Professor and Head, Agricultural Economics Unit at Institute of Economic Growth, Delhi, and Professor of Marketing at Punjab Agricultural University, Ludhiana. He was Visiting Professor at University of Wollongong, NSW Australia (2000) and Visiting Fellow at Institute of Developing Economies, Chiba Shi, Japan (2003). His Ph.D. thesis, submitted to Indian Agricultural Research Institute, New Delhi, was selected for Jawaharlal Nehru Award of Indian Council of Agricultural Research in recognition of its outstanding Research contributions. Dr. Chand has worked as consultant for FAO, ESCAP, OECD, World Bank, Indian Institute of Foreign Trade, Delhi and Government of Punjab. At present he is engaged in research on Trade Liberalisation, WTO and Asian Agriculture, Food Policy and Development Economics. Dr. Chand is author of 7 books and 60 research papers published in reputed national and international journals.

R.S. Deshpande is currently Professor and Head of the Agricultural Development and Rural Transformation (ADRT) Unit of the Institute for Social and Economic Change, Bangalore. He has served on various policy bodies of Government of India and Government of Karnataka. He has to his credit 8 books and 50 research studies. He has published extensively on Agricultural Development, WTO and its impact on Agriculture, Droughts and Drought Mitigation, Farmers' Movements, Irrigation and Watershed Development.

M. Indira is currently working as Reader in the Department of Economics at University of Mysore, Mysore. She has obtained a Doctorate from University of Mysore through Institute for Social and Economic Change, Bangalore. Her interest areas include Plantation Crops, Gender Studies, Micro-Finance and development of Indian Agriculture. She has published over 50 research articles in international and Indian journals, and completed over a dozen research projects.

Dayanatha Jha was Director of the National Centre for Agricultural Economics and Policy Research, New Delhi. After relinquishing office of the Director, he was awarded National Professorship of Indian Council of Agricultural Research. He has worked for more than a decade with the International Food Policy Research Institute, Washington, DC. His contributions are in the area of agricultural research and development policy. He presided over annual conference of the Indian Society of Agricultural Economics in 2001.

R.L. Jogi is Research Associate at the Institute of Development Studies, Jaipur. He has over 22 years of experience in development studies. His field of specialisation is rural and agricultural economics. He has published several papers in reputed journals.

P.K. Joshi is presently Director of the National Centre for Agricultural Economics and Policy Research (NCAP), New Delhi. Prior to this he has served as South Asia Coordinator/Research Fellow at the International Food Policy Research Institute (IFPRI), Washington DC; Principal Scientist and Theme Leader (Technology Policy) at NCAP; and Senior Economist at the International Crops Research

Institute for the Semi-Arid Tropics (ICRISAT), Patancheru, Andhra Pradesh. He is a member of several government and non-government committees and working groups. He is also member of the executive committees and editorial boards of reputed professional societies. Dr. Joshi is a prolific writer and has a number of research articles both in the national and international journals, and books to his credit.

Suresh Pal is Principal Scientist at the National Centre for Agricultural Economics and Policy Research, New Delhi. His research interest is agricultural science and technology policy with special emphasis on investment, IPRs, seed industry and research investment allocations and impacts. He has published research papers in the journal of national and international repute. He has been consultatnt to several international organisations like centres of CGIAR, World Bank etc. He has co-edited the books *Institutional Change in Indian Agriculture* and *Impact of Agricultural Research:Post-green Revolution Evidence from India*.

Sushil Pandey is a Senior Agricultural Economist and Deputy Head of the Social Sciences Division at the International Rice Research Institute, Philippines. His professional areas of expertise include agricultural research and development, institutional aspects of natural resource management, and policy analysis. In addition to this broad area, his research has focused on micro-economic analysis of farmers' livelihood systems in unfavourable rainfed rice environments, risk coping mechanisms, constraints to technology adoption, and the dynamics of land use changes. He has co-authored/edited five books and has published over 50 research papers and book chapters.

Rajeswari S. Raina is a Senior Fellow at the Centre for Policy Research, New Delhi. Her research interest is in the area of science and innovation policy relevant to agricultural and rural development. Her recent publications analyse features of and lessons from successful innovation systems, contest the notion of political neutrality of science, emphasise the need to distinguish between institutional and organisational change in the agricultural sciences, and highlight the role of professional associations in fostering better practices and policies for effective utilisation of knowledge in developing countries. She is an agricultural science graduate with a Ph.D. in economics (Kerala University, Centre for Development Studies, Trivandrum).

K. Prathap Reddy is the former Director of IRMA. He specialised in the areas of Organisational Behaviour, Strategic Management, and Human Resource Development. Prof. Reddy has published a large number of papers in various Indian journals. Prof. Reddy worked for a fairly long period at the National Academy of Agricultural Research Management, Hyderabad. Prof. Reddy has done consulting work for FAO, ILO-COOPNET, World Bank, NDDB, and a large number of co-operatives and development organisations in India.

Sukhpal Singh is faculty member with the CMA, IIM, Ahmedabad. He teaches and trains in agribusiness management and has research interests in vertical co-ordination of agribusiness chains and their governance, contract farming and franchising, presently researching small farmer participation in global food and fibre chains including organic produce. He has to his credit three books and several research papers and articles. He has been a visiting fellow at the IDS, Sussex (UK), and the Chulalongkorn University, Bangkok (Thailand). He is a member of the working group, of the NDC on contract farming policy and, of the Planning Commission on agricultural marketing infrastructure policy for the 11th Five-year Plan.

G. Sridhar is pursuing his Fellowship in Rural Management at Institute of Rural Management, Anand. His area of interest is Rural Marketing. He has two years of experience in sales in Marico Industries Limited and two and half years of experience as Faculty in Marketing at Institute for Technology and Management, Warangal. He has published papers in national and international journals of repute. He was part of a consulting team to study Leadership sponsored by Wharton School of Business, USA.

Rasheed Sulaiman V. is Director, Centre for Research on Innovation and Science Policy, (CRISP) Hyderabad, and Director for the LINK South Asia Rural Innovation Policy Studies Hub. Previously he was Senior Scientist at the National Centre for Agricultural Economics and Policy Research (NCAP), New Delhi. His work focuses on institutional change and poverty relevance with respect to agricultural research and extension. Since 1999, he has been working on the development and application of the innovation systems concepts to explain and plan interventions for agricultural research and rural development. His recent studies focus on understanding innovation capacity in various rural sub-sectors and the role of civil society organisations in promoting pro-poor rural innovation. He has a Ph.D. in Agricultural Extension from the Indian Agricultural Research Institute (IARI).

L. Velasco is an assistant scientist at the International Rice Research Institute. Her field of expertise is Statistics and data management. She has co-authored over a dozen reports on the economics of rice production systems covering aspects of technology adoption, risk analysis, and livelihood systems in rainfed areas.

Preface

In 2004, IRMA launched an ambitious programme of collaborative research on The Governance in Development. The programme culminated into a Symposium on *Governance in Development—Issues, Challenges and Strategies* held during December 14–19, 2004 to commemorate silver Jubilee of the institute. Symposium on the main, had objective to: (i) identify issues and challenges confronting governance in development across different dimension; (ii) identify the role of state, market and civil society organisations in bringing out good governance in development process; and (iii) create new knowledge and strategies for governance in development process that expands human capabilities and opportunities. The Symposium comprised of 16 workshops; each workshop focused on different themes all of which were related to thematic and sectoral issues of governance of rural development processes. The workshop on "Institutional Alternatives and Governance of Agriculture" was one of the 16 workshops. The present book is an outcome of this collaborative processes.

The workshop on "Institutional Alternatives and Governance of Agriculture" was particularly designed to critically examine the various macro issues currently faced by the agriculture sector and to examine the role of State for the development of agriculture in emerging environment of globalisation and liberalisation. The book is divided in four parts. Part I, consisting of three chapters, examines governance framework and macro–development issues and concerns in agriculture sector. Part II discusses issues related to prices and subsidies and role of State in new emerging agrarian economy and global macro–economic environment; Part III discusses issues related to research and development including the role of private sector in development and dissemination of agricultural technology. The final section (Part IV) examines the role of cooperative, new emerging supply chains and institutional alternatives like contract farming in integrating small farmers with the market, their strength and potential threats. Overall concern of the contributors to the present volume has been the impact of agricultural development strategies on the growing number of small and marginal farmers. While we are embarking on higher rate of economic growth (8-9 per cent), the agricultural sector is not doing particularly well and the fact that the share of agriculture in GDP has declined sharply without significant decline of population dependent on agriculture, the issues raised by contributors to this volume have special significance. Present book is a modest contribution to initiate debate about governance of agriculture and identification of institutional alternatives to integrate millions of small and marginal farmers in development process so that impact of growth is widespread and inclusive.

I take this opportunity to thank all the workshop participants for their valuable comments and observations made during the course of presentation and discussion of various papers. Our special gratitude is to the session chairpersons, discussants, rapporteurs and contributors without whose benign cooperation it would have been difficult to conduct the workshop smoothly.

Thanks are also due to Swiss Agency for Development Cooperation (SDC), Sir Dorabji Tata Trust (SDTT), Sir Ratan Tata Trust (SRTT) for providing generous grants for research, conducting the symposium and publication. In particular, I would like to acknowledge the support provided by the Kurt Vogele, Amitabh Behar, Teresa Khanna, Sarosh N. Batliwala, Arun Pandhi, H.D. Malesra and Mukund Gorakshakar. The Institute of Rural Management Anand and School of Business & Human Resources, XLRI Jamshedpur have allowed me time and freedom to edit the book. I have received utmost support from the IRMA Director for conducting symposium in which our colleagues and students at IRMA contributed enormously, their contributions are gratefully acknowledged. Our thanks are also due to Sona Kapila and Sanu Kapila at Academic Foundation for providing all necessary support during the editing.

Last but not the least, I thank Mrs. Padmini Unikrishanan who handled all the administrative chores relating to the workshop and symposium and word-processed the present and earlier versions of this book so meticulously and ungrudgingly. Without her willing cooperation and help, it would have been very difficult for me to finish this work. The views expressed and inferences drawn are those of the respective authors of the chapters of this book and do not represent those of the funding agency or their employing institutions.

Vishwa Ballabh

Part I

Overview of Governance Issues in Indian Agriculture

1

Introduction: Governance Challenges in Agriculture

VISHWA BALLABH and K. PRATHAP REDDY

Introduction

Indian agriculture is at crossroads today from being stagnant for more than two centuries. It became a vibrant sector of economy immediately after Independence. To begin with, land reforms enacted and implemented in 1950s and 1960s played a crucial role in breaking the agrarian impasse. This coupled with investment in irrigation played a crucial role in augmenting agricultural production. Further impetus to agricultural production was received through Green Revolution technology in mid-1960s and 1970s, which by 1990s spread to almost all parts of the country depending upon the conditions suitable for adoption of such technology. Necessary public support was made available through price support and procurement policies. By 1980s, the larger changes in Indian economy began to unfold towards delicensing and deregulation in the Industry. However, agricultural sector continues to remain within the framework of the old policy regime and did not benefit much from the earlier liberalisation of Indian economy; in fact no change has taken place in agricultural policies (Chand, 2004). During this period, which created a lot of confusion, the indirect impact of trade liberalisation is however considered significant. Many scholars believe that Indian agriculture may have comparative advantages but it does not have competitive advantages (see for instance Bhalla, 2004). The purpose of this volume is to examine the current issues confronted in agriculture and identify the role of private sector, cooperatives, and public systems within the framework of new governance paradigm.

Governance Paradigm and Agricultural Development

The notions of governance that have emerged in recent years include not merely institutions of national government but also those of local and global governance. These new definitions are more broad based and consider governance as a process which encompasses state-society interactions and partnership. The definition of governance, thus, includes a range of organisations, public, private and cooperatives, and complex relationship(s) between and among them. Institutions of local government (such as *panchayats*); civil society organisations (ranging from social movements to non-governmental organisations, and from cooperative to civic associations); and private corporations as well as other market institutions are all relevant actors in the context of new governance paradigm. Democracy and civil liberties form an integral part of good governance.

The concept of governance (or good governance) varies widely from a very restrictive World Bank definition which is much more concerned with the economic aspect of governance to include those issues which are concerned with human and civil rights. For example, the World Bank defines governance as "the manner in which power is exercised in the management of a country's economic and social resources for development" (World Bank, 1992). This has been equated with 'sound development management' and emphasises more on economic policies and management of development projects. On the other hand, UNDP defines governance as the exercise of economic, political and administrative authority to manage a country's affairs at all levels. It comprises the mechanisms, processes and institutions, through which citizens and groups articulate their interests, exercise their legal rights, meet their obligations and mediate their differences (UNDP, 1997). Thus, there are several alternative conceptualisations of governance which recognise the plurality of actors involved. Governance in this broader sense includes the legitimate authority exercised in the application of government power and in the management of public affairs. There is greater emphasis on participation, decentralisation, accountability and responsiveness and even broader concerns such as those of social equity and justice. This new emphasis in governance has, in the main, come from the understanding of the development process itself which encompasses expansion of the real freedom that citizens enjoy to pursue the objectives they have reason to value, and in this sense, the expansion of human capabilities is seen as the central feature of the process of development (Dreze and Sen, 2002).

Several alternative models of governance are emerging in India to enlist greater participation of people in the management of public affairs and development process (Jayal, 2001). The first is the imperative to roll back the state, mandated by the agenda of economic reforms and globalisation; the second, the contestation of state projects, practices, and discourses contained in the practices of social movements, arguing for a radical participatory democratic politics. Contrary to these is the third model of governance which identifies the state as the locus of power, and therefore, makes the control of the state the main objective of any political programme. The fourth model of governance is expressed in the phenomenon of NGO, as it seeks to either take on developmental functions in ways that are imitative of state initiatives in this field, or else takes on the work of implementing state policies and programmes as a franchisee or public service contractor. The fifth model of governance brings together the state and community, sometimes in partnership, though with varying degrees of emphasis on one or the other. Finally, the sixth model of governance is that of decentralising the state. The initiative for this has been state-driven, taking the form of a constitutional amendment, for example, Panchayati Raj Institutions and recent changes brought through constitutional amendment of the Panchayati Raj Act.

The purpose of any development process is to increase real pace for social and economic activities for a fair and just society. The current development concerns include food security and alleviation of poverty, equity (especially, gender equity), empowerment, etc. Various institutions and organisations are engaged in addressing these issues in an environment which is ridden with poverty, inequities and dominant development paradigm where liberalisation, privatisation and globalisation are considered a panacea for all developmental problems. Many different linkages need to be considered while looking at governance issues in development, like participation, accountability and transparency and their strategies (Figure 1.1).

Figure 1.1

Framework for Understanding Governance in Development

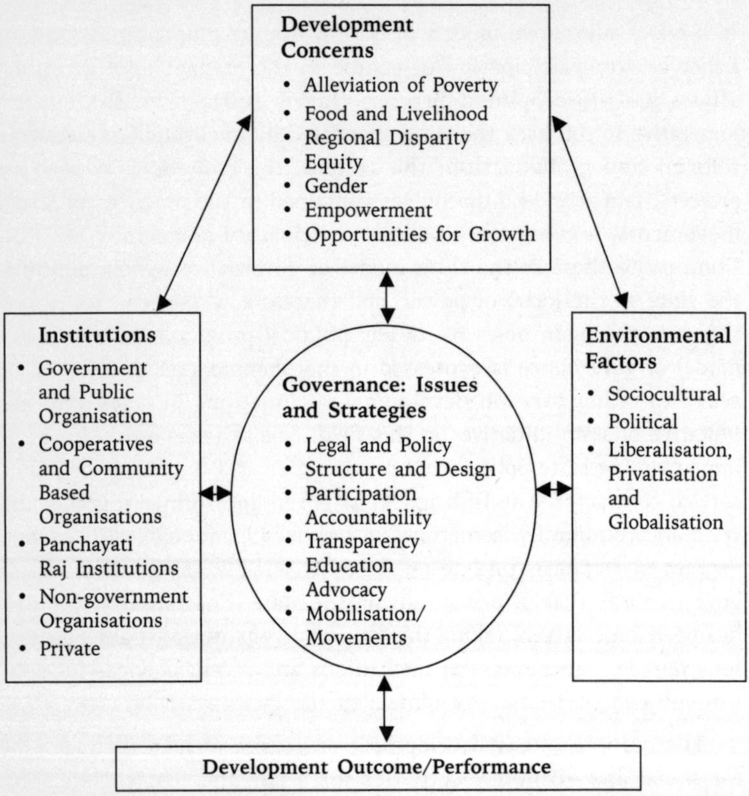

Source: IRMA Symposium Proposal.

The role of 'governance' in agriculture, however, cannot be understood without proper understanding of the changing agrarian structure and the various strategies adopted for augmenting growth and development in agriculture sector and its consequences. The number of small and marginal landholding has increased manifold. The distribution of land ownership and landholding continues to be highly skewed. Although bulk of production and investment decisions remain in the hands of millions of peasant households, the government does influence the legal, material and economic environment in which farmers operate (Vaidyanathan, 1996). Furthermore, the technology, institutions, and infrastructure development in agriculture are inextricably linked and perhaps, it is difficult to separate their impact (Bhalla, 2004). Table 1.1, shows the dominant strategy adopted and the role played by the state and peasants in bringing out changes in agriculture and its consequences. The state has played a major role in breaking the impasse in agriculture through land reforms and investment in irrigation. With the advent of Green Revolution technology, the state actively participated through price support, input subsidies and market regulation. The role of state in recent past, however, is declining. Many scholars believe that agriculture sector is still subjected to a lot of government regulations and has not been liberated. This is one of the important reasons these scholars believe as to why agriculture is not performing as well as other sectors of the economy. Critics however believe that withdrawal of government and reduction of support has led to stagnation and deceleration in agriculture in the post-liberalisation period.

Table 1.1

Agricultural Development Strategies in Different Periods

	1950-1965	*1965-1985*	*After 1985*
A. Strategy			
State-led land redistribution	Vigorous and massive	Slow down (except West Bengal state).	Negligible
Infrastructure	Massive public investment in irrigation	Massive public/ private investment supported by the institutional credit subsidy programmes.	Decline of public investments; but increase in private investments.
Technology	No break-through	HYVs in paddy, wheat etc.	
Extension	State-initiated extension programmes	State-led extension programmes.	Decline.
Price and market development	Regulated and market development of *mandis*	Price support and procurement. Development of commodity cooperatives.	Move towards free trade.
B. Consequences			
	Breaking of agricultural impasse. Regional disparities.	Regional concentration of growth.	Expansion of growth but disparities continue.

The proponents of globalisation on the other hand, believe that the future of Indian farmers depends on how the farm sectors are connected with markets and agribusiness for high-value commodities (HVCs), such as fruits, vegetables, milk, meat, eggs and fish. It is because the per capita demand for these commodities is growing rapidly while those for cereals is declining (Kumar *et al.*, 2003, and Joshi *et al.*, 2004). The rising per capita income, changing demographic profile, and growing urbanisation have ensued the growing demand for high-value and processed commodities as well as convenience foods. Production portfolio is gradually responding to such changes. It is testified by the facts that the share of HVCs in gross value of agricultural output has gone up from 26 per cent in 1981-82 to approximately 40 per cent in 2000 (Birthal *et al.*, 2005). Thus, demand-side factors are driving production of HVCs while lack of infrastructure and market support, and high production and price risk impede their supply (Joshi *et al.*, 2005). The problem is further compounded by the increasingly large number of smallholder farms, for example, more than 80 per cent farms in India are less than two hectares. Being small, their marketed surplus is meagre that escalates their transaction costs. Also HVCs are exposed to additional risk. So there must be risk management or mitigation instruments for the smallholder farms to take advantages from emerging opportunities. This spills over into issues connected with insurance, transaction costs associated with production, marketing and management of exogenous shocks in supply chain of food processing and high-value agriculture.

Whether one supports or opposes liberalisation and globalisation of Indian agriculture, no one denies the rapid changes that are taking place. The changes are bringing both new challenges and opportunities in the governance of Indian agriculture and demands for new institutional structure if growth with social justice has to be realised in Indian agrarian economy. Some of these changes are discussed in the following sections.

Increasing Number of Small Landholdings

Despite the weak implementation of land reforms and the relative ineffectiveness of land ceilings in most parts of the country, a single land tenure approximating the *ryotwari* system has come into prevalence in most parts of the country (Vyas, 1994). This has also been accompanied by a check on further expansion of the large holdings, resulting in an increase in the number of agricultural holdings in the country. Some of these holdings are very small and sometimes operationally unviable, thereby leading to the phenomenon of reverse tenancy (Vyas, 1994).

Changes in the Land Lease Market

The land lease market has also undergone tremendous changes. It is now believed that the small and marginal farmers lease in and lease out much more than their large counterpart (Chand, 2004). The implications for such reverse tenancy and lease market are not understood. There are advocates who argue for liberalisation of lease market. However, issues such as, what would be its consequences and who will gain and who will lose, have not been properly understood. In relatively more fragile and water-scarce regions, the land lease markets are tied with water resources. The rich farmers who own and control water resources gain much more than those who cannot afford to invest in development of water resources, particularly groundwater resources (Prakash and Ballabh, 2004).

Regional Disparities in Indian Agriculture

The regional disparities and inequalities continue to be the main feature of Indian agriculture. The large part of growth in agriculture is contributed by relatively better endowed regions. Although the spread of growth performance has been better in the late 1980s and 1990s, it has not been uniform across regions and states. The central peninsular region continues to have slow growth and suffers from instability in production and productivity (Bhalla and Singh, 2001).

Evolution of Contract/Corporate Farming

Corporate farming refers to farming undertaken by business entities on commercial basis (as opposed to traditional subsistence-based farming that uses a large component of family labour and non-market inputs). Contract farming on the other hand, involves cultivation of a specified crop by farmers with an intention to sell the output to a specified agent or business entity, at mutually agreed upon prices or methods of pricing. The advantages to the business entity is the availability of the produce at consistent and required quantity and quality, while the farmers have the advantage of using technological inputs from the business organisation and also be less dependent on the vagaries of the market. While the current legal environment is not favourable to corporate farming, there have been several experiments in the field of contract farming. However, some of these initiatives have run into problems caused arguably by the lack of perceived value by both farmers and business firms, and the problems in enforceability of contract (Singh, 2004).

Trade Liberalisation and Globalisation

Liberalisation is expected to provide an impetus to trade in agricultural commodities. This in turn, is expected to provide more scope for specialising in crops in which each region has a comparative advantage, and also ultimately, resulting in larger returns to the farmers. However, opening up also brings up issues of dealing with international aspects of trade.

The emerging trade in agricultural commodities is likely to be influenced largely by the provisions of the WTO's Agreement on Agriculture (AoA). The AoA ostensibly tries to promote efficiency through reduction of subsidies and improvement of quality. However, for developing countries (including India), there are provisions for exemptions and certain support to agriculture, especially for the purpose of stabilisation and food security (Bhalla, 2004: 277). The emphasis on market access in international trade has not worked yet in favour of India as several of the developed countries have put in place very high standards of sanitary and phytosanitary requirements that Indian exports are not easily able to comply with, due to technological and market-related reasons.

Liberalisation has also implied provision of better protection for intellectual property rights—which is especially relevant in the context of agricultural biotechnology, new varieties and seeds. While this is argued to be a necessary condition for facilitating technological advances in agriculture, it may also lead to higher input prices for farmers and may especially be problematic for small farmers. Related to liberalisation and globalisation of agriculture sector is emergence of international commodity chains which has deepened the interdependence and the integration of the world economy through foreign direct investment and sub-contracting of production. The gains from such internationalisation of food commodity are generally unevenly distributed (Singh, 2004).

The public sector research and extension has played a major role in generation and dissemination of technology. The public support system was also geared to provide price and market support, particularly through minimum price and procurement policies. While these policies are still continuing, there are reasons to believe that impact of these policies has not been uniform. The Eastern and Central regions were particularly left out. The Food Corporation of India does not have adequate facilities and as such, Eastern India has not gained much from these policies (Pandey *et. al.*, 2002). It is also argued that private and public sectors need to collaborate with each other not only in generation of technology and its dissemination but also in the management of whole commodity chains. The role of cooperatives and other peoples' institutions, needs to be examined in this scenario.

Against these changing dimensions of Indian agriculture, the essays contained in this volume examine the role of state and private sector in the development of Indian agriculture. The chapters in the volume are divided into four parts.

Part 1 consists of three chapters including this introductory chapter. Bhalla (Chapter 2), examines regional pattern of agricultural development and finds that there has been deceleration in agricultural growth in post-liberalisation and globalisation period, particularly after 1995. The chapter highlights that labour productivity is not improving in Indian agriculture which is an indicator of welfare of large masses of landless people. Similar issues are also dealt by Deshpande and Indira (Chapter 3). However, the authors argue that it is not the question of for-or-against globalisation. Indian agriculture cannot remain isolated from the rest of the world in current political environment. Therefore, they argue that we need to identify strategies that meet our needs and requirements best.

Historically, the state has played a major role in the development of agriculture through price support, input subsidies, infrastructure development and provision of development of technology and extension facilities for the farmers. Part II and III, examine the changing role of state in price support, input subsidies, technology generation and dissemination. The chapter by Acharya and Jogi (Chapter 4), examines the extent of the subsidies provided to farm sector, both at aggregate level and by state and they argue that extreme precaution needs to be taken in withdrawing subsidies from the farm sector, particularly those tailored towards small and marginal farmers. They further argue that increasing prices for the farm produce may not help small and marginal farmers since they have very little marketable surplus, even otherwise it has potential to increase inequities in the agrarian economy. Ramesh Chand (Chapter 5) on the other hand, argues that the role of prices policies and state support to agriculture through price support system need to be reexamined. He further argues that the role played by CACP is not sufficient to make Indian agriculture globally competitive.

The technology and extension services were main instruments in breaking the slow growth rate in agricultural productivity in mid-sixties. The technology generation was mainly in the public domain and generated by ICAR-supported research institutes and state agricultural universities. The private sector has played very little role in generation of technology. However, the public research system is besieged with the number of problems including bureaucratic hassles and has very little resources for real research expenditure. With the changing dimension of agriculture and emergence of biotechnology as a new frontier area for agricultural productivity growth, Suresh Pal and Dayanatha Jha (Chapter 6), argue that we need to create favourable conditions for greater participation of private sector in agricultural research and technology. On the contrary, Rajeswari S. Raina and Rasheed Sulaiman (Chapter 7), argue that role of public sector in technology generation and extension should not be undermined. However, they also argue that the current structure of ICAR-led agricultural research system is highly bureaucratic and top-down hierarchal and does not address the need of the farmers, particularly those living in fragile drought-prone areas. They argue that non-linear, flexible and participatory approach may result in better and more adaptive technology. A similar approach needs to be adopted in extension and dissemination of technology. In the Part III (Chapter 8), Pandey *et al.*, prove some of the issues and points raised by Raina and Sulaiman. Pandey *et al.*, found that in homogenous irrigated areas, agriculture has benefited more from technology generated through linear approach in rice production and it has made significant impact on productivity leading to increase in farm income, whereas rainfed lowland and upland rice has not benefited much from such technologies. They also argue for a strong need for changes in the way agricultural technologies are evolved and disseminated.

The final part of the book, deals with emerging new institutional arrangements in agricultural sector, i.e., vertical linkages with industry and farm sector. As argued before, vertical linkages between the industry and farm sector may bring new vistas and usher in Indian agriculture through vertical coordination. Vertical coordination means the synchronisation of the successive stages of production and marketing, regarding the quantity, quality and the timing of product flows. There are three approaches in vogue for the vertical coordination: (i) spot market, (ii) contract production, and (iii) vertical integration. Each of the three approaches has different implications for the transaction cost.

In spot market transaction, cost is determined by the cost of search and negotiation right, product and prices which could be reduced through entering into a contract arrangement before production is completed. Thus, the transaction cost in contract arrangement is related to *ex ante* reaching to the agreement and *ex post* cost associated with enforcement of the agreements. Vertical integration may reduce the cost of contracting and spot market trading but also introduces a new type of cost—cost of governance within the firm like in vertically integrated cooperatives.

In theory, transaction cost economies suggest that there is need to search for those institutional arrangements which minimise the transaction cost and such institutional changes could be accepted by the parties involved in exchange, provided a win-win situation is obtained. Joshi and Birthal (Chapter 9), convincingly demonstrate that the vertical coordination through contract farming has benefited small and marginal farmers in milk, vegetable and broiler productions. They argue that the farmers not only receive higher returns with low production and transaction cost but also benefited in terms of access to new technology, markets, and achieved economies of scale. The industry on the other hand, benefited as they were assured of better quality products. Thus, profitable linkages are possible between industry and small farm holders. On the contrary, reviewing contract farming as practiced by several industries, Singh (Chapter 10), argues that the approach has not penetrated deep in the agrarian economy and benefits also have been limited. He further argues that producers' cooperatives will face new challenges and competition and therefore, they are likely to be adversely affected. Baviskar (Chapter 11) examines the rise and fall of sugar cooperatives in Maharashtra and argues that corruption and bureaucratic hassles have led to the decline of these cooperatives. Sridhar and Ballabh (Chapter 12) on the other hand, argue that both cooperative and private sector have a role to play in vertical coordination between farm sector and industry, but the producers cooperative have an added advantage that most of the decision making remains with farmers and their representatives. However, the benefit of these cooperatives may reach to the farmers only if there is proper design and institutionalisation of processes as in the case of AMUL. Otherwise, as discussed by Baviskar, they will neither serve the interest of the farmers nor will they be effective in ushering growth in the agrarian economy.

The chapters in the present volume though varied in content and nature are unified in their emphasis on elements of both 'sustainability' and 'growth' and their inclusion in agricultural development agenda. Along with 'quantum' of growth, the 'quality' of growth also should be given importance. Due to several reasons, subsidies for agriculture in the country cannot be eliminated and there is a need to adopt a suitable pricing mechanism to ensure a healthy growth in the sector. To help farmers overcome higher cost of production and lower market prices of agricultural products, the need to promote insurance mechanisms and research to come out with alternative crops are emphasised. Cooperatives are identified as the suitable institutions to help farmers earn better returns in a failed market situation or in a market riddled with imperfections. To attain higher agricultural production, there is a need to ensure equity in growth, especially in less-developed regions such as Bihar and Chhattisgarh. As a solution to the malady of 'market failure', it was suggested that contract farming/group contract needs to be adopted. Indian farmers now need a two-pronged support in the form of 'minimum support price' and 'minimum insured price'. There is need to continue with the existing PDS system. However, the quantity of procurement by the government needs to be brought down. The allocation to subsidies needs to be brought down gradually, by transferring subsidies more towards public investment. Budgetary allocations for research and development (R&D) in agriculture sector should be stepped up. In the emerging market scenario, there is a need for a greater partnership between public and private investments for R&D. For developing efficient agricultural extension systems, the need is to encourage systems thinking, and document and analyse processes and outcomes of the technology dissemination. In case of agroprocessing sector, there is a need to create an enabling environment to promote more investment from the private sector and build private-public partnership. The continued need for a proactive role on the part of the state is required in this regard. The state can also create an enabling environment for industry and farm linkages.

It is strongly argued that emerging governance reforms with clear links to the processes of globalisation represent a neoliberal mode of development. Given such a nature, the new governance agenda is bound to affect negatively issues like poverty alleviation, equality including that of gender, interests of farmers and backward sections/ regions, our cultural moorings, and democratic system. The need, therefore, is for adopting suitable policy strategies, both at macro and micro level involving the state, private sector and people's institutions to make the agricultural sector grow broad-based with equity and social justice.

References

Bhalla, G.S. (2004). "Vol. 19: Globalisation and Indian Agriculture", *State of the Indian Farmer: A Millennium Study*, Department of Agriculture, Government of India and Academic Foundation, New Delhi.

Bhalla, G.S. and Gurmail Singh (2001). *Indian Agriculture: Four Decades of Development*, Sage, New Delhi.

Birthal, Pratap S., P.K. Joshi and Ashok Gulati (2005). "Vertical Coordination in High-Value Food Commodities: Implications for Smallholders", *MTID Discussion Paper* No. 81, International Food Policy Research Institute, Washington DC.

Chand, Ramesh (2004). "India's National Agricultural Policy: A Critique", *Discussion Paper* No. 85/ 2004, Institute of Economic Growth, Delhi.

Dreze, Jean and Amartya Sen (2002). *India: Development and Participation*, Oxford University Press, New Delhi.

Jayal, N.G. (2001). "Reinventing the State: The Emergence of Alternative Models of Governance in India in the 1990s", in N.G. Jayal and Sudha Pai, *Democratic Governance in India: Challenges of Poverty, Development, and Identity*, Sage Publications, New Delhi.

Joshi, P. K., Ashok Gulati, P. S. Birthal, and L. Tewari (2004). "Agricultural Diversification in South Asia: Patterns, Determinants and Policy Implications", *Economic and Political Weekly,* Vol. 39(24), June 12-18, pp.2457-2468.

Joshi, P. K., Ashok Gulati; P. S. Birthal, and P. Parthasarthy Rao (2005). "Agricultural Diversification and Vertical Integration in India: Will Smallholders Participate?", MTID, International Food Policy Research Institute, Washington, DC, *Mimeo.*

Kumar, P., Mruthynjaya and P. S. Birthal (2003). "Changing Consumption Pattern in South Asia", Paper presented at the International Workshop on *Agricultural Diversification and Vertical Integration in South Asia* organised by FICCI-ICRISAT-IFPRI on 5-6 November, New Delhi.

Pandey, Sushil, B.C. Barah, and L. Velasco (2002). "Patterns of Rice Productivity Growth in Eastern India: Implications for Research and Policy", *Mimeo,* International Rice Research Institute.

Prakash, Anjal and Vishwa Ballabh (2004). "A Win-some Lose-all Game: Social Differentiation and Politics of Groundwater Markets in North Gujarat", *IRMA Working Paper* No. 183, Institute of Rural Management, Anand.

Singh, Sukhpal (2004). "Governance Issues in Institutional Alternatives for Agricultural Development under Globalisation—A Review and Research Issues", *Mimeo,* Institute of Rural Management, Anand.

UNDP (1997). *Governance for Sustainable Development,* United Nations Development Program, New York.

Vaidyanathan, A. (1996). "Agricultural Development: Imperatives of Institutional Reforms", *Economic and Political Weekly,* Vol. 31(35/37), September, pp.2451-2458.

Vyas, V.S. (1994). "Agricultural Policies for the Nineties", *Economic and Political Weekly,* Vol. 29(26), June 25, pp.A54-A63.

World Bank (1992). *Governance and Development,* The World Bank, Washington, DC.

2

Governance Issues in Agriculture Poverty and Agricultural Development

Regional Perspective

G.S. BHALLA

Introduction

India has witnessed a significant decline in both rural and urban poverty during the recent period specially since the mid-1980s. The growth rate of GDP has also recorded visible acceleration since 1980. Consequently, it is generally inferred that rapid growth rate has made a significant dent on poverty in India. Currently, the proponents of economic reforms have also put forward a theory that the reduction in poverty is because of introduction of economic reforms and structural adjustment policies in 1991. In this context, some scholars have looked at regional performance and have come to the conclusion that the states that have reformed the most have achieved maximum growth and that the laggard states are the ones that have failed to reform (Sachs *et al.*, 2002).

The entire emphasis on these exercises is to look at aggregate growth rate of the economy and growth of GDP at the state level. There is no reference to sectoral patterns of development. Nor has any reference been made to the structure of employment and incidence of rural and urban poverty. Again, no account is taken for the relationship, if any, between agricultural growth and its impact on rural poverty reduction at the state level. This is a reversal of the earlier position taken by some of the scholars who had demonstrated the existence of negative relationship between agricultural growth and rural poverty (Ahluwalia, 1978).

The purpose of this chapter is to revisit some of these issues. In particular, the objective is to look at 'poverty and agricultural development' in a regional perspective and see if agricultural growth has played a significant role in the context of poverty reduction in India. The chapter is divided into five sections. After the Introduction in section one, we very briefly review the performance of Indian economy and Indian agriculture since Independence with a more focused discussion of performance of agriculture at the regional level in section two. Section three is devoted to a discussion of the problem of deceleration of agricultural growth at both the national and regional levels during the nineties as compared with the eighties and the main reasons for it. This is then followed in section four by some analytical exercises that bring out the relationship between agricultural growth and incidence of rural poverty at the state level. It is often argued that it is not agricultural growth but, more so, growth of labour productivity in agriculture that is instrumental in reducing poverty. More important, it is also argued that labour productivity in agriculture becomes instrumental in triggering growth of non-farm sector. These propositions are carefully examined with the help of relevant data. Finally, section five contains main conclusions arrived at in the chapter.

Pattern of National and Regional Growth: Growth of Overall GDP and Major Sectors

Growth of the Indian Economy at the National Level

India achieved a major increase in the growth rates of GDP and per capita income after Independence. Taking the entire period 1950-1951 to 2000-01, whereas gross domestic product (GDP) of India recorded a growth rate of nearly 4.23 per cent per annum at 1993-94 prices, the per capita income grew at an annual rate of 2.12 per cent (Table 2.1 a, b). This was several times higher than the growth rate of GDP of about 1 per cent per annum and that of per capita income 0.22 per cent per annum during 1900-01 to 1946-47 (at 1938-39 prices).

Along with GDP growth, growth rate of agriculture also recorded a notable acceleration. It rose at an annual rate of 0.46 per cent only during 1900-01 to 1946-47 (at 1938-39 prices) compared with a growth rate of 2.54 per cent per annum during the post-Independence period 1950-51 to 2000-01. The growth rates recorded by other sectors of the economy were also much higher (Sivasubramonian, 2000).

For analysis of overall and agricultural growth, it is convenient to divide the entire period into four sub periods, namely, 1950-51 to 1964-65, 1967-68 to 1979-80 and 1980-81 to 1990-91 and the post-reform period of the nineties. Table 2.1 below gives details of GDP growth during various periods.

Table 2.1(a)

Growth Rates of GDP and Per Capita Income 1980-81 Prices

Years	*GDP*	*GDP Agr.*	*Secondary Sector*	*Tertiary Sector*	*Per Capita Income*
1950-51 to 1964-65	4.00	2.65	7.73	4.61	1.69
1967-68 to 1979-80	3.45	2.10	4.43	4.49	1.11
1980-81 to 1990-91	5.46	3.94	6.86	6.58	3.01
1990-91 to 1998-99	6.23	1.95	7.45	8.24	4.30
1950-51 to 1998-99	4.16	2.61	5.61	5.15	2.05

Source: National Accounts Statistics, Various Issues.

Table 2.1(b)

Growth Rates of GDP and Per Capita Income 1993-94 Prices

Years	*GDP*	*GDP Agr.*	*Secondary Sector*	*Tertiary Sector*	*Per Capita Income*
1950-51 to 1964-65	3.94	2.54	6.88	4.76	1.86
1967-68 to 1979-80	3.44	2.05	4.23	4.54	1.23
1980-81 to 1990-91	5.62	3.08	7.10	6.72	3.50
1992-93 to 2000-01	6.19	2.80	6.40	7.80	4.00
1950-51 to 2000-01	4.23	2.54	5.51	5.37	2.12

Source: National Accounts Statistics, 2001 and 2002.

During 1950-51 to 1964-65 (the First, Second and Third Plan periods), the overall GDP recorded a growth rate of about 3.94 per cent per annum and per capita income grew at a rate of 1.86 per cent per annum. The growth rates of income from the primary, the secondary and the tertiary sectors were 2.65 per cent, 7.73 per cent and 4.01 per cent per annum, respectively.

But there took place a marked slowdown in the Indian economy during the second period of 1967-68 to 1979-80, partly because of drought and also because of wars and conflicts with neighbours that resulted in a big decline in pubic and overall investment. The result was that both overall GDP and sectoral GDP growth showed a perceptible deceleration during this period (Table 2.1 b).[1] This period was also characterised by a visible deterioration in agricultural production in general and foodgrains production, in particular. India had to resort to large-scale food imports under PL 480, consequent to two serious droughts during 1964-65 and 1965-66. Although the late 1960s marked the initiation of Green Revolution in some parts of India but its impact in increasing food output was only very limited. It took considerable time for the new technology to expand to new areas.

The eighties mark a watershed in the history of economic development of India; there was a significant acceleration in the growth rate of GDP which rose to 5.62 per cent per annum during 1980-81 to 1990-91 compared with a GDP growth rate of only 3.45 per cent during the seventies. Agricultural GDP also grew at a rate of 3.08 per cent per annum compared with only 2.05 per cent during the 1970s. There was acceleration in the growth of GDP during the post-reform period of 1992-93 to 2000-01. At 1993-94 constant prices, the growth of GDP accelerated from 5.6 per cent to 6.1 per cent per annum during the 1990s. However, there was a deceleration in the growth rate of gross product from agriculture which decelerated from 3.08 per cent per annum during 1980-81 to 1990-91 to 2.8 per cent per annum during 1992-93 to 2000-01. The deceleration of growth rates in agriculture was much steeper in terms of 1980-81 prices.[2]

Crop Production

The data on growth of crop production also brings out similar trends in crop growth during various periods. Taking all crops

---

1. The figures given in Table 2.1(a) at 1980-83 prices, differ from those in Table 2.1(b) where calculations are done by using the recent GDP data at constant 1993-94 prices. However, except for agriculture, the trend rates of growth of GDP and other sectors are similar in the two series.

2. The main reason for the discrepancy in the two estimates is much higher GDP contribution attributed to fruits and vegetables in the 1993-94 series. But the National Statistical Commission (2001), has expressed serious doubts about the validity of the income data from fruits and vegetables.

together, crops registered a growth rate of 3.15 per cent during the first period 19950-51 to 1964-65. The main source of growth during this period was growth of area and the contribution of yield growth was only limited.

Crop output grew at a rate of 3.15 per cent during the first period 1949-50 to 1964-65 (Table 2.2). The growth rates of major cereals except rice decelerated during the second period 1967-68 to 1979-80. But the 1980s saw a real spurt in the growth rates of all major crops and of total crop production. Thus, the growth rate of total crop output increased to 3.19 per cent per annum during 1980-81 to 1990-1991. The yield growth rate was as high as 2.56 per cent per annum. The introduction of new technology and its spread to more crops and to more areas was instrumental in bringing about this momentous change in agricultural growth scenario. One of the main contributions of new seed-fertiliser technology was that yield growth increasingly became the dominant source of growth of output after 1966-67. By the eighties, yield growth accounted for as much as 80 per cent of the growth of total crop output

Sources of Agricultural Growth

The main strategy adopted to increase the growth rate of agriculture in the post-Green Revolution period was to increase yields through the use of modern inputs and improved methods of production, the role of technology as a major input in agriculture was accorded explicit recognition. The new strategy in agriculture which was successfully introduced in a few northwestern states and was confined mainly to wheat, gradually spread to other crops and new areas. The culmination of new technology came about only after the eighties, when it expanded from the irrigation belt to almost all regions of India. The new strategy became successful as a consequence of large-scale investments in irrigation and in scientific research and large-scale use of fertilisers.

Table 2.2

All India Compound Growth Rates of Area Production and Yield of Major Crops

	1949-50 to 1964-65			1967-68 to 1980-81			1980-81 to 1990-91			1990-91 to 2000-01		
Crops	*Area*	*Prod.*	*Yield*	*Area*	*Prod.*	*Yield*	*Area*	*Prod.*	*Yield*	*Area*	*Prod.*	*Yield*
Rice	1.21	3.5	2.25	0.77	2.22	1.46	0.40	3.56	3.47	0.81	1.74	0.92
Wheat	2.69	3.96	1.27	2.94	5.65	2.62	0.46	3.57	3.10	1.03	3.27	2.21
Coarse	0.90	2.25	1.23	-1.03	0.67	1.64	-1.34	0.40	1.62	-2.07	-0.54	1.18
T. Cereals	1.25	3.21	1.77	0.37	2.61	1.70	-0.26	3.03	2.90	-0.06	1.86	1.38
T. Pulses	1.72	1.41	-0.18	0.44	-0.4	-0.67	-0.09	1.52	1.61	-0.79	-0.04	0.55
Foodgrain	1.35	2.82	1.36	0.38	2.15	1.33	-0.23	2.85	2.74	-0.19	1.66	1.28
Sugarcane	3.28	4.26	0.95	1.78	2.6	0.8	1.44	2.70	1.24	1.87	2.70	0.82
Oilseeds	2.67	3.2	0.3	0.26	0.98	0.68	1.51	5.20	2.43	0.88	1.62	1.04
Cotton	2.47	4.55	2.04	0.07	2.61	2.54	-1.25	2.80	4.10	2.33	1.37	-0.94
Non-Foodgrain	2.44	3.74	0.89	0.94	2.26	1.19	1.12	3.77	2.31	1.19	2.41	0.86
All Crops	**1.58**	**3.15**	**1.21**	**0.51**	**2.19**	**1.28**	**0.10**	**3.19**	**2.56**	**0.19**	**1.96**	**1.09**

Source: GoI (2001). *Agricultural Statistics at a Glance*, Ministry of Agriculture.

Figure 2.1

Growth Rates of Yield

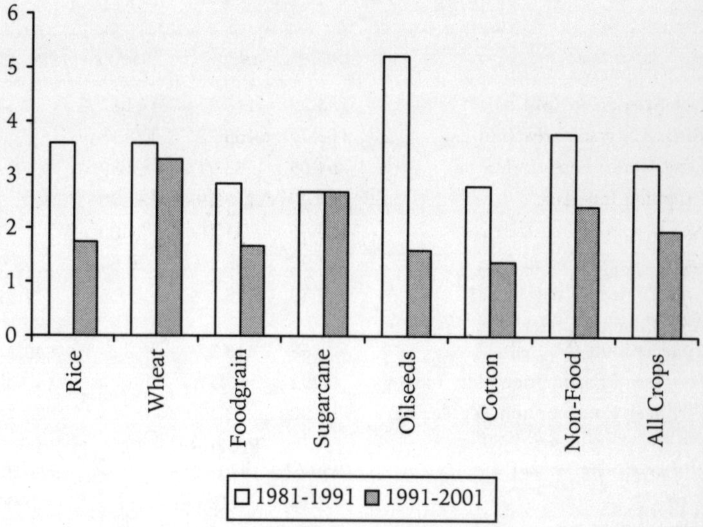

Figure 2.2

Growth Rates of Output

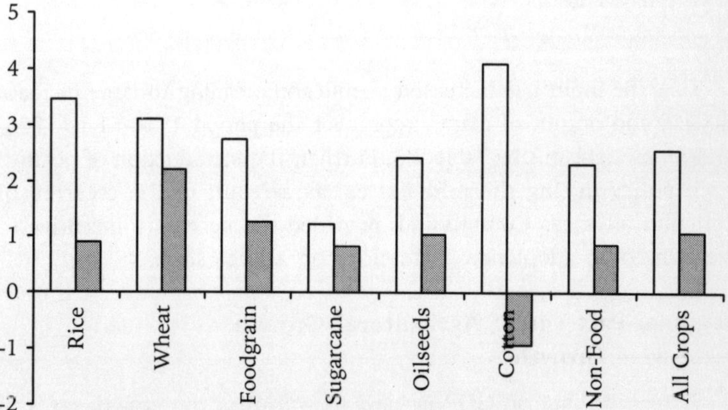

Table 2.3

Use of Major Inputs and Increase in Yields of Major Crops During 1970-71 to 1999-2000

Input Use	*1960-61*	*1970-71*	*1990-91*	*1999-2000*
Net Area Sown (Mn ha)	133.20	140.27	142.82	-*
Gross Cropped Area (Mn ha)	152.77	165.79	188.15	-
Land Under Forests (Mn ha)	54.05	63.91	68.39	-
Cropping Intensity	114.69	118.19	131.70	-
Net Irrigated Area (Mn ha)	24.66	31.10	53.00	-
Gross Irrigated Area (Mn ha)	27.98	38.19	70.64	79.9
Area Under HYV (Mn ha)	1.89	15.38	-	72.11
Area Covered Under Soil Conservation (Mn ha)	1.58	13.37	-	40.23
Fertiliser Consumption (Mn Tonnes)	0.292	2.177	-	14.308
Fertiliser Consumption (Kg Per ha)	1.90	13.13	-	76.75
		Progress		
Yield Levels (Kg Per ha)	*1960-61*	*1970-71*	-	*1999-2000*
Rice	1013	1123	-	1990
Wheat	851	1307	-	2725
Oilseeds	507	579	-	944
Cotton	125	106	-	266
Sugarcane (Tonnes Per Hect)	46	48	-	70
Tea	971	-	-	1787

Note: * Not available.

Source: GoI (2001). *Agricultural Statistics at a Glance*, Ministry of Agriculture.

That the input use increased significantly leading to large increase in yield and output of many crops over the period 1960-61 to 1996-1997 is brought out by Table 2.3. Further, the introduction of positive price policy during the mid-sixties, as a result of the creation of Agricultural Prices Commission, provided the necessary incentive to the farmers to adopt new technology on a large scale.

Regional Patterns of Agricultural Growth: State-wise Growth

State-wise data on GDP is used to work out the growth rates of GDP, per capita income and growth of agriculture industry and services.

The state-wise income data for the eighties are available at the 1980-81 prices and this series terminates in 1997-98. Data from 1993-1994 to 2001 are now available at the 1993-94 prices. We have used both these series. First, 1980-81 constant price data are used for working the state-wise growth rates during 1983-84 to 1993-94. Again, data at 1993-94 prices are used for calculating growth during 1993-94 to 1999-2000. Strictly speaking, to be comparable data should be at the same constant prices. But such comparable series have not been made available by the Central Statistical Organisation (CSO). The two sets of data are therefore, at different constant prices. Nevertheless, while absolute data are not comparable, the comparison of sector-wise and overall growth rates at different constant prices may not lead to a major error.

Table 2.4, brings out that compared with the eighties, there was some acceleration in the growth rate of GDP and per capita income, during the 1990s both at the national level and for most of the states. Again, most of the states also registered a notable rise in the growth rates of the secondary and tertiary sectors during the 1990s. However, one of the disturbing feature of growth during the 1990s was that as compared with the 1980s, the growth rate of gross product form agriculture decelerated significantly for both India as a whole and for most of the states.

During 1983-84 to 1993-94, while total GDP for India grew at 5.32 per cent agricultural product grew at a rate of 3.05 and industry and services at rates of 6.17 per cent and 6.67 per cent per annum, respectively. The growth rate of GDP further accelerated to 6.61 per cent per annum during the period 1993-94 to 1999-2000. The growth rates of the secondary and the tertiary sectors also recorded a visible acceleration during the 1990s compared with the 1980s.

Although most of the states also recorded growth in their GDP during the latter period, a few states also registered deceleration in their growth during this period. The states where growth rates of GDP decelerated were Andhra Pradesh, Assam, Maharashtra, Punjab and Tamil Nadu.

Basing themselves on the growth rates during 1980-81 to 1990-91 and 1990-91 to 1997-98, at 1980-81 prices, Sachs *et al.*, (2002) had come to the conclusion that the best performance in terms of growth of GDP has been recorded by those states that have liberalised their

Table 2.4

Percentage Annual Compound Growth

States	1983-84 to 1993-94					1993-94 to 1999-2000				
	At 1980-81 Prices					At 1993-94 Prices				
	Agriculture	Secondary	Tertiary	GDP	Per Capita Income	Agriculture	Secondary	Tertiary	GDP	Per Capita Income
Andhra Pradesh	3.05	4.79	5.93	4.58	2.42	0.74***	5.64	6.22	4.39	2.53
Assam	2.12	3.24	5.10	3.51	1.25	0.83	3.85	2.87	2.33	0.62
Bihar	0.45***	4	4.9	2.69	1.98	1.04***	9.45*	6.96	4.48	1.62
Gujarat	0.84***	6.9	6.56	5	3.11	2.48***	8.63	8.71	7.39	5.35
Haryana	4.86	7.35	7.36	6.18	3.66	1.64***	7.1	4.10***	6.04	-2.12
Himachal Pradesh	3.08	9.34	6.78	5.89	3.94	0.56**	10.47	8.8	7.06	4.78
Jammu & Kashmir	-	-	-	-	-	4.08	2.25*	7.29	5.05	1.72
Karnataka	3.54	7.15	7.41	5.86	3.99	4.09	9.51	10.18	8.05	5.85
Kerala	4.4	5.63	5.78	5.33	3.94	0.96***	4.74	7.61	5.14	3.12
Maharashtra	5.39*	7.09	8.73	7.42	5.20	1.68**	5.68	7.39	4.93	2.86
Madhya Pradesh	2.82*	8.02	6.4	5.21	2.73	2.17**	6.36	7.15	6.00	3.52
Orissa	-0.57***	5.95	6.04	3.39	1.51	0.33***	5.4	6.76	4.10	1.99
Punjab	4.62	7.1	4.4	5.13	3.11	2.01	6.74	7	4.77	2.36
Rajasthan	3.93	7.85	8.42	6.19	3.71	0.50*	10.86	9.22	8.17	5.27
Tamil Nadu	4.43	5.18	10.29	7.45	6.10	1.39***	5.31	9.32	6.22	4.26
Uttar Pradesh	2.8	6.38	5.95	4.66	2.61	2.89	6.39	5.2	4.62	2.11
West Bengal	4.45	4.57	5.17	4.73	2.47	4.04	6.78	9.52	7.18	12.79.0
India	**3.05**	**6.17**	**6.67**	**5.32**	**3.50**	**2.87**	**6.96**	**8.77**	**6.61**	**4.11**

Note: * Significant at 5-10 per cent; ** Significant at 10-20 per cent; *** Insignificant.

Source: CSO, *State Domestic Product*, Various Issues.

economy the most. The performance of Andhra Pradesh, Gujarat and Maharashtra which registered very high growth during the 1990s was cited as an example (Sachs *et al.*, 2002). However, the evidence to prove the hypothesis was very weak even on the basis of their own data. For example, of the five states that performed better during the 1990s compared with the 1980s, only three had undertaken economic reforms worth the name. Both West Bengal and Kerala which did not undertake any radical reforms had also done better during the 1990s. Growth rates based on GDP growth data at 1993-94 prices brings out that out of the five states, namely, Andhra Pradesh, Gujarat, Maharashtra, Karnataka and Kerala which had done better in terms of GDP growth during 1990-91 to 1997-98 as per the 1980-81 series, only one state, namely, Gujarat performed better during 1993-94 to 1999-2000 as per the revised series at 1993-94 prices. On the other hand, the growth rates of both Andhra Pradesh and Maharashtra decelerated despite the fact that these states were in the forefront of undertaking reforms. It is therefore obvious that there is no connection between the degree of reforms and growth performance.

But this apart, a very disturbing development during 1993-94 to 1999-2000 was that as compared with the 1980s, agricultural growth rates decelerated significantly both at the all-India level and for most of the states (Table 2.4). For India as a whole, growth rate of agricultural GDP decelerated from 3.05 per cent per annum during 1982-83 to 1993-94 to 2.87 per cent per annum during 1993-94 to 1999-2000. The deceleration was very marked in the developed north western states of Punjab, Haryana, and Himachal Pradesh. Many other states also registered decline in growth rates of agricultural GDP. The only states where agriculture product rose during this period were Gujarat (statistically insignificant result) and to a limited extent Kerala and Uttar Pradesh.

Regional Patterns of Agricultural Growth: Crop Output

State-wise data on crop production confirms the above trend. Data on levels and growth of aggregate crop output of 44 crops at the state and the regional levels are available for 1962-1965 to 1996-1999 (Bhalla and Singh, 2001). Table 2.5, gives details about regional pattern of agricultural growth during 1962-1999 and the three sub-periods, namely 1962-1965 to 1970-1973, 1970-1973 to 1980-1983,

1980-1983 to 1990-1993 and 1990-1993 to 1996-1999. Taking the entire period 1962-1965 to 1996-1999, total crop output in India increased at a compound annual growth rate of 2.71 per cent at constant 1990-1993 prices. But important changes took place in the regional pattern of agricultural development during the various sub-periods.

Table 2.5

State-wise Growth of Agricultural Output, 1962-1965 to 1996-1999

States	*1970-1973 Over 1962-1965*	*1980-1983 Over 1970-1973*	*1990-1993 Over 1980-1983*	*1996-1999 Over 1990-1993*
Haryana	4.65	3.02	5.04	1.98
Himachal Pradesh	3.33	0.96	2.74	-0.11
Jammu & Kashmir	5.37	3.47	0.17	0.49
Punjab	6.63	4.74	4.22	0.73
Uttar Pradesh	2.54	2.77	3.06	2.47
North-west Region	**3.60**	**3.21**	**3.55**	**1.91**
Assam	1.85	2.80	2.42	1.31
Bihar	1.12	-0.41	2.12	3.33
Orissa	0.99	2.65	2.92	-5.14
West Bengal	2.37	0.68	5.97	2.99
Eastern Region	**1.57**	**1.09**	**3.63**	**1.25**
Gujarat	1.78	3.12	0.86	6.83
Madhya Pradesh	1.97	1.28	4.53	3.86
Maharashtra	-3.64	6.57	2.12	3.29
Rajasthan	4.29	1.26	6.06	4.90
Central Region	**0.73**	**3.13**	**3.33**	**4.50**
Andhra Pradesh	0.93	3.61	3.42	1.52
Karanataka	2.64	2.32	3.68	3.62
Kerala	4.09	-0.91	1.92	3.60
Tamil Nadu	2.76	-0.57	4.00	3.25
Southern Region	**2.40**	**1.38**	**3.43**	**2.19**
All States	**2.08**	**2.38**	**3.44**	**2.83**
CV	**88**	**89**	**50**	**112**

Source: GoI, *Area and Production of Principal Crops in India*, Various Issues, Ministry of Agriculture.

Firstly, during the first phase of the Green Revolution 1962-1965 to 1970-1973, the new technology was only confined to wheat and the main beneficiaries were the irrigated northwestern states of India, in particular, Punjab, Haryana and western Uttar Pradesh. Another state that benefited from wheat revolution was West Bengal. The new technology had hardly any impact on rice, the main foodgrain crop, with the result that the rice-growing eastern states were not able to derive appreciable gains from the new technology. The southern states of Karnataka, Kerala and Tamil Nadu also registered medium to high growth, but in their case also the new technology could make appreciable contribution only in limited areas. Crop output in the dry rainfed states in the central region was hardly influenced by new technology and agricultural production in that region was characterised by sharp weather-borne year-to-year fluctuations.

The second period from 1970-1973 to 1980-1983 is characterised by the extension of new seed-fertiliser technology from wheat to rice and its spread from Punjab and Haryana not only to eastern Uttar Pradesh but also to the rice-producing states in the southern region. Along with Punjab and Haryana, Uttar Pradesh, the largest state of India, also registered an acceleration in its growth from 2.54 per cent during 1962-1965 to 1970-1973 to 2.77 per cent per annum during 1970-1973 to 1980-1983.

The third period 1980-1983 to 1992-1995 marks a turning point in India's agricultural development. At the all-India level, the growth rate of crop output accelerated from 2.38 per cent during 1970-1973 to 1980-1983 to 3.38 per cent during 1980-1983 to 1990-1993. During this period, not only did agricultural growth accelerate in the few irrigated regions as earlier, it also permeated to all the regions including the rainfed regions of India. Especially creditable was the performance of eastern states, in general and West Bengal, in particular, where the growth rate increased to an unprecedented level of 5.4 per cent per annum. Another important development was a significant acceleration in the growth rates of agricultural output in the rainfed states of Madhya Pradesh and Rajasthan, primarily as a result of large shifts of areas from coarse cereals to oilseeds. Thirdly, Tamil Nadu, which had a negative growth during the seventies, also recorded high growth rate of 4.6 per cent during this period.

One of the important consequences of widespread growth over all the regions was a notable reduction in interstate inequalities in both the yield levels and growth rate of output. The coefficient of variation of yields which had increased from 56.9 in 1962-1965 to 58.2 in 1970-1973 declined to 46.3 during 1990-1993. The coefficient of variation for growth rates declined from 88 during 1962-1965 to 1990-1993 to 50 during 1980-1983 to 1992-1995, but increased again to 112 during 1996-1999.

Deceleration at the National and Regional Levels

The initiation of economic reforms in 1991, with the aim of liberalisation of the economy and its integration with the world economy, marks the beginning of a new policy framework for India. The structural adjustment programme had the objective of bringing macro-economic stability through reducing fiscal deficit, gradually reducing the role of the public sector through privatisation, freeing the labour market through reducing the strength of trade unions and also, bringing reforms in the monetary and fiscal areas.

To begin with, no explicit reference was made to freeing of Indian agriculture and integrating it with the world economy, but the economic policy changes, especially in the external sector and in particular, the devaluation of the rupee, made many tradable agricultural commodities competitive in the world market. Other strands of new economic policy were, gradual withdrawal of input subsidies and raising the output prices with a view to ending discrimination against agriculture and improving the terms of trade of agriculture *vis-à-vis* other sectors of the economy. This was expected to give a big incentive to agriculturists to increase their production and exports.

Contrary to expectations, agriculture failed to show any buoyancy after the introduction of economic reforms. As a matter of fact, both the total crop sector and most major crops recorded a deceleration in their growth rates during the nineties as compared with the eighties (Table 2.4). The growth rate for all crops taken together decelerated to 1.96 per cent per annum during 1990-91 to 2000-01 compared with a rate of 3.19 per cent per annum during 1980-81 to 1990-91. It may be noted that the reported crops taken together account for more than 95 per cent of gross cropped area in the country.

A more serious problem was gradual decline in the yield levels of various crops. Thus, whereas the yield growth for all crops taken together decelerated from 2.56 per cent per annum during the eighties to 1.09 per cent per annum during the nineties, that for rice the yield growth rate decelerated from 3.47 per cent to 0.92 and for wheat from 3.10 per cent to 2.21 per cent per annum. This is a serious development which has arisen as a result of neglect in public investment in research and development and extension in agriculture.

In the case of cotton there have been extreme year-to-year fluctuations in production. Whereas the growth rate of cotton output has declined from 2.33 per cent per annum during the 1980s to 1.37 per cent per annum during the 1990s, its yield growth rate has gone down significantly from 4.10 per cent per annum during the eighties to -0.94 per cent during the nineties. In this case, the effectiveness of pesticides is declining and the spurious nature of these has failed to prevent complete loss of the crop, leading many farmers to a state of distress and driving some of them to commit suicides. A major deceleration in the growth of crop output and yields has adversely affected the farmers by reducing their income and profitability. This also had an adverse impact on employment.

Reasons for Deceleration of Agricultural Growth during the Nineties

There are many reasons for the recent deceleration in the growth of agricultural output and yield of major crops in India. The most important among these was the sharp deceleration in total investment and more so in public sector investment in agriculture since the beginning of 1980s and more so since 1991 (Table 2.6). Although private investment has increased, but this increase has not been able to compensate for the steep decline in public investment. The most serious effect of deceleration in total investment has been on crippling agricultural research and extension.

Secondly, the assumption that increased prices would automatically lead to increase in aggregate supply because of supply response has not proved correct. Although all empirical studies had already rejected this hypothesis, nevertheless after economic liberalisation there emerged a new misplaced faith in the efficacy of price mechanism. This has again proved to be erroneous.

Table 2.6

Capital Formation in Agriculture (at 1993-94 Prices)

(Rs. Crore)

Years	Total	Public	Private	Per Cent Share Public	Per Cent Share Private	Total GCF in Agriculture as % of Total GDP	Total GCF in Agriculture as % of GDP from Agriculture
(At 1980-81 Prices)							
1960-1961	1668	589	1079	35.3	64.7	2.7	5.1
1970-1971	2758	789	1969	28.6	71.4	3.1	6.7
1980-1981	4636	1796	2840	38.7	61.3	3.8	9.9
(At 1993-94 Prices)							
1990-1991	14836	4395	10441	29.6	70.4	1.9	6.6
1991-1992	13389	3871	9518	28.9	71.1	1.7	6.1
1992-1993	14508	4076	10432	28.1	71.9	1.8	6.2
1993-1994	13523	4467	9056	33.0	67.0	1.6	5.6
1994-1995	14969	4947	10022	33.0	67.0	1.6	5.9
1995-1996	15690	4848	10842	30.9	69.1	1.6	6.2
1996-1997	16176	4668	11508	28.9	71.7	1.5	5.9
1997-1998	15942	3979	11963	24.9	75.1	1.4	5.9
1998-1999	14895	3870	11025	26.0	74.0	1.3	5.2
1999-2000	17304	4221	13083	24.4	75.6	1.4	6.0
2000-2001	16906	3927	12979	23.2	76.8	1.3	5.9
2001-2002	17328	4127	13201	23.8	76.2	1.3	5.7
2002-2003*	18657	4538	14119	24.3	75.7	1.3	6.4

Note: * Provisional, now actual figures are available at 1999 prices.
Source: GoI, CSO, *National Accounts Statistics*, Various Issues.

This has resulted in reducing the potential for future growth. A decline in research investment has had more serious consequences and seems to be the main cause for stagnation and deceleration of yields of major crops. The increased private investment has not benefited agricultural research either. The major reason for decline in public sector investment has been fiscal compression, which has mainly fallen on investment. There has been little or no effort to cut on inessential expenditures, like expenditure on salaries, subsidies and defence, etc.

Regional Agricultural Growth, Labour Productivity and Rural Poverty

Agricultural Growth and Rural Poverty

The growth of the economy and that of per capita income is accompanied by a significant reduction of poverty in India over a period of time. This notwithstanding, even now India along with China has the largest number of poor in the world. The following section briefly reviews the performance of Indian economy in general and that of agriculture in particular, with a view to analyse the relationship, if any, between growth and poverty reduction.

Two hypotheses are examined below. The first is that state-wise growth of GDP is negatively related to incidence of poverty. Thus, state-wise incidence of poverty during 1993-94 is regressed against state-wise growth of GDP during 1983-84 to 1993-94.

The results are as follows:

$Y=52.39-3.67x$, $t=1.86$ with a significance of 0.084 i.e. significant at 8.4 per cent probability.

Similar relationship is analysed for growth during 1993-94 to 1999-2000 and incidence of poverty during 1999-2000 is:

$Y=37.68-2.66x$, $t=1.30$ with a significance of 0.214, that is the result is insignificant for the nineties.

It is therefore interesting to note that in spite of the general impression to the contrary, rapid growth during 1993-94 to 1999-2000 did not have a significant impact on reduction of poverty during 1999-2000. Table 2.7 gives the details.

An attempt was made to find the relationship between growth rate of agriculture during 1983-84 to 1993-94 and incidence of rural poverty during 1993-94 by fitting linear and log-linear trend lines. The results for log-linear curve are completely unsatisfactory as the value of correlation coefficient is very low.

The results for linear relationship bring out that growth of agriculture during 1983 84 to 1993-94 made a significant (at 97 per cent level of probability) impact on reduction of rural poverty during 1993-94. However, the relationship between state-level growth of agriculture during 1993-94 to 1999-2000 and incidence of poverty during 1999-2000 is completely insignificant. There seems to be no relationship whatsoever between the two during the 1990s. This needs some explanation (Table 2.8).

Table 2.7

Growth of GDP and Incidence of Poverty

States	*GDP Gr. 1980-81 Price 1983-1993*	*T. Poverty 1993-94*	*GDP Gr. 1993-94 Price 1999-2000*	*T. Poverty 1999-2000*
Andhra Pradesh	4.58	22.19	4.39	15.77
Assam	3.51	40.86	2.33	36.09
Bihar	2.69	54.96	4.45	42.60
Gujarat	5.00	24.21	7.39	14.07
Harayana	6.18	25.05	6.04	8.74
Himachal Pradesh	5.89	28.44	**7.06**	7.63
Karnataka	5.86	33.16	5.05	20.04
Kerala	5.33	25.43	**8.05**	12.72
Madhya Pradesh	5.21	42.52	4.93	37.43
Maharashtra	7.42	36.86	5.14	25.02
Orissa	3.39	48.56	6.00	46.15
Punjab	5.13	11.77	4.10	6.16
Rajasthan	6.19	27.41	4.77	15.28
Tamil Nadu	7.45	35.03	8.17	21.12
Uttar Pradesh	4.66	40.85	6.22	31.15
West Bengal	4.73	35.66	4.62	27.02

Source: CSO, Various Issues.

It is now well known that there are serious problems with regard to the data on growth of gross product form agriculture at 1993-94 prices, primarily because of very high growth attributed to fruits and vegetables during this period compared with the 1980s. We have already commented about this regarding growth of GDP in agriculture at the all-India level. There is strong reason to believe that this error is also present in the state-wise data on gross product data from agriculture at updated 1993-94 prices.

Table 2.8

Agricultural Growth and Rural Poverty

States	*Per Cent Annual Gr. 1983-84 to 1993-94*	*Rural Poverty 1993-94*	*Per Cent Annual Gr. 1993-94 to 1999-2000*	*Rural Poverty 1999-2000*
Andhra Pradesh	3.05	15.92	0.74	11.05
Assam	2.12	45.01	0.83	40.04
Bihar	-0.45	58.21	1.04	44.3
Gujarat	0.84	22.18	2.48	13.17
Haryana	4.86	28.02	1.64	8.27
Himachal Pradesh	3.08	30.34	0.56	7.94
Karnataka	3.54	29.88	4.09	17.38
Kerala	4.40	25.76	0.96	9.38
Madhya Pradesh	2.82	40.64	2.17	37.06
Maharashtra	5.39	37.93	1.68	23.72
Orissa	-0.57	49.72	0.33	48.01
Punjab	4.62	11.95	2.01	6.35
Rajasthan	3.93	26.46	0.50	13.74
Tamil Nadu	4.43	32.48	1.39	20.55
Uttar Pradesh	2.80	42.28	2.89	31.22
West Bengal	4.45	40.8	4.04	31.85
	$y = -3.6197x+44.759$		$y = -0.0392x+22.189$	
	$R^2 = 0.2836$		$R^2 = 0.0000107$	

Source: CSO; GSDP Various Years.

Questions have also been raised regarding the all-India and state level data on incidence of poverty during 1999-2000. The main reason attributed is the fact that the schedule for weekly recall and monthly recall was canvassed to the same household in many cases. This, it is argued, has introduced a non-sampling error in the estimates. Some authors feel that the extent of poverty reduction during 1999-2000, as compared with 1993-94, is much lower than indicated by the official estimates (Sen, 2000).

It is most probably these errors because of which the robust relationship between growth of agriculture and reduction in the incidence of poverty which holds true for the entire period 1973-74 to 1993-94 has been vitiated during the 1990s.

Labour Productivity in Agriculture and Rural Poverty

It is now increasingly appreciated that it is labour productivity in agriculture that plays an important role in making a dent on poverty. Furthermore, per worker productivity in agriculture also becomes a powerful instrument for diversification of the economy. The argument is that increased labour productivity in agriculture results in higher wages and incomes for agricultural workers. Since agricultural workers constitute a very high proportion of workforce, the increased income is very widely spread among a large number of workers. This leads to reduction in rural poverty. Furthermore, higher incomes of this mass of workers result in rapid growth of manufacturing and services sectors because of very strong input, output and consumption linkages. The overall result is both a decline in rural poverty as well as in diversification of the economy. We have tried to look at both these relationships. It comes out that per worker productivity in agriculture does have a significant negative relationship with the incidence of rural poverty. The relationship is significant for both 1993-94 and for 1999-2000 (Table 2.9).

Table 2.9

Per Worker Productivity and Incidence of Poverty

States	*Per Worker Productivity in Rs.*		*Rural Poverty Ratio*	
	1993-94	*1999-2000*	*1993-94*	*1999-2000*
Andhra Pradesh	8505	9497	15.92	11.05
Assam	12240	13917	45.01	40.04
Bihar	5028	5016	58.21	44.3
Gujarat	11946	10438	22.18	13.17
Harayana	41859	42871	28.02	8.27
Himachal Pradesh	9409	11125	30.34	7.94
Jammu & Kashmir	16464	18294	30.34	3.97
Karnataka	11587	13800	29.88	17.38
Kerala	18546	25200	25.76	9.38
Madhya Pradesh	8882	9025	40.64	37.06
Maharashtra	10818	12070	37.93	23.72
Orissa	8272	7841	49.72	48.01
Punjab	43919	51792	11.95	6.35
Rajasthan	9294	11744	26.46	13.74
Tamil Nadu	10345	12001	32.48	20.55
Uttar Pradesh	9915	12389	42.28	31.22
West Bengal	16507	18008	40.8	31.85
India	**11739**	**13495**	**37.27**	**27.09**

Source: CSO; GDP Series (Various Issues) and NSSO, 40th and 55th Rounds.

The linear regression equation for 1993-94 is:

$y = -.00055x+41.67$

$R^2 = 0.255$

$t = -2.16$ significant at 95.2 per cent.

For 1999-2000 the regression equation is:

$y = -0.00059x + 31.75$

$R^2 = 0.26$

$t = -2.38$ significant at 95.6 per cent probability levels.

To conclude, per worker productivity has a significant negative relationship with incidence of rural poverty both during 1993-94 and 1999-2000.

Conclusions

This chapter has briefly reviewed the growth experience of India since Independence with special reference to the growth of agriculture both at the national and state level. India embarked on economic reforms in 1991. The aim of the reforms was to liberalise the economy and gradually integrate it with the world economy. It was expected that the reform package of liberalisation of trade and termination of protection to industry would go a long way in ending discrimination against agriculture and turning the terms of trade in its favour. Furthermore, reversing the policy of low food prices for food security reasons and consequent rise in prices of major foodgrains would go a long way in providing incentive to the farmers to increase their production.

Our analysis has brought out that instead of acceleration of growth, there has taken place a notable deceleration in the growth rate of agricultural GDP as well as crop output. This is true not only at the national level but also at the state level. Our analysis has also brought out a few interesting features regarding the relationship between growth and poverty.

Our state-wise analysis shows that the growth of agriculture during 1980-81 to 1990-91, did have a significant impact on reduction of incidence of rural poverty during 1993-94.

However, agricultural growth during 1993-94 to 1999-2000 had no impact whatsoever in reducing the incidence of rural poverty during 1999-2000. Nineties therefore, mark a departure form all earlier periods wherein agricultural growth was found to be significantly and inversely related to incidence of rural poverty.

Two more results are important. It is found that both during 1993-1994 and 1999-2000 growth of per worker productivity in agriculture is significantly related to poverty reduction in rural India. It is therefore, very important to give more attention to increasing labour productivity in agriculture. The second important result is that, growth of per worker productivity in agriculture not only reduces the incidence of rural poverty, it is also instrumental in diversification of workforce from agricultural to non-agricultural activities.

We also have found that during 1980 to 1993-94 there was a clear relationship between agricultural growth and growth of overall GDP and the correlation coefficient was quite high. But during 1993-94 to 1999-2000, there is a complete disjunction between growth of GDP from agriculture and growth of overall GDP. The only relationship during this period is between growth of tertiary sector and growth of GDP with both the agriculture and the secondary sectors playing a very nominal or negligible role (Appendix A-2.1).

To conclude, despite the fact that as per official data the incidence of rural poverty has declined during the 1990s, the deceleration of agricultural growth during 1993-94 to 1999-2000 is a very serious challenge. This is because, it is only agricultural growth which is going to determine the fortunes of a vast majority of working people in India and that it is only agricultural growth that can enable them to diversify and improve their standard of living. The post-liberalisation policies that have neglected public investment in rural infrastructure are primarily responsible for the steep deceleration in agricultural growth. It would not be possible to regenerate Indian agriculture and enable it to meet the challenges of economic liberalisation and globalisation without accelerating public investment in rural infrastructure and without creating appropriate institutional structures like service cooperatives, trading houses, and market intelligence services that serve the interests of the vast majority of marginal and small farmers. This constitutes one of the biggest challenges of governance for agricultural administration in India.

References

Ahluwalia, M.S. (1978). "Rural Poverty and Agricultural Performance in India", *Journal of Development Studies*, Vol. 14(3), April, pp.298-323.

Bhalla, G.S. and Gurmail Singh (2001). *Indian Agriculture—Four Decades of Development*, Sage, New Delhi.

Government of India (Various Issues). *National Accounts Statistics*, CSO.

———. (Various Issues). *Area and Production of Principal Crops in India*, Ministry of Agriculture and Cooperation.

———. (Various Issues). *Agricultural Statistics at a Glance*, Ministry of Agriculture and Cooperation.

———. (2002). *Report of the Statistical Commission of India*, Ministry of Statistics.

Sachs, Jeffrey D., Nirumam Bajpai and Ananthi Ramiah (2002). "Understanding Regional Economic Growth in India", *CID Working Paper* No. 88, Centre for International Development at Harvard University, USA.

Sen, Abhijit (2000). "Estimates of Consumer Expenditure and its Distribution: Statistical Priorties after the NSS 55th Round," *Economic and Political Weekly*, Vol. 35(51), December 16, pp.4499-4518.

Sivsasubramonian, S. (2000). *The National Income of India in the Twentieth Century*, Oxford University Press, New Delhi.

Appendix Table A-2.1

State-wise Growth of Sectoral GDP and Per Capita Income at 1980-81 Prices

States	1981-1991 GDP	1991-1998 GDP	1981-1991 PCY	1991-1998 PCY	1981-1991 Agriculture	1991-1998 Agriculture	1981-1991 Secondary	1991-1998 Secondary	1981-1991 Tertiary	1991-1998 Tertiary
Andhra Pradesh	4.31	8.50	2.42	6.91	2.24	1.87	5.33	13.74	5.96	9.91
Assam	3.58	3.51	1.25	1.60	2.23	2.23	4.03	5.60	4.69	4.01
Bihar	4.66	2.69	1.98	5.54	2.97	2.15	6.11	3.28	5.57	3.70
Gujarat	5.08	9.57	3.11	5.90	-0.25***	4.67	7.82	13.12	7.26	9.04
Haryana	6.58	5.02	3.66	3.40	4.30	2.70	9.50	6.50	7.71	7.34
Himachal Pradesh	5.03	0.00	3.94	3.59	1.95	3.53	7.45	0.00	6.95	0.00
Karnataka	5.30	5.29	3.99	3.42	2.39	2.88	6.85	5.95	7.47	7.21
Kerala	3.57	5.81	3.94	4.57	2.01	3.51	2.85	6.38	5.23	7.40
Madhya Pradesh	4.56	6.17	2.73	3.82	2.25	3.66	6.55	9.63	6.53	6.50
Maharashtra	6.02	8.01	5.20	5.90	3.67	3.97	6.43	8.89	7.07	8.88
Orissa	4.29	3.25	1.51	1.70	1.37**	-1.06	7.20	4.91	6.11	4.95
Punjab	5.32	4.71	3.11	2.75	4.87	2.39	7.35	7.94	4.70	5.55
Rajasthan	6.60	6.42	3.71	3.78	4.44	6.84	7.93	6.68	8.95	5.50
Tamil Nadu	6.68	9.19	6.10	7.92	3.57	1.40	5.16	7.03	9.35	12.59
Uttar Pradesh	4.95	3.58	2.61	2.07	2.66	2.19	7.92	4.20	6.37	4.70
West Bengal	4.58	6.85	2.47	4.91	5.52	6.27	3.39	5.86	4.86	8.06
All India	**5.62**	**6.23**	**3.50**	**4.30**	**3.08**	**1.95**	**7.10**	**7.45**	**6.72**	**8.24**
CV										
	Ag GDP	*Ag GDP*	*Agr Sec*	*Agr Sec*	*Agr Ter*	*Agr Ter*	*Sec GDP*	*Sec GDP*	*Sec Ter*	*Sec Ter*
Correlation Coeff.	0.453	-0.285	-0.051	0.125	-.0035	0.141	0.589	0.842	0.481	0.713

Note: PSY - Per capita Income.

Source: CSO, *State Domestic Products*, Various Issues.

3

Globalisation and Indian Agriculture: Performance under a New Paradigm

R.S. DESHPANDE and M. INDIRA

Introduction

Indian agriculture has undergone various phases of growth and development during the last five decades. The experience so far indicates a few bright spots as well as phases of stagnation marked by breaks in the process of development. Major impediments faced by Indian agriculture at the time of independence included food insecurity, constraints on resource availability, ill distribution of resources, primitive technology and regional imbalances (Dantwala, 1996). We have been partially successful in overcoming a few of these impediments and today India can pose as one of the food secure nations *albeit* in arithmetic sense (Acharya, 2002). And during the five decades we have also followed a riverine process of development and altered the model of development several times in response to the worldwide trends. The phase of globalisation is one such step that has been ushered in as a new mode of development. Therefore, we have more questions to be answered and issues to be discussed than before.

The travelogue of any development process begins with resource augmentation, productivity enhancement, employment generation, distribution and finally value addition. We have been able to work partially on the impediments faced by the Indian agriculture and now we are at the crossroad of getting into global market as a predominant player (Bhalla, 1995, Ahluwalia, 1996). India has achieved an important position among the producers of many commodities as well as it provides a large market for the purpose of other international players to participate in. There are a few questions that crop up at this juncture and these relate to the structure of internal and external markets with India's response to it (WTO, 1998). The domestic market governance naturally comes as the first issue to be debated and to understand India's preparedness for facing the challenge of globalisation in this context. Hitherto, we have always been making our presence in international markets in response to the residual surplus. It is time now to cultivate a culture of producing for the sake of the international market and marking the presence in the process. It is easily said than done. Our markets as well as farmers will have to be equipped with infrastructure, information along with a full reform package (Pangariya, 1999). This chapter discusses three important issues *viz.*, (i) the pre-setting of globalisation and issues pertaining to governance in agricultural sector during nineties; (ii) the process of globalisation and the impediments in the domestic as well as world market, and (iii) steps needed in order to participate in the process of globalisation through development governance and reforms in allied sectors.

Pre-setting

Macroeconomic crisis of early nineties was the beginning of the process of calibrating trade globalisation in the economy and agriculture was no exception. Even though, the basic current emerged actually during mid-eighties, it could acquire a visible drive only by early nineties (Sen, 2000, Rao, 2001). As is well known, the crisis began when the foreign exchange reserves touched a critical bottom level, adverse balance of payment condition was evident and a near debt trap situation became imminent (Joshi and Little, 1996). An alternate view is about the very necessity of getting into the structural adjustments itself (Ghosh, 1997). If one looks carefully at the data on National Accounts Statistics, it is quite visible that the trigger of the situation leading to the crisis was located in the expansion of non-agricultural sectors during mid-eighties beginning with the historical budget presented by the then Finance Minister. The performance of the agricultural sector during that period was certainly impressive and contributed significantly to the national growth, and agricultural exports were also increasing. However, balance of payment was absolutely in precarious condition and it was felt that the situation was beyond the capacity of the economy to rescue, leading to the launch of structural adjustment programme and globalisation was an unavoidable outcome of the process.

Globalisation means integration of the economy with the rest of the world. The process of integration is facilitated by flow of information, technologies, goods and services, finance, capital and people. Report of the World Commission on Social Dimension of Globalisation observed that the key characteristics of globalisation include: "liberalisation of trade; cross-border financial flows and increased competition in global markets." According to the Report, it has come about due to deliberate policy decisions for free trade and the emergence of information and communication technology. The essential feature of globalisation is connectivity that is facilitated by information technology revolution. This reduced the cost of communication drastically. Globalisation has several dimensions like social, cultural and economic and these impinge on welfare across sectors (Parikh *et al.*, 1997).

The new paradigm of global economy is based on the theory that free trade among countries leads to efficient allocation of resources enhances productivity and social welfare. Under this paradigm, a country's development need not be constrained by insufficient capital resource, if it has potential. Inflow of foreign capital helps development. For example, inflow of foreign capital to Malaysia was 17.4 per cent of its GDP during 1993 and 12.7 per cent in Thailand during 1995. Rapid development of capital market is an essential feature of globalisation, which facilitates easy flow of movement of funds. However, too much dependence on foreign capital that is volatile under free global markets carries the risk of withdrawal at any moment.

Following the crisis, the state of affairs was handled carefully with a battery of macroeconomic tools that included liberalisation of foreign trade, devaluation of the currency and other steps in domestic macroeconomic policy management (Singh, 1995). This period incidentally coincided with a few major changes in the arena of international trade, heralding the establishment of World Trade Organization (WTO) and removal of non-tariff trade barriers. India being one among the founder members of General Agreement on Trade and Tariff (GATT), agreed to abide by the set of regulations given under the various agreements of WTO. The macroeconomic situation in the country was also undergoing a rapid transition along with significant changes in trade scenario, in this process the agricultural sector, sheer by its significance in the economy, became an important player. Naturally growth trends in agricultural sector and the domestic market conditions emerged as the initial issues to signify the frontal impact of globalisation (Rao, 2001).

India's agricultural sector cannot be compared with that of many countries significantly participating in the international trade. Among the major constraints faced by the sector, prominent is the lowest average size of holdings as a base for production. About 80 million small and marginal farmers inhabit the sector with only a small proportion of farmers generating sizeable marketable surplus. Market conditions in factor as well as product markets are far from satisfactory; and finally India never had a sustained presence in the international trade to participate pro-actively in the process of globalisation. These overt constraints provoked the use of terminology like 'level playing field' while analysing comparative performance of India *vis-à-vis* its trading partners. It is quite clear that the production as well as domestic and international trade environment in India is not comparable to many of its competitors but finally that needs to be achieved in the process. Therefore, the significant question crops up, whether agriculture will stand at the receiving end? How this should be avoided, is a major policy issue to wrestle with.

Agriculture and Globalisation

Over the last five decades, Indian agricultural sector performed under various constraints. The exemplary performance during late sixties, mid-seventies and early eighties helped to overcome the problem of aggregate food insecurity. The performance of the last two years of eighties was a landmark and that was not exceeded in the following decade (Figure 3.1). It is argued that the annual growth of agriculture GDP shows a declining trend in the post-reform period. While it has grown at an annual rate of 3.4 percent during 1980s, it registered only 1.8 per cent growth between 1997-98 and 2000-02. Growth rate was 4.7 per cent between 1992-93 and 1997-98. Similarly, it is also argued that there is a decline in area, production and productivity of all crops. While area under all crops has shown a marginal increase in growth rate during 1990s, production and yield have shown a decreasing trend. But as can be seen from Figure 3.1, that the decade of nineties has recorded positive growth in GDP in most of the years except for a few years, but while comparing the aggregate growth analysts tend to conclude with a bad performance during nineties. Probably the peak achieved at the end point in the decade of eighties leads to such a conclusion. One point however is quite clear that the performance of the agriculture sector during eighties was quite supportive.

Figure 3.1

Growth in GDP Originating from Agriculture: Annual Growth Rate of GDP at Factor Cost in Agriculture

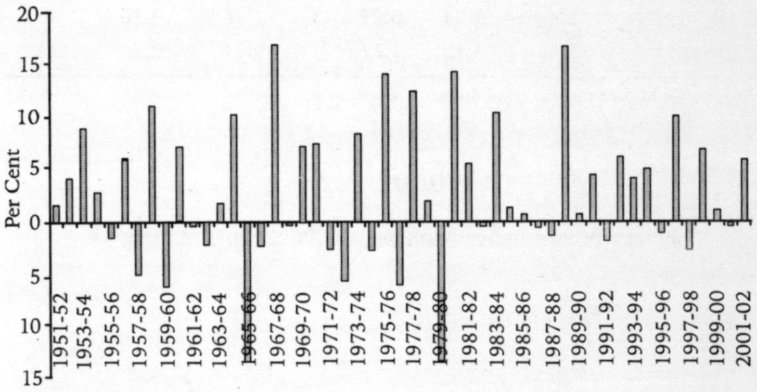

Source: Based on *Agricultural Statistics at Glance*, Various Issues.

The growth rates seen from the Table 3.1 indicate that the long-term performance of the sector is quite satisfactory, though not exemplary. But the growth rates mask a lot than they reveal. What is important to note here is that the growth during recent past as well as during the last three decades has come from the technological inputs. Globalisation may further usher in new technological opportunities. A comparison of the growth rates in the two decades of eighties and nineties can be quite deceptive and therefore we have resorted to view the trends over the entire period. Figures 3.2 and 3.3 present this picture.

If one looks at the performance of the agricultural sector over the five decades in terms of growth in crop productivity, it is quite clear that the sector has witnessed alternative cycles of growth and stagnation. The performance between 1980 and 1995 was quite ideal

Table 3.1

Growth Performance Over Five Decades: 1949-50 to 2001-02

Crops	1949-50 to 1964-65			1967-68 to 2001-02		
	Area	Prod.	Yield	Area	Prod.	Yield
Rice	1.21	3.50	2.25	0.62	2.78	2.20
Wheat	2.69	3.98	1.27	1.38	4.34	2.92
Coarse Cereals	0.90	2.25	1.23	-1.44	0.54	1.90
Cereals	1.25	3.21	1.77	-0.02	2.77	2.32
Pulses	1.72	1.41	-0.18	0.30	0.81	0.74
Foodgrains	1.35	2.82	1.36	0.01	2.51	2.12
Oilseeds	2.07	3.20	0.30	1.31	3.32	1.60
Non-foodgrains	2.44	3.74	0.89	1.36	3.20	1.68
All Crops	**1.58**	**3.15**	**1.21**	**0.34**	**2.78**	**1.90**

Source: GoI (2003). *Agricultural Statistics at a Glance.*

Figure 3.2

Growth in the Index Numbers of All Crop Productivity

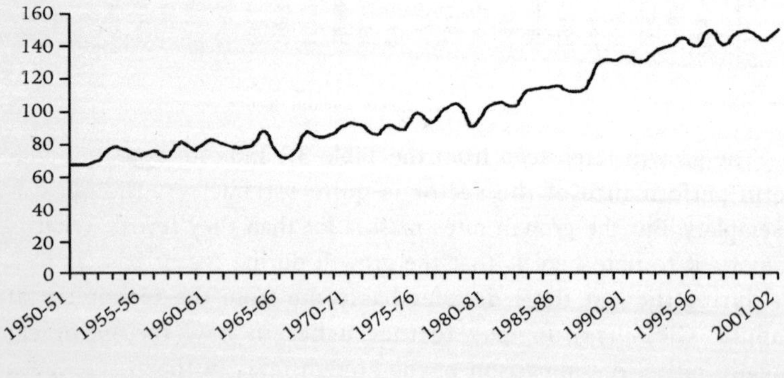

Source: Same as Figure 3.1.

but after that a phase of stagnation seem to have emerged strongly. This is more visible in the non-foodgrain sector than in the foodgrains. This seems to be a matter of serious concern, especially when we are looking at a growth strategy from globalisation and trade angles.

Figure 3.3

Growth in Productivity of Non-foodgrains: 1950-2002

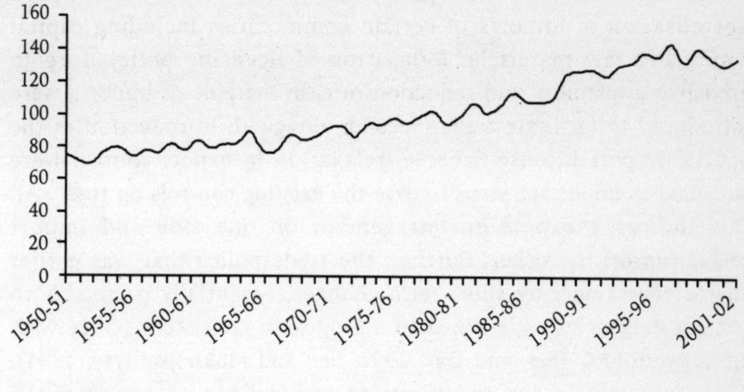

Source: Same as Figure 3.1.

Figure 3.4

Growth in Productivity Index of Foodgrains

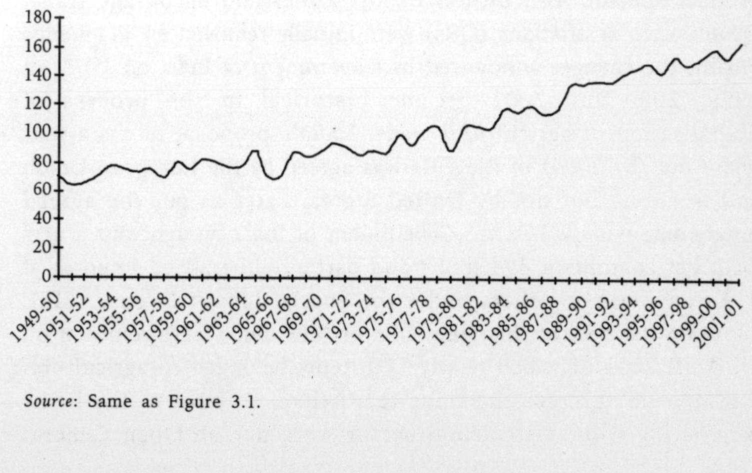

Source: Same as Figure 3.1.

Trade Sector Performance

Among the major changes that took place in the trade policy during nineties, five were of greater significance for agricultural sector. First, the EXIM policy of March 1990, introduced liberalisation of imports of certain commodities including capital goods and raw materials. Relaxation of licensing policy, foreign exchange availability and reduction in cash margins of imports were introduced to facilitate trade. Second, alongwith introduction of the Special Import License Scheme, relaxation in export control were launched as important steps to ease the existing controls on trade. All this indicated export encouragement on one side and import relaxation on the other. Further, the trade policy that was earlier characterised only by short-term changes, essentially protective to combat exigencies, was tuned to a long-term consistent policy with an outward look (Sen and Das, 1992; Sen and Mukhopadhyay, 1994). Third important set of modifications included the extension of the Exim Scrip facilities to a number of agricultural commodities, decanalisation, and significant shifting of commodities from restricted and prohibited lists to free list took place during 1994 (Sen, 2000). Thus the percentage of free trade items increased from 22 per cent in 1995-96 to 58 per cent by 2000. Fourth, the EXIM Policy of 2001, gave special importance to the agricultural sector through the creation of the Special Economic Zones and Agricultural Export Zones wherein the state governments were required to identify product specific Agricultural Export Zones and encourage trade. Quantitative Restrictions (QRs) were initially removed on 111 items. Finally, the changes announced by Government of India on 1st April 1999, 2000 and 2001 became historical in the process of liberalisation of agricultural trade. India's proposal of a six-year phase out (by 2004) of the QRs was agreed by the European Union and Australia but not by United States. Later as per the agreed programme with WTO, the Government of India brought out a new OGL list containing 894 items and partially liberalised imports of 414 items bringing them under the Special Import License (SIL). Close on the heel of this step, QRs on 715 items were removed on 1st April 2001 of which nearly 170 items belonged to agriculture. Through this process the trade restrictions on most of the items originating from agricultural sector were put on Open General

License (OGL) list. This was also recently followed by a long-term policy document on foreign trade. These policies in the process of globalisation brought forth issues dealing with the impact of international markets on agricultural sector.

Globalisation of trade has opened up quite a few concerns for the agricultural sector. On the positive side it is argued that globalisation has unwrapped the prospects for Indian agriculture to make its presence felt in the international market. India has demonstrated comparative advantage in quite a few commodities therefore, it was rightfully expected that India would emerge as a significant player in trade of these commodities. It is expected that globalisation will help to boost up exports and meet the import bills apart from enhancing foreign exchange reserves. But at the same time that will increase import-intensity of exportable commodities. Opening of trade will also help to augment export competitiveness and improve the quality of production. In these circumstances a clear long-term export oriented production strategy can be chalked out. The demand for processed agricultural products will increase and that will have a substantial value addition to the farmers' produce.

Table 3.2

Growth Rates in Agricultural Exports

Region	*Average Annual Growth Rates (%)*					
	1955-60	*1960-70*	*1970-80*	*1980-90*	*1990-95*	*1955-95*
World	3.5	5.2	16.6	3.6	6.9	6.7
Developed country	2.7	5.4	14.9	4.3	6.2	6.4
Developing countries	4.7	4.7	24.0	2.7	8.8	8.2
(a) Developing Asia	6.4	4.4	23.5	3.9	11.1	8.7
(b) India	1.5	1.7	13.4	3.5	12.5	5.5

Source: Bhalla (2004); Originally from: 1. UN, *Yearbook of International Trade Statistics*, various issues. 2. UNCTAD, *Handbook of International Trade Statistics*, various issues.

The export performance of the agricultural sector during the decade of nineties has been quite satisfactory (Table 3.2). There are some commodities that have recorded positive growth performance, and at the same time we have witnessed declining exports of a few important commodities (Table 3.3). Marine products, cashew, tea, *basmati* rice and spices have shown significant increase in exports. But at the same time oil meals, non-*basmati* rice, coffee, meat preparations, fresh vegetables and fruits have shown decline in exports. On the negative side, it is feared that sudden shortages and hoardings of certain important commodities may be deleterious impact on economy. This however, could be managed provided through long-term market intelligence strategies and development of appropriate institutions to meet such contingency.

Table 3.3

Export Performance of Agricultural Products: 1995-2000

(Exports in US$ millions)

Items	*1995-96*	*1996-97*	*1997-98*	*1998-99*	*1999-00*
Marine Products	1012.31	1129.86	1208.72	1038.15	1181.55
Cashew	369.97	362.41	377.13	386.76	566.42
Tea	350.63	292.38	505.47	538.23	407.99
Basmati Rice	254.69	351.74	454.10	446.03	401.10
Spices	237.58	338.92	379.76	387.96	393.23
Castor Oil	222.31	176.84	155.21	159.72	245.37
Guar Gum Meal	68.02	100.40	146.82	172.93	189.15
Tobacco Unmanufactured	113.38	186.21	247.17	136.00	184.87
Processed Fruits and Juices	61.25	59.05	73.51	69.12	113.29
Pulses	39.47	37.10	97.22	53.00	93.56
Sesame and Dairy Products	77.02	77.61	81.51	79.07	85.88
Tobacco Manufactured	20.40	27.15	41.51	45.03	44.55
Poultry and Dairy Products	17.59	34.90	31.80	23.04	22.76
Floriculture Products	18.01	17.87	23.37	25.18	20.94
Shellac	18.78	14.75	15.65	15.52	18.85
Fruits/Vegetables Seeds	12.32	11.86	14.41	15.32	15.55
Share of these Commodities in Total Agriculture Exports (per cent)	47.29	46.88	58.11	59.52	72.40

Source: Bhalla (2004).

Import Performance

Increase in imports of the agricultural commodities is one of the possibilities of globalisation. It makes available goods and services on competitive prices to the consumers, but at the same time unabated imports may cause severe disincentives to the domestic producers. On the negative side it is feared that sudden import surges may occur in the market. Increased intensity of exports may facilitate entry of new-private traders and the market margins as well as undue profiteering will increase. These can act as strong disincentives to the producers. Such a situation will be common in the case of the commodities, which have higher income elasticity of demand. The process of increased trade will not only generate export-import price parity but also integrate the world market prices with domestic prices. Therefore, the prices in the domestic market of these commodities are likely to increase to keep pace with international prices. In other words, the international prices may normatively guide domestic price movements. This in turn may lead to price instability and increased price fluctuations. The worst consequence of such situation is the likely disincentive it will create among the domestic producers.

Overall Trade Performance

According to the average shares in total import bill pulses, soybean oil, silk, rice, natural rubber, rapeseed mustard oil, cotton lint, milk and cream and cereals are at the top of our import list. Among the imports of processed products sugar, resins, milk and cream, cheese, curds, jute and fibres and vegetable oils top the share of total imports. The commodity composition of imports and exports along with the earlier growth rates indicate the likely trends in import demand across products. In order to assess the possible trends in import demand, we have grouped the commodities by cross classification based on the share of imports and exports. The groups are indicated below.

These four groups indicate different categories under import and export scenario. Commodities having higher share in the import bill indicate constraints on domestic availability and hence are likely to continue in future provided these do not feature under higher export share group. From Table 3.7, we can get four groups based on the past import and export performance and their characteristics.

If we categorise the commodities in the above groups, it becomes possible to indicate the commodities which have high potential in changing the import shares. The last group with low share of exports

Table 3.4

Agricultural Products Showing Decline in Export Growth during 1995-96 to 1999-2000

Exports in US$ million (1999-2000 prices)

Items	*1995-96*	*1996-97*	*1997-98*	*1998-99*	*1999-00*
Oil Meals	703.18	985.44	925.44	461.43	370.43
Non-*Basmati* Rice	1113.00	542.20	454.03	1046.54	316.41
Coffee	449.98	402.20	456.93	410.63	315.17
Meat and Preparations	187.73	199.86	217.77	217.77	180.44
Fresh Vegetables	89.04	94.27	84.31	84.31	81.63
Fresh Fruits	68.92	68.90	74.58	74.58	66.59
Misc. processed items	161.81	215.41	68.85	60.62	62.39
Groundnuts	68.62	91.86	152.56	33.19	42.34
Processed vegetables	42.74	32.93	31.39	39.75	38.17
Cotton raw including wastes	60.94	443.90	221.41	49.17	18.64
Spirit and beverages	13.37	56.75	19.83	16.80	16.21
Suger and Molasses	151.62	303.89	68.68	5.81	8.74
Other cereals	5.08	13.71	3.39	2.06	1.88
Wheat	109.81	196.91	0.11	0.32	0.00
Share of these commodities in total Agriculture exports (per cent)	52.71	53.12	41.89	40.48	27.6

Source: Bhalla (2004).

and low share of imports indicates possibilities of increased imports. In this group we have grapes, copra, oilseed cake, groundnut oil and milk and condensed cream. Presently we have low shares of imports of these commodities probably due to low domestic demand or the domestic production just adequately meeting the domestic demand. It is expected that the demand for these products may increase due to increase in incomes and as the production does not yield any exportable surplus the import demand will increase. The second group of commodities, where the import demand is likely to increase, comprise the commodities with higher share of exports coupled with higher share of imports. Here, even though the domestic production

Table 3.5

India's Import of Selected Agricultural Commodities: 1990-91 to 2001-02

(In US $ Million)

Commodities	*1990-90*	*1991-92*	*1993-94*	*1994-95*	*1998-99*	*1999-00*	*2000-01*	*2001-02*
Rice		4	18	3	0	6	3	2
Wheat		0	40	0	266	179	1.8	1.4
Cereals & prep	102	66	35	26	25	222	19.4	18.2
Pulses	268.2	121	186	199	322	82	109.2	662.6
Sugar	5.2	0	0	727	127	256	7	7
Fruit & nut*	41	41	69	11	155	136	176	158
Milk/Cream*	3	3	5	2	1	25	2	2
Cashew nuts	75	108	154	220	207	276	211	90
Crude Rubber	126	74	109	118	160	143	152	174
Wool raw	102	80	119	112	161	114	100	131
Cotton raw	0	2	6	161	22	289	259	430
Jute raw	11	2	11	20	14	32	18	20
Vegetable Oils	181.6	101	53	199	745	1857	1334	1356
Pulp & W paper	255	121	151	202	284	256	282	295
Agri Imports	915	598	805	1884	3292	3432	2388	3045
Agri Exports	3354	3203	4028	4226	6626	5773	6256	6154
Total Imports	24075	19411	23306	28654	41484	49671	50536	51413

* For fruits & nuts and milk/cream source is—Director General of Statistics and Commercial Intelligence (DGSCI) for respective years.

Source: Bhalla (2004).

Table 3.6

Share in Import-Export

Share of Import/Export	*Imports*	*Exports*
Below 0.10 per cent	Groundnut oil, Cheeseand Curd, Soyabean Cake, Sunflower Seeds, Cereals, NES, Coffee Green, Canned Meats, Onions	Lemons, Limes, Tomatoes, Pineapple, Copra, Citrus Fruits, Bananas, Cotton Seed, Soyabean, Milk & Cream, Canned Meat, Soyabean Oil, Potatoes
0.10 to 0.50 per cent	Coconut Oil, Pepper (Black, White, Long), Milk and Cream, Evaporated and Condensed Tobacco Unmanufactured, Tea, Linseed Oil, Grapes, Copra, Oilseed Cake.	Grapes, Sugar, Cereals, Wheat, Silk, Linseed Cake and Meal, Jute and Fibres, Cotton Seed Cake, Apples, Eggs in Shells, Sugar Raw, Centrifugal, Oranges, Tangerines.
0.50 to 2.00 per cent	Wheat, Jute and Blast Fibres, Wheat and Meslin, Sugar Total, Sugar Raw	Soyabean Cake and Meal, Sesame Seed, Coffee Green, Pulses, Sunflower Seed Cake
Above 2.00	Pulses, Soyabean Oil, Silk, Rice, Natural Rubber and Gum, Rapeseed Mustard Oil, Cotton Lint, Milk and Cream Dry, Cereals	Tea, Rice, Cotton Lint, Tobacco, Unmanufactured, Castor Oil, Pepper, Rapeseed and Cake, Onions, Cereals, Oilseed Cake and Meal, Groundnuts.

Source: Based on FAO data taken from *www.fao.org*.

meets the domestic demand and generates exportable surplus there are four reasons for increasing import demand: (1) There is a possibility of qualitative differences in the commodity that is exported as well as imported (forming substantial share in both). (2) The time lag between and emergence of domestic demand for consumption and production may also create such a situation. In such cases imports are resorted to satisfy the domestic demand initially and as the domestic production generates exportable surplus, the commodity is exported. (3) High share in exports and high share in imports occur when there are high fluctuations in the relative prices (price ratios between world and domestic prices). Imports are resorted to when the world prices are below the domestic prices and exports in the opposite situation. (4) The import demand increases if the import contents in the factors of production of an exported commodity increases. In such case the situation of high import and high exports can prevail.

Table 3.7

Import-Export Category, Commodity Characteristics and Prices

Share of Exports or Imports	*Group Characteristic*
i. High Exports–Low Imports	- Domestic production satisfies domestic demand. - Exportable surplus exists - External demand pull. - World price higher than domestic price. - High domestic demand–Low export demand.
ii. Low Exports–High Imports	- Domestic production not sufficient to meet demand. - Negligible exportable surplus. - Domestic price higher than world price. - High domestic demand–High export demand.
iii. High Exports–High Imports	- Exportable surplus exists. - Import intensive exports. - Fluctuating world and domestic prices. - Low domestic demand–Low export demand. - Exportable surplus does not exist.
iv. Low Exports–Low Imports	- Inconsistency in relative price advantages between world prices and domestic prices.

Source: Same as Table 3.6.

Trade Balance

Trade balance reflects a one-stroke performance of the trade scenario. We tried here to look into the performance of the sector in terms of trade balance. On the count of trade performance, the agricultural sector did not under perform during eighties. The macroeconomic crisis that emerged at the beginning of nineties was largely the creation of the non-agricultural sector. The trade performance of agricultural sector picked up in 1988 significantly. What is striking in the decade of nineties is the increased trade balance in agricultural sector in the later period and that has a positive sign. If this is read along with the overall trade balance of the economy, the role of agricultural sector becomes clear. Figure 3.5 shows the satisfactory position of the trade performance of the agricultural sector during nineties.

Figure 3.5

Trade Performance of Agricultural Sector during Nineties

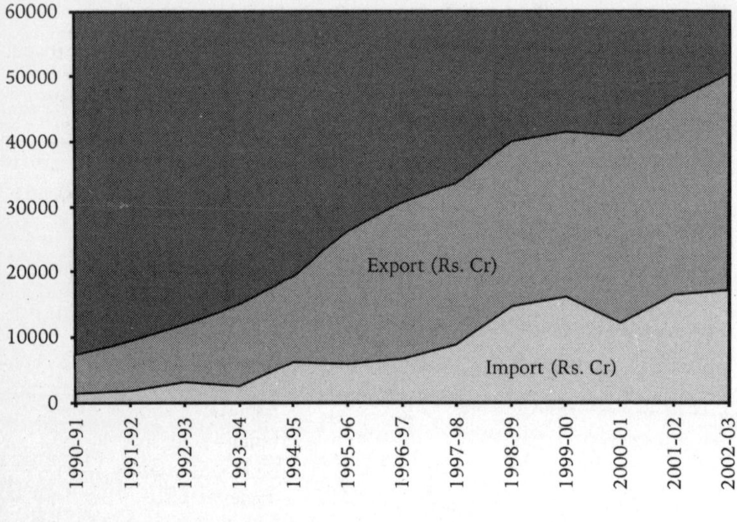

Source: GoI (2005). *Agricultural Statistics at Glance*, 2005.

Impact Concerns

The process of globalisation has spurred strong debates about its feasible impacts on the agricultural sector. Several views are expressed beginning from a possibility of significant destruction to our philosophy of rural development to the emergence of market as the sole correcting mechanism. It is argued that the flow of capital to the rural sector will reduce, preference will be more towards the market-oriented crops impinging the food security, poor farmers may face hard situation to sustain in farming, corporatisation of agriculture may take place (for detailed discussion see Deshpande, 2002). According to many, agriculture sector is the last sector to witness any changes induced by globalisation. This is partially due to delay in making appropriate policy changes and due to the forward and backward linkages of agriculture sector with other sectors. There is a time lag in 'trickle down'. On the other hand the proponents of the globalisation vouch that most of the maladies will be rectified through market process and that is under the assumption that markets have the capability of correcting the imperfections in the Indian context. Reality however, lies somewhere in between.

Changes in Cropping Pattern

Diversification of agriculture in order to meet the changing demand is adopted as one of the important strategies by several countries to cope up with the volatile prices through deliberate policy changes and encouragement of private participation. Diversification is in favour of high value export-oriented crops under contract or buyback system. According to a recent study (Joshi *et al.*, 2004), agricultural diversification increased in all south Asian countries. Fruits and vegetables have shown good performance during 80s and 90s. The study revealed the shift from crops to livestock sub-sector during 80s and 90s in all regions of India except Eastern and North-eastern states. Within the crop sub-sector, non-foodgrain crops have gradually replaced foodgrain crops. The shift is more towards non-foodgrain crops like oilseeds, fruits, vegetables, spices and sugarcane. Regional pattern of diversification showed that southern region is highly diversified followed by western region (Gulati and

Figure 3.6

Area Share of Foodgrains and Non-foodgrains

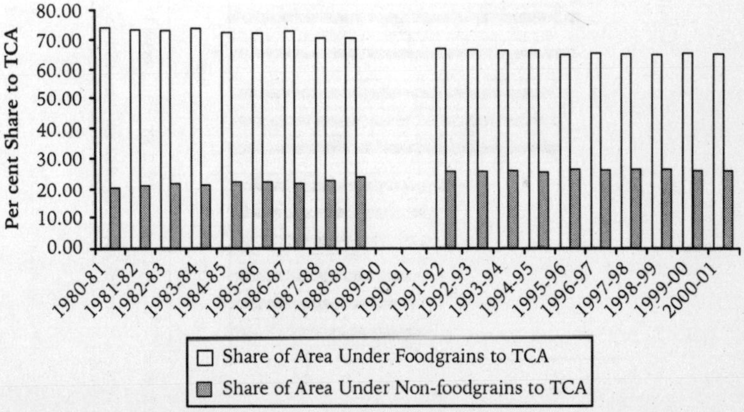

Source : Same as Figure 3.5.

Figure 3.7

Changes in Area Allocated for Major Crops

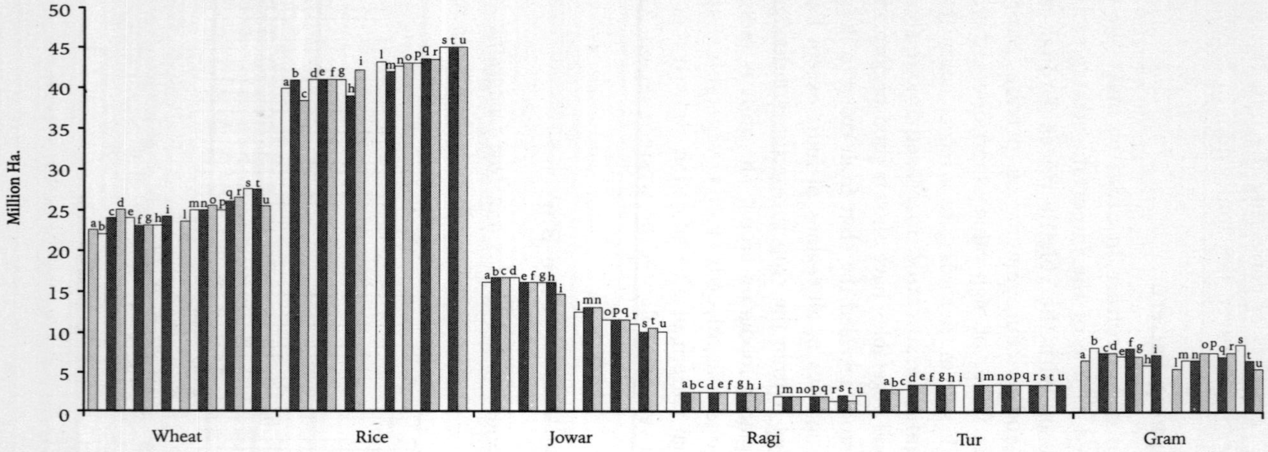

a: 1980-81	b: 1981-82	c:1982-83	d: 1983-84	e: 1984-85	f: 1985-86	g: 1986-87	h: 1987-88	i: 1988-89	j: 1989-90	k: 1990-91
l: 1991-92	m: 1992-93	n: 1993-94	o: 1994-95	p: 1995-96	q: 1996-97	r: 1997-98	s: 1998-99	t: 1999-00	u: 2000-01	

Source: Same as Figure 3.5.

Kelly, 1996). It was observed that crop diversification results in increased employment opportunities. For example, it was estimated that one hectare shift in area from wheat to potato would generate 145 additional man-days. Similarly, one hectare from coarse cereals to onions would generate 70 man-days of employment. According to the authors, diversification has not affected the food security adversely because there is a change in the consumption basket and the shift is more towards non-cereal food in both rural and urban areas. Crop diversification has a positive impact on non-traditional items.

Employment and Poverty

Employment in agricultural sector registered a negative trend. Employment on usual status basis has registered a growth rate of 1.54 per cent during 1983-1993 but showed a meagre growth rate of 0.18 per cent during 1993-94 and 1999-00. Same is the case with current daily status (2.23 per cent and 0.21 per cent) respectively. Real agricultural wages also increased at a lower growth rate in 1990s (2.5 per cent per annum) compared to 80s (5 per cent). Wages of female casual labour in agriculture increased by 3.09 per cent in 80s and 2.93 per cent in 90s. There are differences across states in the growth of real wages. While Kerala and Tamil Nadu registered highest growth (7.9 per cent and 6.7 per cent) between 1900 and 2000, Assam and Rajasthan registered negative growth rate of -0.7 and -0.8 per cent respectively (Table 3.9).

Table 3.8

Growth of Employment in Agriculture (Usual Status) in India

Period		*Growth of Employment in Agriculture*
1983-1984 to 1993-94	Rural	1.38
	Urban	1.54
1993-1994 to 1999-00	Rural	0.18
	Urban	-3.4

Source: Jha, Brajesh (2004). *Economic Policies for Augmenting Rural Employment in India*, Institute of Economic Growth, Delhi.

Figure 3.8

Changes in Area Allocated to Commercial Crops

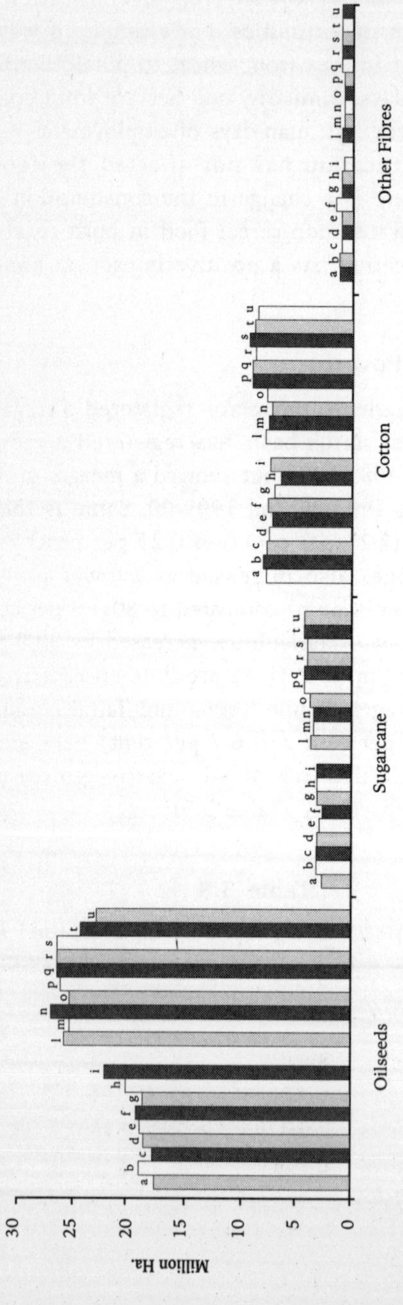

a: 1980-81	b: 1981-82	c:1982-83	d: 1983-84	e: 1984-85	f: 1985-86	g: 1986-87	h: 1987-88	i: 1988-89	j: 1989-90	k: 1990-91
l: 1991-92	m: 1992-93	n: 1993-94	o: 1994-95	p: 1995-96	q: 1996-97	r: 1997-98	s: 1998-99	t: 1999-00	u: 2000-01	

Source: Same as Figure 3.5.

Table 3.9

Growth Rates of Real Agricultural Wages across the States between 1990 and 2000

State	*Growth Rate (%)*
Andhra Pradesh	1.3
Assam	-0.7
Bihar	0.3
Gujarat	5.1
Haryana	2.7
Karnataka	3.2
Kerala	7.9
Madhya Pradesh	1.8
Maharastra	1.6
Orissa	0.7
Punjab	-0.8
Rajastan	2.8
Tamil Nadu	6.7
Uttar Pradesh	2.5
West Bengal	1.6
All India	**2.5**

Source: Dreze and Sen (2002).

It is clearly borne out by the data that employment has not been increasing despite growth in agricultural sector. That provokes investigation into the search for a connection between the process of globalisation and typologies of employment. The experience of the last decade brings out that the growth in the agricultural sector has been generating more forces for casualisation of employment and the trends in casualisation are quite bold across the country. These trends are sharper in the agriculturally lagging regions. That leads us to the question of the quality of growth in the agricultural sector in the wake of globalisation in addition to the location of growth across regions. At the same time one cannot deny the influence of the quality of growth in the non-agricultural sector also. The trends in capital formation suggest that the employment scenario is a direct derivate of capital formation in the sector. In that context, a pragmatic policy is needed which is pointedly focused on efforts to correct the trends in capital formation and especially inducing the private capital formation at a higher rate of growth. Directing the growth inducing factors towards important components in agricultural sector is an undisputable prerequisite of such a policy.

Emerging Scenario

The impact of globalisation on agricultural economy involves both governance as well as analytical issues. The first set of issues address to the basic analytical concern namely: Can one take the decade of nineties as the period representing globalisation in the agricultural sector? Have all the significant changes in the governance of market took place during 1990-91 to facilitate globalisation? And such other queries derive no satisfactory answers. This is pertinent on the face of the fact that a large number of steps in governance were taken at distinct points of time during the decade of nineties and all of it did not happen at any one point of time. The globalisation of trade in agricultural sector was significant probably only in the post 1995. Moreover, one has to assume some gestation period for settling down the impact parameters. Second question points towards the data on trade of agricultural commodities at sub-national level. This is a major issue in governance while analysing the impact of globalisation. We have not yet developed a foolproof method to record commodity-wise data on trade originating from individual states. Commodities move towards ports of destination mostly by road or rail. These are unrecorded in the statistical system by their place of origin and purpose of movement. Therefore, the reliability of data at sub-national level is quite questionable. Third issue relates to the question about testing the hypothesis related to changes due to globalisation by adopting the usual 'before and after' approach. A good number of changes take place independent of the trade related factors. Lastly, one must be wary about the level of aggregation across commodities and regions while computing various trade related parameters like trade sensitivity, market access, aggregate measures of support etc. (Datta and Deodhar, 2000). It is necessary to discuss how one goes about these in terms of methodology.

The second set of issues relate to the study of growth behaviour across crops and regions in the face of the changes in the trade policies. It is essential to identify the crops and regions that have lagged or performed well in this period, and the reasons for such differential growth behaviour. The location of the trade sensitive commodities in the Indian context will help to monitor the changes that occur in their trade pattern (following WTO, 2003). There are a few methodological problems in the computation of commodity-region specific trade sensitivity indices. It is necessary to map these and discuss about the variables that will enter into such computations. Lastly, where and how do we set the trigger for activating the ameliorating measures, in the case of an alarming situation caused by import surges? Such situation can be confronted in these trade sensitive commodities.

The third set of issues deals with the impact of globalisation on the domestic prices. The methodological questions about the measurement of market and price integration between the world and domestic market need to be discussed carefully (Nayyar and Sen, 1994 and Deshpande and Naika, 2004). It is also necessary to decide the appropriate price data from among the available price series (FHP, WSP, MSP, Averages of selected markets, etc.) to be used for arriving at the measures of integration. This is more pertinent in view of the lack of domestic market integration. The character of the world market, the mechanism of price formation and the likely changes in price policy are a few important concerns for discussion (Chand and Jha, 2001). Even when we have problems about the intra-regional, inter-market integration, the global integration of the domestic markets needs to be understood carefully. In the face of this, how one should look at global integration, is an intriguing question. Similarly, the choice of the border prices across trading partners *vis-à-vis* that of the countries is also a ticklish issue. The concern about the food security in the context of globalisation has been voiced vociferously (Sharma, 1994, 2000, Shiva, 1999). While one cannot sideline the importance of food security in the context of India and the probable vulnerability, it will be imprudent to keep away from the forces of change in the present context. It is quite possible that any attempt to shy away from 'pro-active trade led growth' policy may land us into another worst situation.

References

Acharya, S.S. (2002). "Food Security and New International Trade Agreement: Perspectives from India", in G.S. Bhalla, J.L. Racine and F. Landy (Eds.), *Agriculture and The World Trade Organisation: Indian and French Perspectives*, Èditions de la Maison des sciences de l'homme, Paris.

Ahluwalia, Montek S. (1996). "New Economic Policy and Agriculture: Some Reflections", *Indian Journal of Agricultural Economics*, Vol. 51(3), July-September.

Bhalla, G.S. (1995). "Globalisation and Agricultural Policy in India", *Indian Journal of Agricultural Economics*, Vol. 50(1), January-March.

———. (2004). "Globalisation and Indian Agriculture", *State of the Indian Farmer: A Millennium Study*, Academic Foundation and Ministry of Agriculture, Government of India, New Delhi.

Chand, Ramesh and Dayanath Jha (2001). "Trade Liberalisation, Agricultural Prices and Net Social Welfare", in S.S. Acharya and D.P. Chaudhry (Eds.), *Indian Agricultural Policy at the Crossroads*, Rawat, Jaipur.

Dantwala, M.L. (1996). *Dilemmas of Growth–Indian Experience*, Sage, New Delhi.

Datta, Samar K. and Satish Y. Deodhar (Eds.) (2000). *Impact of WTO Agreements on Indian Agriculture*, Oxford and IBH, New Delhi.

Deshpande, R.S. (2002). "Agriculture, Natural Resource Management and Rural Development", Proceeding of a Seminar on *Developmental Reforms for Resurgent India: A Nodal Strategy*, Ministry of Culture and Tourism, Government of India (eds.), New Delhi.

Deshpande, R.S. and P. Thippiaiah (2000). *Impact of Removal of Quantitative Restrictions on Import of Agricultural Produce*, ISEC, Bangalore.

Deshpande, R.S. and T. Raveendra Naika (2004). "Moon in the Mirror: Farmer and the Minimum Support Prices in Karnataka", *Monograph* No. 7, Institute for Social and Economic Change, Bangalore.

Dreze, Jean and Amartya Sen (2002). *Development and Participation*, Oxford University Press, New Delhi.

Ghosh, Jayati (1997). "India's Structural Adjustment: An Assessment in Comparative Asian Context", *Economic and Political Weekly*, Vol. 32(20&21), May 17-30.

Government of India (2005). *Agricultural Statistics at a Glance*, Directorate of Economics and Statistics, Department of Agricultural and Cooperation, Ministry of Agriculture, New Delhi.

Gulati, Ashok and Tim Kelly (1999). *Trade Liberalisation and Indian Agriculture: Cropping Pattern Changes and Efficiency Gains in Semi Arid Tropics*, Oxford University Press, New Delhi.

Jha, Brajesh (2005). "Economic Policies for Augmenting Rural Employment in India", Paper presented at the Technical Workshop of ADB-MOF Project on *Policy Research Networking to Strengthen Policy Reforms*, ISEC, January.

Joshi, Vijay and IMD Little (1996). *India's Economic Reforms-1991-2001*, Oxford University Press, New Delhi.

Joshi, P.K., Ashok Gulati, Pratap S. Birthal, Laxmi Tewari (2004). "Agriculture Diversification in South Asia. Patters, Determinants and Policy Implications", *Economic and Political Weekly*, Vol. 39(24), pp.2457-2467.

Nayyar, Deepak and Abhijit Sen (1994). "International Trade and the Agricultural Sector in India", *Economic and Political Weekly*, Vol. 29(19), May 14.

Pangariya, Arvind (1999). "The Millennium Round and Developing Countries: Negotiating Strategies and Areas of Benefits", Paper Presented at the Conference on *Developing Countries and the New Multi-lateral Round of Trade Negotiations*, Harvard University, Harvard, November 5-6.

Parikh, Kirit S., N.S.S. Narayana, Manoj Panda and Ganesh Kumar (1997). "Agricultural Trade Liberalisation: Growth, Welfare and Large Country Effect", *Agricultural Economics*, Vol. 17, pp.1-20.

Rao, C.H. Hanumantha (2001). "WTO and Viability of Indian Agriculture", *Economic and Political Weekly*, Vol. 36, September 8.

Sen, Sunanda (2000). *Trade and Dependence: Essays on the Indian Economy*, Sage, New Delhi.

Sen, Sunanda and R. Upendra Das (1992). "Import Liberalisation as a Tool of Economic Policy in India since Mid-Eighties", *Economic and Political Weekly*, Vol. 27(12), March 21, pp.585-594.

Sen, Sunanda and Hiranya Mukhopadhyay (1994). "Devaluation, Liberalisation and Structural Linkages between India's Foreign Trade as National Income", *Economic and Political Weekly*, July 31.

Sharma, Devinder (1994). *GATT to WTO–Seeds of Despair*, Konark Publications, New Delhi.

———. (2000). "WTO and Agriculture: The End Result is Zero", *Hindu Business Line*, New Delhi, September 30.

Shiva, Vandana (1999). *Stolen Harvest: Hijacking of the World Food Supply*, South End Press, New Delhi.

Singh, Manmohan (1995). "Inaugural Address, Indian Society of Agricultural Economics", 54th Annual Conference, *Indian Journal of Agricultural Economics*, Vol. 50(1), January-March.

World Trade Organization (1998). *India Should Keep up with its Trade Reforms to Ensure Strong Economic Growth*, Press Release, April.

———. (2003). *Negotiations on Agriculture*, Report by the Chairman, Mr. Stuart Harbinson, July 7.

Part II

Prices and Subsidies

4

Input Subsidies and Agriculture

Future Perspectives

S.S. ACHARYA and R.L. JOGI

Introduction

Subsidies, as welfare augmenting instrument of fiscal policy, have been a common feature of economic management in most of the economies. In India, direct and indirect subsidies have been pervasive in several economic and social sectors including trade, transport, industry, agriculture, education and health. The objective of this chapter is to present the status of farm input subsidies in Indian agriculture and analyse the related issues in the emerging scenario. The chapter has been divided into seven sections. The first introductory section includes concept and methodology for estimation of subsidy. The trend in the level of major input subsidies during the last two decades (1980-81 to 2000-01) is analysed in the second section. This section includes growth rates, changes in composition and sources of growth in subsidies. State-wise distribution of subsidies is discussed in the third section. In the fourth section, crop-wise bifurcation of input subsidies has been attempted. The estimates pertaining to the share of different size groups of farms in total input subsidies are presented in the fifth section. The issues relating to the input subsidies and implications of their continuance or withdrawal are discussed in the sixth section. Concluding observations are given in the last section.

The chapter has been built on our earlier work in this area (Acharya, 1997a, 2000; Acharya and Jogi, 2004). Input subsidies in Indian agriculture are of two broad categories *viz.*, direct or explicit subsidies and indirect or implicit subsidies. Direct or explicit subsidies are in the nature of payments to the farmers to meet part of the cost of input and include subsidy on seeds of improved or high-yielding varieties, plant protection chemicals or equipments, crop-specific minikits and improved farm implements. These are usually made available to specified target groups such as, small and marginal farmers or those belonging to scheduled castes and tribes. Contrary to direct subsidies, indirect or implicit subsidies arise on account of pricing policy of certain inputs. There is no direct payment to farmers but as the inputs are supplied at a price or user charge lower than the cost of production, it amounts to implicit subsidisation of the input for the farmer. Direct or explicit subsidies account for a very small fraction of total input subsidies in Indian agriculture. A recent study based on a sample survey of farmers in Haryana has reported that direct input subsidies account for only about 1 per cent of the total subsidies accruing to the farmers. Implicit or indirect subsidies on fertilisers, electricity for agriculture and canal water account for 99 per cent of total input subsidies in Indian agriculture (Tuteja, 2003). The focus in this chapter is, therefore, on the subsidies on fertilisers, electricity and canal water. The methodology for estimation of subsidies on these key inputs has been extensively discussed and reported in the literature (Gulati, 1989; Gulati and Narayanan, 2000, 2003; Acharya and Jogi, 2004). The subsidy on fertilisers is the difference between farmers' price and normative cost of production (for domestic fertilisers) or its landed cost (for imported fertilisers). In the case of decontrolled fertilisers (phosphatic and potassic), the subsidy component is directly released by the central government to the states. The estimates of fertiliser subsidy are available in centre's budget documents. In the case of electricity for agriculture and canal water, the estimates of subsidy depend on the method of estimation. The subsidy on electricity for agriculture is estimated as the difference between the unit cost of generation, transmission and distribution and user charges collected from the farmers, multiplied by the reported electricity supply to this sector. The subsidy on canal water is the difference between the water charges collected from the farmers and cost of operation and maintenance of public irrigation systems. Some argue for inclusion of some capital cost also in computation of subsidy on canal water. Contrary to fertiliser subsidy, which is borne by the central government, the subsidy on electricity for agriculture and canal water is borne by the respective state governments.

All-India estimates of electricity subsidy for agricultural purposes are available in the annual reports of electricity departments, brought out by the Power and Energy Division of the Planning Commission, Government of India. These Planning Commission estimates are higher than the estimates of electricity subsidy reported by the Ministry of Agriculture (Government of India, 2003), quoting Central Statistical Organisation on page 147 of *Agricultural Statistics at a Glance*, 2003. We have used Planning Commission figures, which are, overestimates of electricity subsidy to the agricultural sector.

The all-India subsidy on canal irrigation was estimated as per the method suggested by Gulati and Narayanan (2003). According to this simple method:

$$CIS = OME + DEP - IIC$$

where CIS is canal irrigation subsidy; OME is the total cost of operation and maintenance of government irrigation systems; DEP is the depreciation on irrigation works computed as the difference of GDP (gross domestic product) and NDP (net domestic product) of the irrigation sector; and IIC is irrigation charges collected from the farmers of irrigation command areas. The information on OME, GDP, NDP and IIC was collected from National Accounts Statistics.

Trends in Input Subsidies and Sources of Growth

The estimates of major input subsidies in Indian agriculture during the last two decades are shown in Table 4.1. There has been a consistent increasing trend in the fertiliser subsidy which went up from Rs. 505 crore in 1980-81 to Rs. 4,389 crore in 1990-91 and further to Rs. 13,800 crore in 2000-01. There are three important aspects of trend in fertiliser subsidy which need to be noted. First, the growth rate of fertiliser subsidy has decelerated during the nineties. The subsidy on fertilisers, which during the eighties had recorded a compound growth rate of 24.1 per cent per annum, increased at the rate of 12.1 per cent per annum during the nineties. Second, the deceleration in the growth of fertiliser subsidy during the nineties was observed mainly due to the lower base during the eighties. The rate of increase in fertiliser subsidy in absolute terms during the nineties was considerably higher than that during the eighties. The rate of increase in fertiliser subsidy during the eighties was Rs. 388 crore per year, whereas it was Rs. 941 crore per year during the nineties. And third, the share of subsidy on imported fertilisers in the total fertiliser subsidy has consistently declined during the last two decades. During 1980-81, out of a total fertiliser subsidy of Rs. 505 crore, as much as 66.3 per cent (Rs. 335 crore) was on imported fertilisers. In 1990-1991, the share of subsidy on imported fertilisers declined to 15.0 per cent (Rs. 659 crore out of Rs. 4,389 crore). In 2000-01, the share of fertiliser subsidy on imported fertiliser further declined and became almost negligible.

Table 4.1

Trends in Major Input Subsidies in Indian Agriculture

Particulars	*Fertiliser*	*Electricity*	*Canal Water*	*Total*
Subsidy (Rs. in Crore)				
1980-81	505	334	581	1420
1990-91	4389	4605	2468	11462
2000-01	13800	26950	9690	50440
Compound Growth Rate (Point to Point)				
1980-81 to 1990-91	24.1	30.0	15.6	23.2
1990-91 to 2000-01	12.1	19.3	14.7	16.0
Rate of Absolute Increase (Per Year)				
1980-81 to 1990-91	388	427	189	1004
1990-91 to 2000-01	941	2234	722	3897
Share in Total Subsidies (Per Cent)				
1980-81	35.6	23.5	40.9	100.0
1990-91	38.3	40.2	21.5	100.0
2000-01	27.4	53.4	19.2	100.0

Source: For first three rows: Government of India, *Economic Survey*, Various Annual Issues; Planning Commission (2000, 2002), Acharya (2000); Gulati and Narayanan (2003); and Acharya and Jogi (2004).

The subsidy on electricity supplied to the agricultural sector also shows a consistent increasing trend during the last two decades. The electricity subsidy in Indian agriculture went up from Rs. 334 crore during 1980-81 to Rs. 4,605 crore during 1990-91 and further to Rs. 26,950 crore during 2000-01. As observed in the case of fertiliser subsidy, the growth of electricity subsidy has also decelerated during the nineties from 30.0 per cent per annum during the eighties to 19.3 per cent per annum during the nineties. However, in absolute terms, the rate of increase in electricity subsidy during the nineties was considerably higher than that during the eighties. While, during the eighties, the electricity subsidy in Indian agriculture increased at the rate of Rs. 427 crore per year, during the nineties, it went up by Rs. 2,234 crore per year. An important aspect of the trend in electricity subsidy that needs to be noted is that the growth of electricity subsidy, both in absolute and percentage terms, during the eighties as well as during the nineties, has been higher than that for the fertiliser subsidy.

Similar to the trend in fertiliser and electricity subsidy, the subsidy on canal irrigation has also been consistently going up in the country. The canal irrigation subsidy went up from Rs. 581 crore in 1980-81 to Rs. 2,468 crore in 1990-91 and further to Rs. 9,690 crore in 2000-2001. The growth in canal irrigation subsidy during the eighties was 15.6 per cent per annum and during the nineties was 14.7 per cent per annum. In absolute terms, the average incremental subsidy on canal irrigation was Rs. 189 crore per year during the eighties and Rs. 722 crore per year during the nineties.

Considering all the three major inputs together, the input subsidies in Indian agriculture went up from Rs. 1,420 crore during 1980-81 to Rs. 11,462 crore during 1990-91 and further to Rs. 50,440 crore during 2000-01. The growth rate of total input subsidies, which was 23.2 per cent per annum during the eighties, decelerated to 16.0 per cent per annum during the nineties. However, in absolute terms, the increase in total subsidies during the nineties at Rs. 3897 crore per annum was more than 3.8 times of the rate of increase during the eighties (Rs. 1,004 crore per annum).

One other aspect of trend in the major input subsidies in Indian agriculture is the change in the relative shares of three key farm inputs in total subsidy. During 1980-81, canal water subsidy accounted for 40.9 per cent, fertiliser subsidy 35.6 per cent and electricity subsidy accounted for only 23.5 per cent of the total subsidies in Indian agriculture. During the eighties, the increase in electricity subsidy was at a considerably higher rate and of canal irrigation subsidy was at considerably lower rate. As a consequence, while the share of electricity subsidy in the total subsidy went up to 40.2 per cent, that of canal irrigation subsidy declined to 21.5 per cent. During this period, the share of fertiliser subsidy in the total subsidy increased marginally to 38.3 per cent. During the nineties, while the share of electricity subsidy in the total subsidy went-up further, that of fertiliser and canal irrigation subsidies declined. During 2000-01, electricity subsidy accounted for 53.4 per cent of total subsidy, with fertiliser subsidy accounting for 27.4 per cent and canal irrigation subsidy 19.2 per cent of total input subsidies in Indian agriculture.

The observed increasing trend in input subsidies needs to be related to the growth of use of these three inputs, because even if the per unit subsidy remains the same over time, the total subsidy bill may increase owing to the increase in the consumption of fertilisers, increase in the use of electricity for irrigation and expansion in canal irrigated areas. It is, therefore, important to bifurcate the incremental subsidy on these three inputs according to the two trivial sources of growth *viz.*, increase in the use of inputs and increase in per unit subsidy. The results presented in Table 4.2, reveal that it was mainly the increase in per unit subsidy, which contributed to the expansion of subsidy bill during the last 20 years (Acharya and Jogi, 2004). The increase in the use of fertilisers contributed around one-fourth of the total increase in fertiliser subsidy, with three-fourths being contributed by increase in per unit fertiliser subsidy. In the case of electricity subsidy, increase in electricity use in agriculture contributed 37.4 per cent of the incremental electricity subsidy, with 62.6 per cent being contributed by the increase in per unit electricity subsidy. There has been very little expansion in canal irrigated area during the last 20 years. While the O&M expenses of canal systems have been going up, the increase in the irrigation rates has been negligible. Therefore, as much as 98.5 per cent of the incremental subsidy on canal irrigation during the last 20 years was attributed to increase in per hectare subsidy, with expansion in canal irrigation contributing only 1.5 per cent of the incremental subsidy. Combined for all the three inputs, 81 per cent of the incremental subsidy is attributed to growth in rate of subsidy and only 19 per cent to the expansion in the use of these inputs.

Table 4.2

Sources of Growth in Input Subsidies (1980-81 to 1999-00)

Particulars	*Expansion in Input Use*	*Increase in Per Unit Subsidy*	*Total*
Fertiliser	24.5	75.5	100.0
Electricity	37.4	62.6	100.0
Canal Irrigation	1.5	98.5	100.0
All Three	**19.0**	**81.0**	**100.0**

Source: Acharya and Jogi (2004).

State-wise Subsidy on Farm Inputs

For estimating the input subsidy at the state level, total subsidy on fertilisers at all-India level was distributed among states on the basis of states' share in total fertiliser consumption in India. The state-level fertiliser-use data are available in official publications. The state-wise electricity subsidy estimates for the period beginning 1992-93 are available in Annual Reports of State Electricity Boards and Electricity Departments, published by the Planning Commission, Government of India (2000, 2002). For the earlier period, the national-level estimates of electricity subsidy were apportioned to the states according to the state shares in total electricity, reportedly consumed in agricultural sector. The state-level estimates of canal irrigation subsidy were generated on the basis of share of each state in total canal irrigated area at the all-India level.

The state-wise distribution of input subsidies at three points of time during the last 20 years (1980-81, 1990-91 and 2000-01) is given in Table 4.3. The state-wise analysis of subsidies is quite revealing. In the case of fertiliser subsidy, there are four important observations. First, Uttar Pradesh has the highest share in all-India fertiliser subsidy throughout the 20-year period. Its share in total fertiliser subsidy was 20.8 per cent in 1980-81, 17.9 per cent in 1990-91 and 18.4 per cent in 2000-01. Second, the share and rank of Punjab in total fertiliser subsidy has been consistently declining during the last 20 years. The share of Punjab in total fertiliser subsidy, declined from 13.7 per cent in 1980-81 to 9.5 per cent in 1990-91 and further to 7.9 per cent in 2000-01. The rank of Punjab in terms of fertiliser subsidy came down from two in 1980-81 to four in 1990-91 and further to five in 2000-

2001. Third, during 2000-01, the first four states in terms of the highest share of fertiliser subsidy were Uttar Pradesh, Andhra Pradesh, Maharashtra and Karnataka, which together accounted for around 49.3 per cent of the total fertiliser subsidy in the country. And fourth, contrary to the general perception, the share of Punjab and Haryana together, in the total fertiliser subsidy was only 13.4 per cent during 2000-01.

Table 4.3

State-wise Input Subsidies in Indian Agriculture

(Rs. in Crore)

States	Fertiliser			Electricity			Canal Irrigation		
	1980-81	1990-91	2000-01	1980-81	1990-91	2000-01	1980-81	1990-91	2000-01
Andhra Pradesh	53	567	1797	22	591	3685	64	273	880
Bihar	19	209	816	10	134	586	42	159	612
Gujarat	33	247	620	31	520	4577	14	69	324
Haryana	21	205	768	22	248	1896	44	195	776
Karnataka	32	291	1114	9	405	1899	21	126	535
Kerala	9	85	143	2	19	97	4	16	46
Madhya Pradesh	18	284	794	8	231	3134	39	224	971
Maharashtra	38	442	1361	40	604	2586	16	66	566
Orissa	7	68	264	1	17	*	30	132	511
Punjab	69	419	1086	43	466	2251	54	223	698
Rajasthan	12	130	550	23	217	2056	36	198	872
Tamil Nadu	45	291	796	55	371	2443	34	112	467
Uttar Pradesh	105	784	2535	64	710	1257	121	466	1674
West Bengal	26	263	896	2	42	390	36	105	386
Others	18	104	260	2	30	93**	26	104	372
All India	**505**	**4389**	**13800**	**334**	**4605**	**26950**	**581**	**2468**	**9690**

Note: * Not available.

** Includes for Orissa also.

In the case of electricity subsidy, the share of Uttar Pradesh was the highest during 1980-81 as well as during 1990-91. During 1990-1991, the first four states in order of the share in the total electricity subsidy were Uttar Pradesh, Maharashtra, Andhra Pradesh and

Gujarat, which together accounted for 52.7 per cent of the total electricity (for agriculture) subsidy in the country. The share of Punjab in total electricity subsidy was only 10 per cent during 1990-91. There has been considerable increase in the electricity subsidy during the nineties. The increase in electricity subsidy between 1990-91 and 2000-01 was estimated as Rs. 22,345 crore (from Rs. 4,605 crore to Rs. 26,950 crore). Of the total incremental subsidy during this period, Gujarat accounted for 18.1 per cent, Andhra Pradesh 14.1 per cent, Madhya Pradesh 13.0 per cent, Tamil Nadu 9.3 per cent, Maharashtra 8.9 per cent and Rajasthan accounted for 8.2 per cent. These six states together accounted for 72.2 per cent of the incremental electricity subsidy in Indian agriculture during the nineties. The share of Haryana in total electricity subsidy during 2000-01 was only 7 per cent.

As regards canal irrigation subsidy, in 1980-81, out of a total subsidy of Rs. 581 crore, Uttar Pradesh accounted for 20.8 per cent, Andhra Pradesh 11.0 per cent and Punjab accounted for 9.3 per cent. In 1990-91, Madhya Pradesh improved its share in canal irrigation subsidy to 9.1 per cent from only 6.7 per cent in 1980-81. During 1990-91, Uttar Pradesh, Andhra Pradesh, Madhya Pradesh and Punjab, together accounted for 48 per cent of the total canal irrigation subsidy in the country. During 2000-01 Madhya Pradesh, Rajasthan and Haryana improved their ranks and share in total canal irrigation subsidy. The share of Uttar Pradesh in total irrigation subsidy continued to be the highest (17.2 per cent) in the country. It was followed by Madhya Pradesh (10.0 per cent), Andhra Pradesh (9.1 per cent), Rajasthan (9.0 per cent) and Haryana (7.9 per cent). These five states together accounted for 53.2 per cent of total canal irrigation subsidy in the country during 2000-01. It may be mentioned here that the share of Punjab in total canal irrigation subsidy during 2000-01 was only 7.2 per cent.

The state-wise break-up of total subsidies (combined for all three major inputs) is shown in Table 4.4. There are several aspects of state-wise distribution of subsidies in Indian agriculture, which are evident from this analysis. First, Uttar Pradesh, which topped the list of states in terms of share in total subsidies in 1980-81 and 1990-91, came down to third rank in 2000-01. Second, Andhra Pradesh, continuously improved its rank from third in 1980-81 to second in 1990-91 and occupied the first rank in 2000-01. Third, the rank of Punjab dropped from second in 1980-81 to fourth in 1990-91 and further to sixth in 2000-01. Fourth, Gujarat and Madhya Pradesh states recorded continuous improvement in their ranks in terms of their shares in total subsidies during the last two decades. And fifth, there has been a consistent decline in the share of Bihar, West Bengal and Orissa in total subsidies in Indian agriculture.

Table 4.4

State-wise Shares in Total Input Subsidies

*States**	*1980-81*		*1990-91*		*2000-01*	
	Rs. in Crore	*%*	*Rs. in Crore*	*%*	*Rs. in Crore*	*%*
Andhra Pradesh	139 (3)	9.8	1431 (2)	12.5	6362 (1)	12.6
Gujarat	78 (7)	5.5	836 (5)	7.3	5521 (2)	11.0
Uttar Pradesh	290 (1)	20.5	1960 (1)	17.1	5466 (3)	10.8
Madhya Pradesh	65 (10)	4.6	739 (8)	6.4	4899 (4)	9.7
Maharashtra	94 (5)	6.6	1112 (3)	9.7	4513 (5)	8.9
Punjab	166 (2)	11.7	1108 (4)	9.7	4035 (6)	8.0
Tamil Nadu	134 (4)	9.4	774 (7)	6.8	3706 (7)	7.3
Karanataka	62 (12)	4.3	822 (6)	7.2	3548 (8)	7.0
Rajasthan	71 (8)	5.0	545 (10)	4.7	3478 (9)	6.9
Haryana	87 (6)	6.1	648 (9)	5.6	3440 (10)	6.8
Bihar	71 (9)	5.0	502 (11)	4.4	2014 (11)	4.0
West Bengal	64 (11)	4.5	410 (12)	3.6	1672 (12)	3.3
Orissa	38 (13)	2.7	217 (13)	1.9	775 (13)	1.6
Kerala	15 (14)	1.0	120 (14)	1.0	286 (14)	0.6
Others	46 (-)	3.3	238 (-)	2.1	725 (-)	1.5
Total	**1420**	**100.0**	**11462**	**100.0**	**50440**	**100.0**

Note: Figures in the parentheses are ranks in descending order.
* States arranged according to their rank in 2000-01.

The results pertaining to the share of different states in total subsidies in Indian agriculture need to be interpreted with caution because of wide interstate differences in cropped area. The gross cropped area (GCA) across states varies from 3 million hectares in Kerala to 26.20 million hectares in Madhya Pradesh. It is, therefore, advisable to look at the interstate differences in input subsidies on per hectare of GCA basis. These estimates are given in Table 4.5. At the all-India level, the input subsidy per hectare of GCA is estimated at Rs. 2,658. Per hectare input subsidy is the highest in Haryana at Rs. 5,705 per hectare. The subsidy per hectare is also relatively higher in Tamil Nadu (Rs. 5,683), Gujarat (Rs. 5,440), Punjab (Rs. 4,896), and Andhra Pradesh (Rs. 4,886). In Kerala and Orissa, the subsidy per hectare of GCA was the lowest at below Rs. 1000 per hectare. In other states, the subsidy varied between Rs. 1,753 and Rs. 2,932 per hectare. The interstate disparity in the subsidy available to the farmers is obviously quite glaring.

Table 4.5

State-wise Input Subsidies Per Hectare of Gross Cropped Area (2000-01)

States	*Total Input Subsidies (Rs. in Crore)*	*Gross Cropped Area (Million Ha)**	*Subsidy (Rs./Ha)*
Andhra Pradesh	6362	13.02	4886
Bihar	2014	9.98	2018
Gujarat	5521	10.15	5440
Haryana	3440	6.03	5705
Karnataka	3548	12.10	2932
Kerala	286	3.00	954
Madhya Pradesh	4899	26.20	1870
Maharashtra	4512	22.35	2019
Orissa	775	8.52	909
Punjab	4035	8.24	4896
Rajasthan	3478	19.29	1803
Tamil Nadu	3706	6.52	5683
Uttar Pradesh	5466	26.15	2090
West Bengal	1672	9.54	1753
Others	725	8.65	839
Total	**50440**	**189.74**	**2658**

Note: * Pertains to 1999-2000.

Crop-wise Input Subsidies

The subsidies being analysed in this chapter are by definition input-specific and not product-specific. Nevertheless, on the basis of information available on crop-wise use of these inputs, it is possible to bifurcate the input subsidies into major crops of India. All-India Input Survey of 1991-92 (Government of India, 1991-92), provides information on share of different crops in the total fertiliser used in the country. These shares were used to assign fertiliser subsidy to different crops. The subsidies on electricity for irrigation and canal water were allocated to different crops in proportion to their share in the gross irrigated area in the country. The crop-wise estimates of input subsidies during 2000-01 are given in Table 4.6. According to these estimates, paddy (rice) accounts for 32.1 per cent of total input subsidies in Indian agriculture. Wheat, another staple food crop, accounts for 27.5 per cent of total subsidies. These two major staple crops, together account for 59.6 per cent of the total input subsidies in Indian agriculture. With *jowar, bajra* and maize, together accounting for 4.8 per cent, it is evident that 64.4 per cent of the total input subsidies are being used in the production of cereals. The share of pulses in the total subsidies is around 2.2 per cent. Two major oilseeds of the country *viz.*, groundnut and rapeseed/mustard account for 6.4 per cent and sugarcane accounts for 5.1 per cent of total input subsidies. Cotton, a fibre crop, accounts for only 4.4 per cent of total subsidies. Obviously, the bulk of the input subsidies are being used in the production of staple cereals and other food crops, thus helping in improving the food security base of the country's population.

The crop-wise share in total input subsidy conceals quite a bit of information because of large variation in area under different crops. Input subsidy per hectare of cropped area is, therefore, more revealing in terms of incidence of input subsidies across crops. Per hectare input subsidies for different crops are also shown in (the last column of) Table 4.6. There is considerable intercrop variation in per hectare input subsidy. Sugarcane has the highest input subsidy of Rs. 6,099 per hectare followed by wheat (Rs. 5,039), paddy (Rs. 3,587), rapeseed/mustard (Rs. 3,306) and cotton (Rs. 2,573). *Bajra, jowar* and *tur*, mostly grown under rainfed or retained moisture conditions, have the lowest per hectare subsidy.

Table 4.6

Crop-wise Distribution of Input Subsidy (2000-01)

Crops	*Per Cent of Fertiliser Use*	*Per Cent of Electricity & Canal Use*	*Subsidy (Rs. Crore)*				*Subsidy Per Ha of Crop Area (Rs.)* *
			Fertiliser	*Elect. + Canal*	*Total*	*Per Cent*	
Paddy	35.05	31.01	4838	11362	16200	32.12	3587
Wheat	19.29	30.54	2662	11190	13852	27.46	5039
Jowar	3.55	1.01	490	370	860	1.71	839
Bajra	1.39	0.94	192	344	536	1.06	603
Maize	2.64	1.87	364	685	1049	2.08	1634
Gram	0.61	2.28	84	835	919	1.82	1495
Tur	0.83	0.19	115	70	184	0.37	537
Groundnut	4.69	1.66	647	608	1255	2.49	1827
Rape & Mustard	1.54	4.86	213	1781	1993	3.95	3306
Sugarcane	5.51	4.95	760	1814	2574	5.10	6099
Cotton	5.86	3.91	808	1433	2241	4.44	2573
Others	19.04	16.78	2627	6148	8775	17.40	1564
Total	**100.00**	**100.00**	**13800**	**36640**	**50440**	**100.00**	**2658**

Note: * Crop-wise areas for the year 1999-2000 were used.

The analysis was extended to look at the input subsidies per quintal of output. For this purpose, the crop-wise input subsidy per hectare was divided by the average yield of crops. The estimates are presented in Table 4.7. Per quintal input subsidy was relatively higher for cotton (Rs. 451) and rapeseed/mustard (Rs. 354). For rice, wheat, gram and groundnut, the subsidy was in the close range of Rs. 186 to Rs. 201 per quintal. For *kharif* cereals and *tur*, it varied from Rs. 87 to Rs. 110 per quintal. For sugarcane, due to the bulky nature of the crop output, the input subsidy per quintal was the lowest at Rs. 9 per quintal.

It was also tried to relate the input subsidies to product prices. The minimum support prices for these crops were used for this purpose. For rice, the support price was derived by multiplying the support price of A-gradc paddy by 1.5, assuming the rice-paddy ratio of 67 per cent. For sugarcane, the statutory minimum price linked to the recovery of 8.5 per cent was used. The results presented in the last column of Table 4.7 reveal that input subsidy as a percentage of prices was around 30 for wheat and rapeseed/mustard and between 15 to 25 for other crops except pigeon pea. In the case of pigeon pea, the ratio was as low as 7.2.

Table 4.7

Crop-wise Per Quintal Subsidy on Inputs in Indian Agriculture (2000-01)

Crops	*Yield (kg\ha)*	*Subsidy (Rs.\ha)*	*Subsidy (Rs.\Qtl.)*	*Subsidy as Percentage of Support Price*
Rice	1901	3587	189	35.0 (540)
Wheat	2708	5039	186	30.5 (610)
Jowar	764	839	110	24.7 (445)
Bajra	688	603	88	19.8 (445)
Maize	1822	1634	90	20.2 (445)
Gram	744	1495	201	18.3 (1100)
Tur	618	537	87	7.2 (1200)
Groundnut	977	1827	187	15.3 (1220)
Rape & Mustard	935	3306	354	29.5 (1200)
Sugarcane	68577	6099	9	15.1 (59.50)
Cotton (Kapas)	570	2573	451	27.8 (1625)

Note: Figures in parentheses are support price for the crop year 2000-01.

The crop-wise bifurcation of input subsidies, presented earlier in this section revealed considerable tilt in favour of irrigated crops. This is not surprising. Subsidies on electricity for irrigation and canal water, are obviously subsidies going to irrigated crops. As regards fertiliser subsidies, the results of input survey for 1991-92 reveal that 68.4 per cent of the total fertiliser used in the country is applied to irrigated areas, with 31.6 per cent going to unirrigated areas. The bifurcation of total input subsidies based on these facts, as shown in Table 4.8, reveals that 91.4 per cent of the total input subsidies are going to irrigated areas, with unirrigated areas accounting for only 8.6 per cent. The value of input subsidies accruing to unirrigated areas was estimated as Rs. 385 per hectare of GCA as against Rs. 6039 per hectare for irrigated areas.

Table 4.8

Input Subsidies for Unirrigated and Irrigated Areas (2000-01)

Particulars	*Unirrigated Area*	*Irrigated Area*	*Total*
Proportion of Total Fertiliser Use (%)	31.6	68.4	100.0
Input Subsidies (Rs. in Crore)			
Fertiliser Subsidy	4361	9439	13800
Electricity Subsidy	-	26950	26950
Canal Irrigation Subsidy	-	9690	9690
Total Subsidy	4361	46079	50440
Per Cent of Total Subsidy	8.6	91.4	100.0
Gross Cropped Area (Million Ha)*	113.4	76.3	189.7
Per Hectare Subsidy (Rs.)	385	6039	2658

Note: * Pertains to 1999-2000.

Farm Size and Input Subsidies

The information pertaining to the share of different farm size groups in input subsidies is not directly available. Some approximate estimates were generated for the year 2000-01, by following the approach used by Acharya and Jogi (2004). The fertiliser subsidy was apportioned to different size groups as per the share of different size groups in total fertiliser use in the country, as available from *All-India Report on Input Survey*, brought out by the Ministry of Agriculture, Government of India (1991-92). This survey reveals that out of the total fertiliser used in the country, 20.6 per cent is used by marginal farmers, 21.1 per cent by small farmers, 24.2 per cent by semi-medium farmers, 23.9 per cent by medium farmers and only 10.2 per cent is used by the large farmers.

As regards the share of different size groups of farms in electricity subsidy, we used the estimates of share of each group in total irrigated area by electrified wells, generated by Acharya and Jogi (2004). According to these estimates, out of the total irrigated area by electrified wells, marginal farms accounted for 14.1 per cent, small farms 17.9 per cent, semi-medium farms 25.3 per cent, medium farms 29.9 per cent and large farms accounted for 12.8 per cent.

Agricultural Census Report (Government of India, 1998) provides information on share of different size groups of farms in total canal-irrigated area in the country. This information was used to allocate the total canal irrigation subsidy, for the year 2000-01, to different size groups. Out of total canal irrigated area in the country, marginal farms account for 21.4 per cent, small farms 19.5 per cent, semi-medium farms 23.3 per cent, medium farms 24.6 per cent and large farms account for 11.2 per cent.

Based on these assumptions, the estimates of input subsidies accruing to different size groups of farms are given in Table 4.9. According to these estimates, marginal farms account for 17.3 per cent and small farms account for 19.1 per cent of total input subsidies in Indian agriculture. The combined share of marginal and small farmers (36.4 per cent) in total input subsidies is not lower than their share in the total operated area (36 per cent) in the country. As regards the semi-medium and medium farms, their share in total input subsidies at 51.8 per cent was marginally higher than their share in total operated area (49.1 per cent). Contrary to general perception, the share of large farms in total input subsidies at 11.8 per cent was considerably lower than their share in total operated area (14.8 per cent).

Table 4.9

Share of Marginal and Small Farms in Input Subsidies (2000-01)

(Rs. in Crore)

Farm Size Groups	*Fertiliser Subsidy*	*Electricity Subsidy*	*Canal Water Subsidy*	*Total Subsidy*
Marginal	2840	3807	2071	8718 (17.3)
Small	2917	4822	1893	9633 (19.1)
Semi-Medium	3337	6810	2254	12402 (24.6)
Medium	3293	8071	2382	13745 (27.2)
Large	1413	3439	1090	5942 (11.8)
Total	**13800**	**26950**	**9690**	**50440 (100.0)**

Note: Figures in the parentheses are percentages to total subsidy.

The analysis was extended further to compare the input subsidies per unit area operated by different size groups of farms. The details shown in Table 4.10, reveal that subsidy accruing on per hectare basis on marginal, small and semi-medium farms did not differ significantly and was in the range of Rs. 3,100 to Rs. 3,184 per hectare. On medium farms, it was little higher at Rs. 3,320 per hectare. It was the lowest on large farms at Rs. 2,459 per hectare.

Table 4.10

Estimated Subsidy Per Hectare for Different Size Groups of Farms (2000-01)

Farm Size	*Total Subsidy (Rs. in Crore)*	*Operated Area (Million Ha)**	*Subsidy Per Hectare (Rs.)*
Marginal	8718	28.12	3100
Small	9633	30.72	3136
Semi-Medium	12402	38.95	3184
Medium	13745	41.40	3320
Large	5942	24.16	2459
All	**50440**	**163.35**	**3088**

Note: * Pertains to 1995-96.

Issues and Implications of Continuation or Withdrawal

Farm input subsidies in Indian agriculture have remained one of the most important debated aspects of Indian agricultural policy, since the launch of economic reforms programme in 1991. The debate mainly revolved around the following inter-related issues:

(i) The role of input subsidies in achieving foodgrain self-sufficiency, improving food security and in the growth of agricultural production.

(ii) The method of estimation of subsidies, particularly those relating to computation of normative cost of domestic fertiliser manufacturing; accounting for the inefficiencies in generation, transmission and distribution systems of electricity; and handling of inflated capital costs and inefficiencies in operation and management of public irrigation works.

(iii) The extent to which the estimated input subsidies can be considered to have accrued to the farmers and alternatively, how much of these are on account of the inefficient supply systems.

(iv) Ever-rising level of input subsidies and erosion in the capacity of central and state governments to bear these subsidies.

(v) Level of farm input subsidies *vis-à-vis* the hidden subsidies (including concessions and exemptions) prevalent in other sectors of the economy like transport, education, health, trade and industry.

(vi) Implications of the rise in input prices/user charges for farm incomes, food security and poverty levels of small and marginal farmers.

(vii) Possible compensation to farmers for rise in fertiliser prices and user charges for electricity and canal water by hike in support prices and implications of such a compensation on the rest of the economy.

(viii) Other possible options to contain the level of input subsidies and to reduce inefficiencies in the use of these critical inputs.

While looking at the implications of continuation or withdrawal of input subsidies, it is important to recall the genesis of these subsidies which can be traced to the philosophy and objectives of agricultural development strategy pursued in the country since the middle of 1960s. The philosophy was based on the recognition that even if the farmer produces efficiently after applying modern technology, he may be put to the undeserved loss by the market place, which is characterised by several imperfections and thus, lose the enthusiasm for increasing production. Therefore, along with the provision of a production technology package and an efficient system of delivery of modern inputs and services, a remunerative and stable price environment was considered an important prerequisite to build a sound agricultural economy in the country. The strategy was designed and pursued to achieve the twin objectives of augmenting the production of agricultural commodities by assuring remunerative prices to the farmers and simultaneously, providing staple food to the masses at reasonable and affordable prices. The simultaneous achievement of these twin objectives required balancing of the interests of farmers and consumers, which, in the short-run, obviously conflict with each other. Both input subsidies and output price support programmes were, therefore, used as complementary instruments of the policy aimed at promoting production/productivity and holding the price line.

It is, therefore, advisable to look at the input subsidies not merely from the angle of finances of electricity departments/boards and canal irrigation units but their overall role in agricultural/rural development and food security of the country. While looking at the implications of presence or withdrawal of input subsidies, the following needs to be kept in view.

First, input subsidies enabled the country to keep the food prices low and yet helped in providing reasonable returns to the farmers to motivate them to increase the production of food and other agricultural commodities. The country has become quite comfortable in terms of foodgrains availability. This could be achieved even by keeping the food prices at affordable levels, mainly owing to the continuation of input subsidies in the agricultural sector. Lower foodgrain prices not only helped in increasing the economic access of the masses to food but also enabled the industry, organised sector and the government to provide employment at lower wage bills. Rise in fertiliser prices and user charges for electricity and canal water may negatively affect economic access to food and also, economic conditions of farmers, which continue to be a matter of concern. The production and employment in rural areas may decline.

Second, the volumes and levels of input subsidies presented in this chapter and elsewhere, are not net transfers to the farmers using these inputs. The kind of output price policies pursued in the country did not allow all the benefits of technology and input subsidies to be retained by the farmers. Further, a large part of fertiliser subsidy is the cost of maintaining some degree of self-reliance in fertiliser production. The estimated electricity subsidy includes inefficiency of some power plants, high transmission and distribution losses, pilferage in electricity, non-recovery of electricity dues and inflated consumption of electricity attributed to the agricultural sector. Similarly, the canal irrigation subsidy includes, inflated costs and inefficient management of public irrigation systems. Thus, the actual subsidies accruing to the farmers for use of these inputs is considerably lower than the estimated subsidies. Therefore, improving the efficiency in the production and management system of these key farm inputs can reduce a substantial part of burden of input subsidies on central or state governments.

Third, as regards the part of the estimated subsidies which really accrues to the farmers, it ought to be recognised that the kind of output price policies pursued in the country and inefficiencies in the output marketing system did not enable the farmers to retain all the benefits of lower input prices or user charges. The economic conditions of several sections of farmers continue to be well below the minimum desired level, because the benefits of input subsidies have been shared by all the sectors of the economy, as mentioned earlier.

Fourth, the argument that withdrawal of input subsidies will increase the use-efficiency of these inputs by reducing their overuse is untenable because it challenges the rationality of Indian farmers. In general, Indian farmers do not operate in the third stage of production function. If some farmers, due to ignorance, use higher than technically recommended levels of fertilisers and water, educating them in better on-farm water management practices and expanding soil-testing facilities is a better option than raising the user charges and squeezing farm incomes further. Overdrawal of groundwater in certain areas is not on account of availability of cheaper electricity. If the reasons for overdrawal of groundwater are irregular and uncertain availability of electricity or early transplantation of paddy in May requiring additional water for irrigation in dry months of May and June, raise in user charges for electricity may hardly help in reducing overdrawal of water.

Fifth, some analysts suggest that while withdrawing the input subsidies (by raising user charges), raising the output prices should suitably compensate the farmers. However, these arguments do not recognise several limitations of this option. Raising output prices cannot compensate marginal and small farmers, or those farmers, who have no or very little marketed surplus (nearly 80 per cent of farmers). For these farmers, input prices are critical for their livelihood security. Further, as majority of these farmers are net buyers of foodgrains, they would end up in paying higher prices for both inputs and outputs. Moreover, output prices of most farm products are not administered prices and markets will not automatically compensate the growers of these products. Such a compensatory mechanism does exist for rice and wheat, but in these products also, the price support operations are required to be carried out only in few states and that too for a part of the produce. Rise in support prices would not help rice and wheat growers of those areas where support operations are not required.

Sixth, a rise in support prices of rice and wheat should not be considered a preferred option over continuation of input subsidies because it would (a) lead to rise in the level of food and other prices, (b) lead to rise in wages and wage bills because wages are linked to the consumer price index (CPI) and these two staples have a considerable weightage in CPI, (c) require government to acquire large quantities of grains at unduly enhanced support prices, and (d) raise subsidy outgo on food, thus, not only nullifying the savings on input subsidies but also increasing the overall subsidy burden of the economy.

And seventh, subsidies on key farm inputs should not be seen in isolation of the subsidies in other sectors of the economy. A recent study on 'Budgetary Subsidies in India', conducted by the National Institute of Public Finance and Policy, has estimated that during 1998-99, the subsidies given by the central and state government amounted to more than Rs. 1,07,842 crore. Unofficial estimates suggest that direct and indirect (hidden) subsidies in other sectors are many times more than that in the agricultural sector. During 2002-03, the subsidy on LPG was Rs. 3,691 crore and on kerosene for PDS was Rs. 3,018 crore. The financial institutions have lost around Rs. 70,000 crore to the industry. The water supply in urban areas is highly subsidised. The subsidy and/or concessions on industrial promotion, trade facilitation, higher education and specialised health care are not insignificant. For improving the financial health of central and state governments, there is a need for carefully prioritising the entire gamut of subsidies for withdrawal, phasing-out or retention.

Owing to such far-reaching implications of withdrawal of input subsidies for the entire economy, a cautious and gradual approach in handling or containing the level of farm subsidies is necessary (Acharya, 1997a, 1997b; Acharya, 2000; Singh, 2004). Indeed the approach to input subsidies so far has been cautious and gradual, which is befitting to the needs of the country in attempting to bridge the rural-urban divide.

Conclusions

Analysis of subsidies on fertilisers, electricity and canal water during the last 20 years has been the focus of this chapter. The input subsidies in Indian agriculture increased from Rs. 1,420 crore during 1980-81 to Rs. 50,440 crore during 2000-01. The growth rate in subsidies decelerated during the nineties but the annual absolute rate of increase during nineties was higher than that during the eighties. The rate of increase in subsidy on electricity for irrigation has been higher than that in subsidy on fertilisers and canal water both during the eighties and nineties. In 2000-01, out of the total input subsidies, electricity subsidy accounted for 53.4 per cent, fertiliser subsidy 27.4 per cent and canal irrigation subsidy accounted for 19.2 per cent. Combined for all the three inputs, 81 per cent of the incremental subsidy is attributed to the growth in per unit subsidy and only 19 per cent to the expansion in the use of these inputs. State-wise analysis of subsidies at three points of time (1980-81, 1990-91 and 2000-01), reveals that Andhra Pradesh, Gujarat and Madhya Pradesh continuously improved their shares in all-India input subsidies. The states, which recorded decline in their ranks in terms of share in subsidies, include Uttar Pradesh, Punjab, Bihar, West Bengal and Orissa. During 2000-01, Punjab accounted for 8 per cent of total subsidies on these three inputs. Interstate variation in input subsidy per hectare of GCA is quite glaring. It was the highest at Rs. 5705 per hectare in Haryana and the lowest at Rs. 909 per hectare in Orissa during 2000-01. The subsidy per hectare was higher in Tamil Nadu and Gujarat than that in Punjab.

Input subsidies in Indian agriculture are mainly going to food crops. Out of the total input subsidies, rice accounted for 32 per cent, wheat 28 per cent, coarse cereals 5 per cent and pulses accounted for around 2 per cent. The subsidy on per hectare basis is the highest for sugarcane followed by wheat and rice. On the basis of output, the subsidy is the highest for cotton (Rs. 392 per quintal), followed by mustard (Rs. 354 per quintal). The crop-wise subsidy as a percentage of price (support) was around 30 for wheat and mustard and in the range of 15 to 25 for other crops except *tur*. By and large, the input subsidies accruing to irrigated lands (Rs. 6039 per ha) was around 15 times of that accruing to unirrigated lands (Rs. 385 per ha).

Across farm size groups, the distribution of subsidies follows the pattern of share of operated area, with small and marginal farms having larger share and large farms having smaller share in subsidies than their respective shares in operated area. The subsidy per hectare of operated area is Rs. 3088 per hectare and it is close to this level across farm size groups except for large farms where it is considerably lower.

Input subsidies should not be looked merely from the angle of finances of electricity or irrigation departments but more importantly from their overall role in food security and agricultural development of the country. Input subsidies enabled the country to improve food security and to keep food prices low for improved economic access of the masses to food and yet helped in providing reasonable returns to farmers. The estimated subsidies do not represent net transfer to farmers. A considerable part of input subsidies is due to inefficient production and distribution systems. The burden of subsidies can be reduced, without raising user charges, by improving the efficiency in the production and distribution systems of key farm inputs. The economic conditions of farmers continue to be well below the minimum desired level because the benefits of the input subsidies were distributed over all the sectors of the economy. The rise in input prices or user charges may not help in improving use-efficiency of these inputs. The option of compensating the farmers for rise in user charges is not feasible for small and marginal farmers and that too is not available for all the crops. Wherever available, the option is likely to be a costlier proposition. Further, subsidies on farm inputs cannot be seen in isolation of the subsidies in other sectors of the economy, which are many times more, and consequence of their withdrawal are less painful.

A great caution is, therefore, needed in handling the issue of input subsidies in Indian agriculture. It is quite satisfying that, despite pressures from several national and international quarters, the approach to the farm input subsidies has continued to be cautious and gradual. The subsidies in Indian agriculture, given the current situation, can be contained only after providing an alternative in the form of profitable technology package to farmers, better inputs, farmer-friendly trade and tariff environment and farm credit on soft terms. A well thought out, properly sequenced, gradualist and regionally differentiated approach to containing the economy-wide subsidies appears to be the most suitable option to resolve the issue of growing input subsidies in Indian agriculture. However, even in this approach, the ultimate objective of improving food and nutritional security at household level and improving the livelihoods of small and marginal farmers and other rural poor households should not be lost sight of.

References

Acharya, S.S. (1997a). "Input Subsidies in Indian Agriculture: Some Issues", in V.S. Vyas and Pradeep Bhargava (eds.), *Policies for Agricultural Development*, Rawat Publications, New Delhi, pp.87-119.

———. (1997b). "Agricultural Price Policy and Development: Some Facts and Emerging Issues", *Indian Journal of Agricultural Economics*, Vol. 52(1), January-March, pp.1-47.

———. (2000). "Subsidies in Indian Agriculture and their Beneficiaries", *Agricultural Situation in India*, Vol. LVII(5), Special Number, August, pp.251-60.

Acharya, S.S. and R.L. Jogi (2004). "Farm Input Subsidies in Indian Agriculture", *Agricultural Economics Research Review*, Vol. 17, January-June, pp.11-41.

Government of India (1991-92). *All-India Report on Input Survey 1991-92*, Ministry of Agriculture, New Delhi.

———. (1998). *All-India Report on Agricultural Census 1990-91*, Ministry of Agriculture, New Delhi.

———. (2002, 2003), *Agricultural Statistics At a Glance*, Ministry of Agriculture, New Delhi.

———. (Various Years). *Economic Survey*, Various Annual Issues, Ministry of Finance, New Delhi.

Gulati, A. (1989). "Input Subsidies in Indian Agriculture—A Statewise Analysis", *Economic and Political Weekly*, Vol. 24, pp.A57-A65.

Gulati, A. and S. Narayanan (2000). "De-mystifying Fertiliser and Power Subsidies in India", *Economic and Political Weekly*, Vol. 35(10), March 4, pp.784-94.

———. (2003). *The Subsidy Syndrome in Indian Agriculture*, Oxford University Press, New Delhi.

Planning Commission (2000, 2002). *Annual Report on the Working of State Electricity Boards and Electricity Departments*, Government of India, New Delhi.

Singh, Richa (2004). "Equity in Fertiliser Subsidy Distribution", *Economic and Political Weekly*, Vol. 39(3), January 17, pp.295-300.

Tuteja, Usha (2003). "Agricultural Input Subsidies in India: Quantum of Subsidies to Scheduled Caste Farmers in Haryana", Agricultural Economics Research Centre, University of Delhi, *Research Study* No. 2003/02, November.

5

Role of State in Agricultural Prices in Liberalised Era

RAMESH CHAND

Introduction

Government intervention in agricultural prices began in a big way in the mid-1960s. The intervention was meant to create a favourable incentive environment for the adoption of new technology based on high yielding varieties (HYV) of wheat and rice which was seen to possess vast potential for raising grain production. India was then facing severe food shortage and mass hunger which were causing lot of distress to the nation. The new technology provided a ray of hope to tackle the problem of food shortage and hunger. Adoption of the new technology involved use of non-conventional inputs and investments on the part of the farmers. This made it necessary to create stable and remunerative environment for the farmers adopting new seeds. At the same time, it was to be ensured that increase in production benefits consumers. Several measures were initiated to achieve the twin objectives of raising food production and improving food availability to consumers. These include: (a) price assurance to producers through the system of minimum support prices implemented through obligatory procurement, (b) inter- and intra-year price stability through open market operations, (c) maintaining buffer stocks, and (d) distribution of foodgrains at reasonable prices through public distribution system.

This policy has been helpful in several ways. From a situation of massive shortages, India has emerged as a grain surplus country, and food security has been attained at national level. A strong base has been created for grain production and for meeting grain demand in medium term. Prices of basic food have remained relatively stable. The policy has had positive impact on farm income and has led to economic transformation in well-endowed, mainly irrigated, regions. However, there have been adverse effects also. The food policy has been highly favourable to rice and wheat production and has resulted in a shift of good quality land and other resources to these crops away from pulses, oilseed and coarse grains. This has created serious imbalances in demand and supply of several agricultural commodities in the country. The country has been facing large shortages of pulses and edible oils and has now to meet about one-tenth of demand for pulses and close to half of the demand for edible oil from imports. These imports are in turn, causing adverse impact on producers in the unfavourable dryland areas, whereas, exports of wheat and rice have been pushed at a huge cost to the state exchequer. Another ominous consequence of government intervention in agricultural prices is the rising burden of food subsidy.

These problems indicate that state intervention in agricultural prices needs to be reoriented and changed. Moreover, economic environment in the country has undergone a sea-change after 1991, when India initiated economic reforms. Government controls and regulations in the economy have been dismantled or relaxed to pave the way for increased participation of private sector in economic activities. The country has adopted policy of economic liberalisation to reduce the role of government in various economic activities. Internal and external liberalisation of economy is providing new options and instruments for achieving various goals, earlier met through government intervention.

The present chapter examines these various issues related to government intervention in the agricultural prices. The chapter examines the system of administered prices, procurement and buffer stock in relation to their underlying objectives and to the emerging scenario of demand, supply and trade. It suggests changes in government price policy to make it more relevant to the current and the future requirements of the country leading to a discussion of various options and alternatives to ensure guaranteed prices to producers, maintenance of inter-year price stability, and the genuine boundaries for government intervention in the prices.

The chapter is organised into five sections. After this brief introductory section, the second section discusses the role of

Commission on Agricultural Costs and Prices (CACP) and the system of minimum support prices (MSP) followed in the country. The third section discusses the consequences and implications of state intervention in grain prices since the beginning of economic reforms. It also examine the factors underlying the accumulation of grain stocks in the recent years and analyses its implications for food security, fiscal burden, future production, private trade and policy. Regional aspect of foodgrain surplus and procurement are also briefly examined in this section. The fourth section covers changes needed in state intervention in price administration, procurement and price stability and also, the concluding section of the chapter and it is argued that government intervention in foodgrain market has become radically different in post-liberalised and globalised era.

CACP and System of Minimum Support Prices

In order to ensure a remunerative and stable price environment for adoption of new technology, there was a need to know what is the minimum level of prices that should be guaranteed to farmers as assured prices. Towards that end, the Agricultural Prices Commission (APC) was set up in 1965 to advise the government about minimum support prices for selected commodities on a regular basis. While making its recommendation, the Commission was required to keep in view the need to provide incentive to the producers for adopting the new technology and maximising production.

The policy was effective in encouraging adoption of new technology in the areas well-endowed with irrigation, and helped in achieving high growth in the production of wheat and rice. During less than 15 years following 1965, wheat production trebled while rice production increased by more than 50 per cent. This helped considerably in overcoming food shortage then prevailing in the country. With the easing of strain on foodgrain production the terms of reference of APC were changed in 1980 to shifting the emphasis from maximising production to developing a production pattern based on balanced allocation of resources and one that was consistent with the overall need of the economy. Subsequently, in 1985 the Commission was renamed as Commission for Agricultural Costs and Prices (CACP) mainly to satisfy the demand from various farmer groups, that full account ought to be taken of cost of production while making recommendation on support/procurement price.[1]

The change in terms of reference of APC in 1980, did not help to promote balanced production pattern in any way. On the contrary, shift in area towards rice and wheat became more pronounced after 1980.[2] Among factors that can be held responsible for continuing shift of area to rice and wheat, farm price policy has been a major one. Though minimum support prices are announced for all major crops, their effective implementation has been ensured only in the case of rice and wheat, and to some extent in the case of cotton and sugarcane. Moreover, MSPs for wheat and paddy were fixed with higher margin over cost of production than for other crops (*Report of the High Level Committee on Long-Term Grain Policy, 2002*, para 3.4 c).

Besides ensuring remunerative prices, government intervention has also affected price stability. As would be seen from Table 5.1, prices of rice and wheat in major markets deviated from trend by 6.64 and 8.82 per cent, whereas prices of the other crops show 14.09 to 28.75 per cent annual instability. This way, farm price policy provided strong support to rice and wheat to guard against price risk.

The strong policy support to rice and wheat and relative neglect of pulses and oilseeds has created large imbalances in demand and

1. The adoption of new technology brought in strong element of commercialisation in farm production and farmers in the Green Revolution areas started aspiring for increase in crop income. This led to emergence of strong farmers pressure groups, which started influencing farm price policy to get higher prices for farm produce to earn higher income. The clout of these pressure groups grew so strong that in 1980, government set up a committee under the chairmanship of Dr. C. H. Hanumantha Rao to look into the cost concepts which serve as a basis for minimum support price. The committee recommended that cost of production used as a basis for MSP should include 10 per cent of paid out cost as an allowance for risk taking and entrepreneurial ability of producers and introduced the new concept, Cost C3, inclusive of risk allowance and managerial functions performed by farmers. The pressure of farmers groups was so strong that government not only accepted this recommendation promptly but also decided to take 10 per cent of total cost rather than paid out cost as allowance for risk taking—this small change almost doubled the absolute amount of 'allowance for risk and managerial function'. This brought in serious distortion in the system of MSP.

2. Wheat and paddy occupied 34.92 per cent of gross sown area of the country during the decade of 1970s which increased to 36.18 per cent during the decade of 1980s. There was a further increase in area share of rice and wheat to the level of 36.62 per cent during 1990s. So much so, wheat and rice cultivation has been extended to areas and soils which were not basically suitable for these crops. Rice cultivation was extended to sandy lands and semi-arid regions basically suitable for crops like cotton and groundnut. For instance, in a district like Bathinda in Punjab state paddy was grown on 1.6 per cent of net cultivated area in 1980-81, which increased to 33 per cent during 1998-99.

Table 5.1

Instability in Domestic Prices of Selected Crops, 1980-81 to 1998-99

Crops	*Market*	*Deviation from Trend Price (Per Cent/Year)*
Wheat	Hapur	8.82
Rice	Delhi	6.64
Sorghum	Nagpur	23.30
Maize	Kanpur	19.87
Cotton	Broach	26.88
Chick Pea	Jabalpur	28.75
Tur	Aurangabad	19.94
Groundnut	Rajkot	14.09
Rapeseed/Mustard	Kanpur	19.41

Source: *Agricultural Prices in India*, various issues, Ministry of Agriculture, GoI.

supply of various commodities in the country, becoming quite serious during the last decade. This can be seen from import dependence of India for edible oil and pulses on one hand, and accumulation of grain stocks with the government, on the other. In early 1990s, India imported less than half million tonne of edible oil to meet domestic demand. The imports rose to more than four million tonne by the end of 1990s and are further growing. India is currently meeting close to half of its domestic consumption of edible oil from imports. In the case of pulses, per capita availability has been declining ever since the beginning of Green Revolution, and current availability is only 32 gram/person/day, which is less than half of what it was in early 1960s. Despite this decline, India has been importing pulses to meet domestic requirement. Average import of pulses during the triennium 1999-2000 to 2001-2002 was 9.32 lakh tonne which constituted about 8 per cent of domestic demand for pulses.

In contrast to deficiency of edible oil and pulses, India has been producing grains which could not be disposed of, either in domestic market or in international market. This is evident from the accumulation of grain stocks held by government before the drought year of 2002-03. In the year 2001-02, government stocks increased to 62.5 million tonne at peak time and did not go below 44.7 million tonne even during the lean months. More than 27 per cent of output of rice and wheat remained piled up with the government, which was about three times the norm of stock requirement for the country.

Table 5.2

Import Dependence of Edible Oils, Pulses and Grainstock with Central Government

Year	*Import '000 Tonne*		*Grain Stock: Million Tonne*	
	Edible Oils	*Pulses*	*Minimum*	*Maximum*
1991-1992	226	313	13.9	20.9
1992-1993	103	383	11.1	13.8
1993-1994	114	628	12.7	24.2
1994-1995	347	554	20.5	30.7
1995-1996	1062	486	26.8	35.6
1996-1997	1416	692	19.8	27.0
1997-1998	1265	1084	15.3	22.4
1998-1999	2622	629	18.2	28.5
1999-2000	4196	269	21.9	33.1
2000-2001	4177	350	21.7	45.7
2001-2002	4213	2177	44.7	62.5

Sources of basic data:

1. *Monthly Statistics of Foreign Trade of India*, Volume I and II, Annual Number, DGCIS, Ministry of Commerce, Calcutta, Various Issues.
2. *Economic Survey*, Ministry of Finance, Various Issues, GoI, New Delhi.
3. *Agricultural Statistics at a Glance*, Various Issues, Ministry of Agriculture, GoI, New Delhi.

Two important inferences follow from the above discussion. One, mere announcement of MSP for those crops for which effective mechanism to ensure MSP is not provided, is merely an exercise on paper. Two, CACP has failed in its role to influence farm price policy to evolve balanced production pattern in the country.

Price Intervention during 1990s

Cost of cultivation was the principal criteria used for arriving at level of MSPs till 1991, when India initiated economic reforms. With the liberalisation policy, strong pressure built up to integrate domestic prices with global agriculture prices. Domestic prices of cereals were lower than international prices at that time. Successive devaluation in exchange rate, further increased the gap between domestic and international prices. Hefty increases in prices were announced to reduce the so called disprotection to Indian agriculture. This can be seen from Figures 5.1 and 5.2, which show movement of MSP for paddy and wheat in relation to wholesale prices of all commodities and fruits and vegetables, respectively. MSPs of paddy and wheat in real terms declined during 1980s but then took sharp upward turn in the beginning of 1990. Growth rate in MSPs of these two food crops remained much higher than increase in overall prices in the economy during the decade of 1990s except a few years. This affected consumption pattern and nutrition in the country as would be seen in the subsequent sections. Likewise, MSP of paddy and wheat relative to prices of horticultural crops declined till late 1980s, creating favourable prices environment for diversification towards horticulture crops. After that, relative prices moved somewhat in favour of paddy and wheat which goes against the diversification of agriculture sector contemplated as a major strategy for growth of agriculture sector in the country. Major implications of increase in MSP of paddy and wheat during the decade of 1990s are discussed below.

Figure 5.1

MSP of Paddy and Wheat Deflated by WPI Base, 1981-82=100

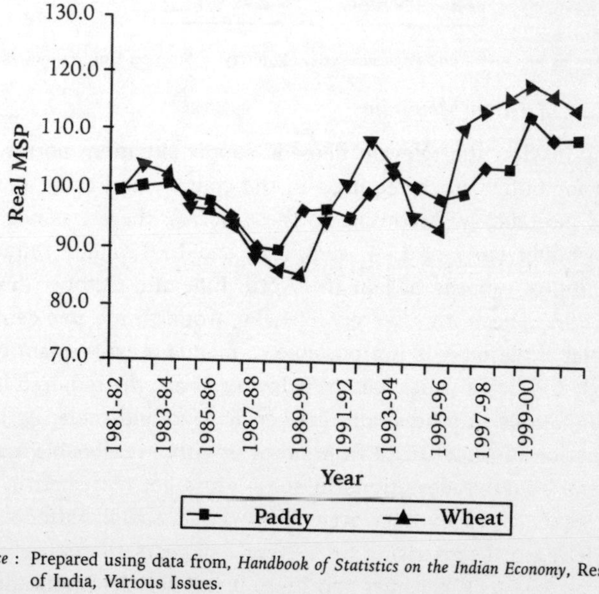

Source : Prepared using data from, *Handbook of Statistics on the Indian Economy*, Reserve Bank of India, Various Issues.

Figure 5.2

MSP of Paddy and Wheat in Relation to WPI of Fruits and Vegetables, 1981-82=100

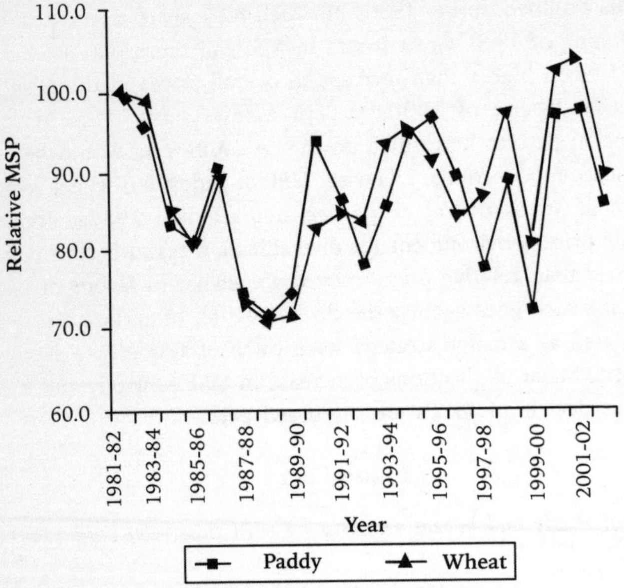

Source : Same as Figure 5.1 and *Economic Survey*, Ministry of Finance, GoI, Various Issues.

Accumulation of Grain Mountain

Keeping in view the relevant demand-supply situation, norms are laid down for buffer stock required in the country and these norms are revised periodically. According to these norms, there was need to maintain a buffer stock of 15.4, 15.8, 24.3 and 16.6 million tonne at the beginning of months of January, April, June and October during 1992 to 1998. The norms were raised by around nine per cent in 1999. In real situation it is not possible to maintain exact quantity of buffer stock and actual stock can go below or above the required level due to fluctuations in production, market demand and trade. As long as the deviation in actual stock from norm is within reasonable limits, and, positive/negative deviations in some years get corrected in the following year, it causes no worry. However, if actual buffer stock keeps depleting or keeps rising for a couple of years successively, or, if level of actual stock becomes too high, it has serious implications, particularly for food availability, fiscal resources, future production and trade.

Actual position of foodgrain (rice and wheat) stock held by government since 1990 is shown in Table 5.3. The stocks do not show any rising or declining trend up to 1997, temporary fluctuations apart. Although actual stock rose much higher than the norm occasionally, it returned to the norm within one to two years. However, since 1998 foodgrain stocks have shown a continuous and sharp increase, at all the times of every year. As a result, grain stock had accumulated to 60.4 million tonne by 1 June 2001, which is two and a half times the required level of stock. Similarly, the stock position in October 2001, and in April to June 2002, was three and half times the buffer stock norm.[3]

Table 5.3

Central Foodgrain Stocks Since 1990: Actual and the Norm

(Million Tonne)

Year	*January*	*April*	*June*	*October*
Actual Stock				
1990	11.7	12.9	18.9	16.5
1991	18.0	17.1	19.8	14.2
1992	13.9	11.1	13.9	9.5
1993	11.8	12.6	24.2	20.9
1994	22.0	20.5	30.7	26.5
1995	30.1	26.8	35.6	29.8
1996	28.5	20.9	27.0	19.8
1997	20.0	16.4	22.4	15.3
1998	18.3	18.2	28.5	24.2
1999	24.4	21.9	33.1	28.0
2000	31.4	21.7	42.2	40.0
2001	45.7	44.7	60.4	58.3
2002	58.0	51.0	62.5	NA
Norm: 1992 to 1998	15.4	14.5	22.3	16.6
Norm: 1999 to Date	16.8	15.8	24.3	18.1

Source: 1. *Economic Survey*, Government of India, Various Issues, 2001-2002.
2. *Monthly Bulletin of Food Statistics*, Ministry of Consumer Affairs, Food and PDS, Various Issues.

3. These stocks correspond to more than one-third of total cereal consumption in the country.

Carrying these stocks has involved huge cost to the state exchequer, in terms of their storage, interest charges, maintenance, and quality and value deterioration. It is useful to examine why huge quantity of grains are accumulated in government stock and what are its implications.

If the stock is showing increase over time, it can result either from increase in output or decrease in consumption or decrease in net import (export-import) or some combination of these changes. Long-term information on these aspects in respect of total of all cereals is presented in Table 5.4. To find out the exact nature of change in cereal demand and its causes, we may well look into the trends in per capita production and availability of cereals for consumption. For the sake of proper correspondence between production and consumption and agricultural year and financial year, production of *rabi* and *kharif* harvested in the same calendar year are added together.[4] As there were sharp year to year fluctuations in cereal production and consumption, the series on per capita cereal production and amount available for actual consumption are presented using three years moving average in Figure 5.3. It reveals that cereal production increased at a faster rate than population during the decades of 1970s and 1980s. During 1990s, per capita cereal production fluctuated around a fixed level (518 gram) devoid of any trend either way because growth rate of cereal production remained more or less the same as the growth of population. Therefore, increase in cereal stock during late 1990s, did not result from growth in cereal production.

Similarly, trade in cereals did not cause accumulation of foodgrain stocks because India remained net exporter since 1995 with magnitude of net export higher than the earlier period (Table 5.4). Finally, the only explanation for large and increasing accretion to cereal stock from 1998 onwards, is the decline in per capita cereal consumption in that period which is evident from the national-level

---

4. For example, 1971 includes *kharif* output of 1971-72 and *rabi* output of the year 1970-1971. *Rabi* output of cereals shown under year 1970-71, as per the official documents, includes *rabi* crops whose harvest normally starts in March and extends to the month of May. *Kharif* cereal output put under year 1971-72 in the official data refer to the output almost all of which is harvested in 1971. Thus, to study the relationship between different variables reported on the basis of financial year (April–March) on the one hand and cereal output on the other, it seems reasonable to include cereal output harvested during March to December of the same year rather than taking output harvested during July to June as followed in the official statistics.

data on per capita availability of cereals for human consumption as shown in Table 5.4 and Figure 5.3.

Figure 5.3

Trend in Per Person Cereal Production and Availability for Consumption

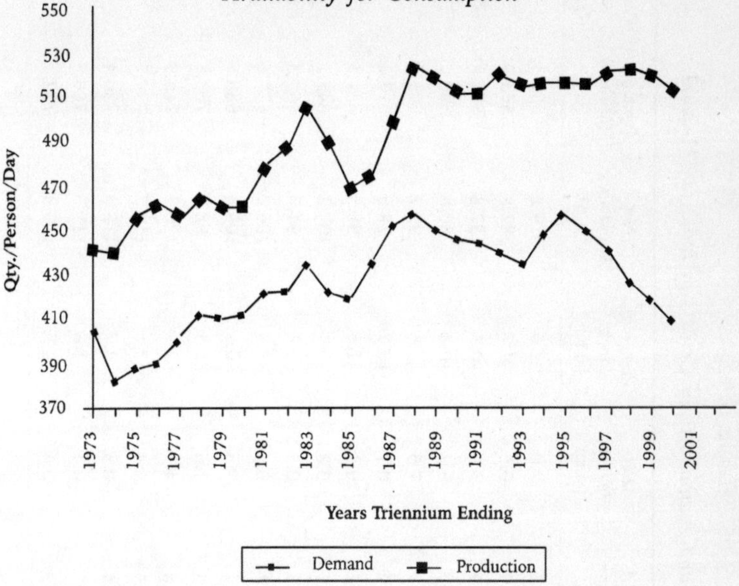

Source: Economic Survey, Government of India, Various Issues.

A close look at per person availability of cereals at national level shows that, up to the triennium ending 1991, per person availability closely followed the trend in per person production. If similar trend had continued during 1990s, then per capita availability of cereals should have fluctuated around 454 grams.[5] However, during 1990s, per capita availability followed sharp decline, rather than remaining stagnant in response to trend in production, which created a big gap between production and availability or consumption (Figure 5.3). This takes us to the larger issue of food security and the causes underlying the decline in cereal intake. Why cereals have gone into stocks rather than being consumed by people?

5. This is computed based on ratio of cereal consumption and production. During 1970s and 1980s, 88 per cent of production was used for consumption, whereas this ratio declined to 85 per cent during 1990s.

Table 5.4

Trend in Production and Availability of Cereals in India, 1971-2001

Year	Cereal Output: Million Tonne (m.t.)			Net Import (m.t.)	Change in Stock (m.t.)	Net Availability (m.t.)	Population (Million)	Per Person Availability (gm/day)	Production Per Person (gm/day)
	Kharif	Rabi	Total						
1971	59.65	31.56	91.2	2.0	2.6	79.2	551.3	393.6	453.3
1972	55.46	34.42	89.9	-0.5	-4.7	82.8	563.9	402.5	436.7
1973	64.21	31.66	95.9	3.6	-0.3	87.8	576.8	417.0	455.4
1974	55.53	30.44	86.0	5.2	-0.4	80.8	590.0	375.3	399.2
1975	69.45	34.28	103.7	7.5	5.6	92.7	603.5	420.7	470.9
1976	62.64	38.54	101.2	0.7	10.7	78.5	617.2	348.6	449.1
1977	73.48	37.17	110.7	0.1	-1.6	98.5	631.3	396.2	445.0
1978	74.13	40.96	115.1	-0.8	-0.3	100.2	645.7	425.2	488.3
1979	59.90	45.59	105.5	-0.3	0.4	91.6	660.3	380.1	437.7
1980	73.89	41.23	115.1	-0.5	-5.8	106.0	676.6	429.3	466.1
1981	75.05	45.08	120.1	0.5	-0.2	105.8	688.5	421.1	478.0
1982	65.77	46.74	112.5	1.6	1.3	98.7	703.8	384.4	438.0
1983	83.86	51.89	135.8	4.1	2.7	120.2	718.9	458.0	517.3
1984	79.75	55.62	135.4	2.4	7.1	113.7	734.5	424.3	504.9
1985	81.54	53.83	135.4	-0.3	2.7	115.4	750.4	421.5	494.2
1986	76.00	55.99	132.0	-0.1	-1.6	117.0	766.5	418.2	471.8
1987	70.20	55.70	125.9	-0.4	-9.5	119.3	782.7	417.5	440.7

Contd...

Contd....

Year	Cereal Output: Million Tonne (m.t.)			Net Import (m.t.)	Change in Stock (m.t.)	Net Availability (m.t.)	Population (Million)	Per Person Availability (gm/day)	Production Per Person (gm/day)
	Kharif	Rabi	Total						
1988	90.00	59.20	149.2	2.3	-4.6	137.5	799.2	471.2	511.5
1989	95.50	66.10	161.6	0.8	2.6	139.6	815.8	468.8	542.7
1990	94.50	62.70	157.2	0.0	6.2	131.4	832.6	432.2	517.3
1991	87.2	68.1	155.3	-0.6	-4.4	139.7	851.7	449.3	499.6
1992	95.8	69.2	165.0	-0.7	-1.6	145.3	867.8	458.6	520.9
1993	95.0	70.8	165.8	2.6	10.3	137.4	883.9	425.8	513.9
1994	96.4	75.9	172.3	0.5	7.5	143.8	899.9	437.7	524.6
1995	90.5	81.1	171.6	-3.0	-1.7	148.9	922.0	442.3	509.9
1996	98.4	77.6	176.0	-3.5	-8.5	159.0	939.5	463.7	513.2
1997	97.3	86.8	184.1	-0.6	-1.8	162.3	955.2	465.5	528.0
1998	97.7	82.0	179.7	-2.9	6.1	148.2	970.9	418.3	507.1
1999	99.9	90.9	190.8	-1.5	7.5	158.0	986.6	438.6	529.8
2000	98.4	95.6	194.0	-1.4	13.9	154.5	1002.1	422.3	530.5
2001	100.4	86.6	187.0	-2.9	12.5	148.2	1027.0	395.4	498.8

Source: *Economic Survey*, Various Issues.

Causes for Decline in Cereal Consumption

Consumers meet their demand for cereals from purchases in the open market and from supply through public distribution system. About 91 per cent demand is met from open market and remaining 9 per cent from PDS supply. As would be seen from Table 5.5, per capita daily availability of cereals from open market was 428.5 gram in 1995-96 and 423.1 gram during 1996-97. After that, cereal availability from open market steadily declined to 367.6 gram by the year 2000-01. PDS supply also followed sharp decline after 1998-99. We further explored whether this decline in cereal intake resulted due to the increase in cereal prices or due to diversification in consumption pattern resulting from shifts in consumer preference from cereal foods to non-cereal foods.

Table 5.5

Per Capita Availability of Cereals in Open Market and Under PDS

(Unit: Gram)

Year	*Total*	*Open Market*	*PDS*
1990-91	449.3	414.8	34.59
1991-92	458.6	416.4	42.28
1992-93	425.8	387.6	38.24
1993-94	437.7	403.0	34.71
1994-95	442.3	412.9	29.38
1995-96	463.7	428.5	35.18
1996-97	465.5	423.1	42.40
1997-98	418.3	381.8	36.48
1998-99	438.6	393.9	44.68
1999-00	422.3	383.4	38.92
2000-01	395.4	367.6	27.73

Source: Same as in Table 5.3.

Price Trends

Procurement price of wheat was raised by more than 20 per cent continuously for three years during 1990-91, 1991-92 and 1992-93. This raise was almost double the highest raise in procurement price recorded during 1980s. Once again procurement price of wheat was jacked up by 25 per cent during 1996-97. As has been the case with wheat, procurement price of rice also witnessed much higher increase during 1990s than in 1980s. During the five years from 1989-90 to 1993-94, rice procurement price was raised by about 11 to 17 per cent in different years.

In order to have a clear idea about the price increase during 1980s and 1990s, their trend growth rates are presented in Table 5.6. Procurement prices of wheat increased by 10.53 per cent annually, during 1990s, which is more than double the growth rate recorded during 1980s. Similarly, procurement price of paddy shows annual growth rate of 9.65 per cent during 1990s compared to 5.42 per cent during the preceding decade. Wholesale prices of wheat and rice, which were strongly influenced by government intervention, also showed much higher growth during 1990s than in 1980s. As a matter of fact during 1980s, increase in procurement prices was quite small compared to the increase in prices of food and other commodities, whereas during 1990s, growth rate of procurement prices outpaced the general rate of inflation.

Table 5.6

Growth Rates in Different Types of Prices of Rice and Wheat

(Per Cent/Per Annum)

Commodity	*Price*	*1980-1981 to 1989-1990*	*1990-1991 to 1999-2000*
Wheat	Procurement Price	4.36	10.53
	Wholesale Price	5.67	9.48
	Retail Price	6.62	8.88
	PDS Price	3.74	11.85
Rice	Procurement Price	5.42	9.65
	Wholesale Price	5.24	9.24
	Retail Price	7.36	8.69
	PDS Price	5.80	12.96
CPI	Food	8.38	9.39
	General	8.58	9.31

Source: Same as in Table 5.3.

Though different prices are correlated with one another, the most relevant prices in determining consumption of cereals are retail prices and PDS prices of cereals. As can be seen from Table 5.6, retail prices of rice and wheat increased annually by 8.88 and 8.69 per cent respectively, during 1990s, which is higher than their growth rates during 1980s. This would surely be a crucial factor in explaining why cereal consumption did not keep pace even with the stagnant per capita production.

The rate of increase in PDS prices during 1990s, was more than three times in the case of wheat and more than double in the case of rice compared to that in 1980s. Hike in PDS prices for above poverty line consumers was particularly high during 1997-98 and 1998-99 (see Table 5.7) when rice prices were raised by 60 per cent and wheat prices by 56 per cent. This caused adverse impact on demand and reduced the difference between retail prices in open market and PDS price, which reduced the attractiveness to buy foodgrains from PDS. Thus, despite greater allocation of grains through PDS, there was sharp decline in foodgrains offtake. It is noteworthy that despite a very large drop in foodgrain output during 2000-01, PDS offtake declined sharply. On the other hand, despite normal output, PDS offtake went up during 2001-02, if only because PDS prices of rice and wheat were decreased by about 27 per cent in this year.

Table 5.7

PDS Supply and Retail and PDS Prices of Rice and Wheat

Year	*Rural Retail Price Rs./Quintal*		*PDS Offtake of Rice and Wheat (Million Tonne)*	*PDS Price Rs./Quintal*		*Foodgrain Production (Million Tonne)*
	Rice	*Wheat*		*Rice*	*Wheat*	
1991-1992	501	407	19.0	377	280	168.4
1992-1993	582	450	17.4	377	280	179.5
1993-1994	587	439	14.8	437	330	184.3
1994-1995	689	479	12.9	537	402	191.5
1995-1996	733	489	14.8	537	402	180.4
1996-1997	807	690	19.7	537	402	199.4
1997-1998	820	655	17.0	700	450	192.3
1998-1999	900	684	18.7	905	650	203.6
1999-2000	995	746	17.1	905	682	209.8
2000-2001	–	–	11.7	1130	830	195.9
2001-2002	–	–	13.7	830	610	211.3

Source: 1. *Agricultural Prices in India*, Ministry of Agriculture, GoI.
2. *Bulletin of Food Statistics*, Ministry of Agriculture, GoI.

Besides causing direct impact, price movements during 1990s also affected cereal demand indirectly. During 1980s, growth rate in rural retail prices was higher than the growth rate in wholesale and procurement prices. In contrast to this, during 1990s, growth rate in retail prices of rice and wheat turned out to be lower than the growth rate in wholesale and procurement prices. Obviously, increase in procurement prices and consequent increase in wholesale prices, was not supported by demand side factors. Second, growth rate in retail prices falling short of growth rate in wholesale and procurement prices squeezed the margin of the private trade. Because of this, private sector withdrew from purchasing rice and wheat from farmers. This affected release of quantity for consumption in the subsequent lean months. Private sector normally buys during harvest period and sells the same produce in the subsequent months, and does not withhold produce from the market for more than a year. However, the same principle is not applicable to public sector agencies which can procure, and have the capacity to keep the produce in buffer stock for a long time. Both the burgeoning government stocks during the last five years and the reduced participation of private sector have affected availability of grains to consumers.

To conclude, rising trend in per capita production of cereals during 1970s and 1980s was accompanied by the rising trend in per capita consumption. One important reason for this was that cereal prices during this period, both in open market and in PDS, increased at a relatively much lower rate than the rate of increase in general price level. In other words, in real terms cereal prices were declining. During 1990s, demand did not keep pace even with stagnant per capita production because government induced hikes in procurement prices and wholesale prices. The consequent increase in retail and PDS prices caused adverse impact on cereal consumption. The ultimate impact of these changes has been, huge accumulation of grain stock with government despite stagnation in per capita production of cereals.

Food Security and Food Subsidies

The most serious implications of accumulation of very large quantity of rice and wheat in government stocks are on food security and fiscal resources. Apart from these, accumulation of grain stock beyond reasonable limits affects export performance and participation of private trade in marketing.

The impact on fiscal resources can be seen from the mounting food subsidy (Table 5.8). Food subsidy at current prices increased from below Rs. 3000 crore in early 1990s to Rs. 9200 crore by 1999-2000. In the next three years, food subsidy rose to Rs. 25000 crore. Food subsidies at constant prices increased four-fold their average level during 1991-92 and 1992-93. About 2.5 per cent of total government expenditure was spent on food subsidy during 1991-92 and 1992-93, which increased to more than 5 per cent in the next 10 years. The amount of food subsidy per unit of foodgrain production has risen four times in real terms in the last 10 years. The country is now spending close to 1 per cent of total GDP and 3.70 per cent of agricultural GDP on food subsidies.

Table 5.8

Growth in Food Subsidies During 1991-92 to 2001-02

	Food Subsidy Rs. Crore		*Food Subsidy as Per Cent of*			*Subsidy/kg Foodgrain Production*	
Year	*Current Price*	*Deflated by WPI Foodgrains*	*GDP Agri.*	*GDP Total*	*Total Govt. Expenditure*	*Current Price*	*Constant Price*
1991-1992	2850	3444	1.67	0.48	2.56	0.17	0.20
1992-1993	2800	3020	1.46	0.42	2.28	0.16	0.17
1993-1994	5537	5537	2.50	0.71	3.90	0.30	0.30
1994-1995	5100	4435	2.00	0.56	3.17	0.27	0.23
1995-1996	5377	4407	1.94	0.50	3.02	0.30	0.24
1996-1997	6066	4396	1.82	0.49	3.02	0.30	0.22
1997-1998	7500	5396	2.12	0.54	3.40	0.39	0.28
1998-1999	8700	5724	2.14	0.54	3.26	0.43	0.28
1999-2000	9200	5227	2.18	0.52	3.17	0.44	0.25
2000-2001	12010	6902	2.76	0.57	3.70	0.61	0.35
2001-2002	17494	10171	3.70	0.78	4.85	0.83	0.48
2002-2003	24176	13894	-	0.96	6.01	1.39	0.80
2003-2004	25160	14295	-	-	-	-	-

Source: *Economic Survey*, Ministry of Finance, Government of India, New Delhi, Various Issues.

Still, the bigger question is whether this increase in food subsidy during the last decade benefited consumers? Answer to this lies in looking at how and to whom this subsidy gets paid. Central government pays food subsidy to FCI to meet (a) the difference between economic cost of foodgrains and their sales realisation at the central issue prices fixed for PDS and other welfare schemes, and (b) carrying cost of buffer stock as a measure of food security. During 1990s, government announced hefty increase in procurement prices and to reduce the wide gap between central issue prices and economic cost, the former was also increased sharply and frequently. Similarly, through its control over substantial part of supply, the government procurement at hiked MSPs also resulted in large increase in wholesale price. However, demand side factors did not justify this increase in cereal prices. This is evident from the monthly wholesale prices of wheat and paddy presented in Tables 5.9 and 5.10, respectively. In the case of wheat, open market prices could be kept at the level of MSP only during harvest time when government agencies were buying the produce. The moment official procurement got over and official agencies withdrew from market, prices fell below MSP. This was true for the states of Punjab and Haryana where official agencies ensure MSP through effective procurement. In other states, UP for instance, where effective procurement system is missing in most of the markets, price of wheat remained below MSP during harvest time during the last three years. Actual market price during April to June varied between Rs. 500 to Rs. 532 as against MSP of Rs. 610 for the year 2001. Similarly, during the year 2002 wheat prices in harvest period remained below Rs. 570 compared to MSP of Rs. 620.

Exactly similar situation holds in the case of paddy (Table 5.10). Market prices could be maintained at the level of MSP in the harvest season only in Punjab and Haryana. In UP and West Bengal per quintal market prices of common paddy varied between Rs. 350 to Rs. 400 in the harvest months during 2000-01, whereas MSP was, Rs. 510. Similarly, during the year 2001-02, market prices in harvest months in these two states varied between Rs. 370 to 515 as compared to MSP of Rs. 530.

Table 5.9

MSP/Procurement Price and Actual Market Price of Wheat During Harvest and Lean Months

(Rupees/Quintal)

Market	Year	MSP	Harvest Period			Lean Period					
			April	May	June	July	Aug.	Sept.	Oct.	Nov.	Dec.
Karnal	2000	580	580	580	580	582	545	528	535	580	560
(Haryana)	2001	610	610	610	600	585	580	590	605	605	608
	2002	620	620	625	600	-*	-	-	-	-	-
Ludhiana											
(Punjab)	2000	580	580	581	587	589	591	557	547	542	550
	2001	610	610	610	565	580	585	603	605	610	612
	2002	620	620	620	615	-	-	-	-	-	-
Hardoi											
(UP)	2000	580	585	582	540	565	-	515	515	570	548
	2001	610	510	500	532	525	560	580	610	622	616
	2002	620	555	525	570	-	-	-	-	-	-

Note: * Not available.

Source: Department of Agriculture and Cooperation, Ministry of Agriculture, GoI.

Table 5.10

MSP/Procurement Price and Actual Market Price of Paddy During Harvest and Lean Months

(Rupees/Quintal)

Market	Year	MSP	Harvest Period			Lean Period					
			Oct.	Nov.	Dec.	Jan.	Feb.	March	April	May	June
Karnal	2000-01	540	540	540	480	-*	485	472	468	-	-
(Haryana)	2001-02	560	560	560	535	-	510	525	-	-	-
Amritsar	2000-01	540	550	545	555	540	515	500	515	-	571
(Punjab)	2001-02	560	560	570	560	560	-	610	-	570	570
Bahraich	2000-01	510	350	370	350	375	365	425	425	415	410
(UP)	2001-02	530	425	410	425	400	415	450	400	400	410
Santhia	2000-01	510	390	380	400	390	440	475	490	480	475
(West											
Bengal)	2001-02	530	515	400	410	405	395	380	375	320	360

Note: *Not available.

Source: Department of Agriculture and Cooperation, Ministry of Agriculture, GoI.

Open market prices turning lower than MSP, or not showing adequate margin over MSP, created serious problem for the produce procured by government at MSP. It forced the government either to keep produce in stock or sell it in open market at heavy discount. Either of these options involved heavy cost/loss which has resulted into a substantial increase in food subsidy.

Inability of open market to absorb hikes in procurement price and inability of consumers dependent on PDS to absorb hikes in PDS price, caused the produce to accumulate in government stocks and forced the government to sell produce at heavy discount. Thus, substantial increase in carrying cost of buffer stock, and rising difference between price at which produce could be sold and economic cost of produce to FCI, resulted in fast growth in food subsidies, particularly during late 1990s and early years of current century. The main beneficiaries of this subsidy are those producers who could sell their produce to government agencies. Rather than being benefited, consumers have been hurt by the system of administered prices in the recent years which resulted in increase in food subsidy.

Perverse Incentives to Private Trade

In order to achieve various goals of food policy, government has been procuring substantial part of marketed surplus from selected food surplus states. Procurement by government constituted 10 to 15 per cent of total rice output and 15 to 22 per cent of total wheat output during 1985-86 to 1989-90 (Table 5.11). When India initiated economic reforms in the year 1991, a move towards increased participation by private sector in various spheres of economic activities was started, which naturally implies reduced role of government in marketing. Government started gradually reducing its participation in industry and services sector. In the case of agriculture, particularly the foodgrain trade, some reduction in the role of government took place after 1992-93. Between 1992-93 and 1996-97, wheat output procured by government declined from 22.3 per cent to 13.41 per cent. Similarly, government procurement of rice declined from 17 per cent in 1993-94 to about 14 per cent in 1996-97. However, this decline turned out to be the part of cyclical variation resulting from production fluctuations, as experienced in the past, and government procurement witnessed steep increase in the recent years.

Table 5.11

Production and Procurement of Rice and Wheat by Official Agencies, 1985-86 to 2000-01

Year	Production (Lakh Tonne)		Procurement (Lakh Tonne)		Procurement as Per Cent of Production	
	Rice	Wheat	Rice	Wheat	Rice	Wheat
1985-1986	638	471	99	105	15.51	22.32
1986-1987	606	443	92	79	15.19	17.82
1987-1988	569	462	69	66	12.13	14.30
1988-1989	705	541	77	89	10.92	16.45
1989-1990	736	499	118	111	16.04	22.27
1990-1991	743	551	127	78	17.09	14.15
1991-1992	747	557	102	64	13.66	11.49
1992-1993	729	572	130	128	17.84	22.37
1993-1994	790	591	143	119	18.10	20.12
1994-1995	818	658	137	123	16.75	18.70
1995-1996	770	621	100	82	12.99	13.21
1996-1997	817	694	130	93	15.90	13.41
1997-1998	825	663	155	127	18.78	19.14
1998-1999	860	708	126	141	14.65	19.92
1999-2000	895	756	182	164	20.34	21.70
2000-2001	849	687	208	206	24.50	29.99
2001-2002	907	735	202	190	22.27	25.80

Source: *Agricultural Statistics at a Glance*, Various Issues, Ministry of Agriculture.

Indeed, government procurement was stepped up despite comfortable food stock situation. During the year 2000-01, government had to procure all time high share of wheat and rice produced in the country. The increase took place despite two odds. One, production during year 2000-01 was low compared with the past two years and second, buffer stock with government was already double its normative requirement. The private trade participation in grain trade reduced as a result. Strong evidence of reduced private sector participation in foodgrain trade can be found in the relative shares of marketed surplus purchased by official agencies and private sector. During the marketing year 1995-96, official agencies purchased about one-third of market arrivals of rice and less than half of wheat. Since then, share of official agencies steadily increased and share of private sector declined. During the year 2001-02, official agencies have bought more than three-fourths of wheat and nearly two-thirds of rice sold in various markets.

There are several reasons for reduction in purchases made by private sector from farmers in the market place. One, lower rate of increase in retail prices compared to procurement prices and wholesale prices gave a signal that demand side factors did not support increase in procurement and wholesale prices. This discouraged private trade to buy produce at official procurement prices and to participate in the grain marketing. Two, build up of huge buffer stock with government meant that it would be forced to reduce the level of excessive stock, which would dampen the domestic prices and might cause losses to those who bought grains before this happened. Third, there was an opportunity to buy some quantity at lower price in lean period compared to prices during the harvest period. Apart from lower price, this also meant shorter period for carrying stock. Fourth, as expected, government offered produce for open market sale and for export at a heavy discount in lean months. Private trade found it cheaper to buy rice and wheat from the government then, rather than buying from market and paying statutory and other charges. For instance, wheat was offered for sale under open market sale scheme during July 2001 to January 2002 at a price of Rs. 650/quintal in North, Rs. 695 in West, Rs. 720 in South and Rs. 705 in East zone (GoI, 2002). MSP/procurement price for this year was Rs. 610/ quintal. Including statutory charges and labour and material charges, purchase of one quintal of wheat from market in surplus states of Punjab would cost Rs. 707.65 (Table 5.12) in harvest season.

The cost in subsequent months including interest and storage cost and transport cost to other zones is shown in Table 5.12. In July, wheat directly purchased from market cost Rs. 719/quintal in North, Rs. 910 in West, Rs. 980 in South and Rs. 966 in East zone. Comparing this cost with the price at which government sold its stock in open market, shows that purchase of wheat from market cost Rs. 69 to Rs. 261 more than the purchase from government. Similarly, by the month of January, disincentive to those who purchased from market increased to Rs. 132 to Rs. 323 in different zones.

Table 5.12

Cost and Benefit of Buying Wheat from Market and Government, 2001-02

(Unit: Rupees/Quintal)

Particulars	*North Zone Punjab*	*West Zone Mumbai*	*East Zone Calcutta*	*South Zone Hyderabad*
1. MSP/Procurement Price	610.00			
2. Purchase Tax @ 4 Per cent	24.40			
3. Surcharge @ 1 Per cent	6.10			
4. Market Fee and RDF @ 4 Per cent	24.40			
5. Commission @ 2.5 Per cent	15.25			
6. Cost of Bag	20.00			
7. Bag Filling/Stitching	2.50			
8. Weighing	1.00			
9. Labour and Transport Cost from *Mandi* to Godown	4.00			
10. Reference Cost Price in Surplus State April–June	707.65	707.65	707.65	707.65
11. Monthly Interest on Working Capital @16 Per cent/Year	9.44	9.44	9.44	9.44
12. Storage Cost @ Rs. 1/Month/Bag	1.00	1.00	1.00	1.00
13. Forwarding Charges	1.00	1.00	1.00	1.00
14. Transport Cost by Road	-	191.50	247.00	261.00
15. Cost of Acquisition of 1 Quintal Produce:				
a. In July (Sum of Items 10 to 14)	719.09	910.59	966.09	980.09
b. In Next January (Item 15a+Interest and Storage Cost for 6 Months) + Item 11 & 12 for 6 Months + 13+14	781.70	973.20	1028.70	1042.70
16. Issue Price Under Open Market	650.00	695.00	705.00	720.00
17. Benefit to Private Sector in Buying from Government Instead of Direct Market				
a. In July	69.09	215.59	261.09	260.09
b. In Next January	131.70	278.20	323.70	322.70

Source: Primary Survey based on information collected from Punjab markets.

The incentive to depend on government supply for export was even bigger. Government supplied rice for export at a price of Rs. 565 to 600 during the year 2001, which were purchased at procurement price of Rs. 765 to Rs. 810 per 1.5 quintal of paddy which is equivalent to one quintal of rice. Similarly, wheat was supplied to private trade for export at a price more than 30 per cent lower than the MSP/procurement price. Clearly, the market conditions and perverse incentives created by government intervention in rice and wheat markets caused decline in the role of private trade in rice and wheat marketing, which is not a healthy trend for long run development of grain trade in the country.

Price Intervention in the New Context

The system of government intervention in agricultural prices has come of age. India has become marginally surplus in production of staples. Demand for staples has reached the level from where consumers are now diversifying their diets towards horticultural and livestock products. However, cereals continue to be the predominant and the cheapest source of energy and nutrition in the country (Chand *et al.*, 2004). Government intervention in agricultural prices must take cognizance of both; the diversification in diet and predominance of cereals in food and nutrition security. This requires that price policy should encourage diversification of production without causing serious setback to cereals production. In other words, production of high- value food crops should increase at a faster rate than cereals. Liberalisation of internal and external policy has thrown new options and challenges for achieving various goals of price intervention.

Trade liberalisation necessitates emphasis on efficiency due to competition from import and in export. It also provides for using trade as an option to stabilise domestic prices. Private sector now is in a better position to undertake spatial and temporal marketing of farm produce. Markets at the wholesale level are found to be integrated for several products (Wilson, 2001; Jha *et al.*, 1997) and market infrastructure has improved a lot to respond to gluts, scarcities, and price signals. Theses changes have made it imperative to redefine the goals for government role in price determination and develop new mechanisms and instruments to achieve those goals. Also, there is rich experience of past four decades that can be used to make the intervention more relevant, effective and meaningful.

Objectives of Price Intervention

The main objectives of price intervention would remain as (1) ensuring remunerative returns to producers, (2) price stabilisation and (3) food security. These objectives should not be pursued in isolation of the challenges facing Indian agriculture. These challenges relate to growth, efficiency, equity and sustainability. Addressing these challenges requires efforts on several fronts, and prices are only one of the instruments to address agricultural challenge. The price intervention needs to be suitably dovetailed with other instruments to attain the objectives of price policy and to address the challenges facing Indian agriculture.

Ensuring Remunerative Returns

In the past, government has ensured guaranteed prices to producers by procuring produce at MSP/procurement price. This could be done on a limited scale and only for a few commodities. The demand and pressure to ensure guaranteed prices to other crops and in other regions, through procurement mechanism, are mounting. Such demand is genuine but it is just not feasible to procure every commodity produced and sold everywhere in the country to prevent prices falling below the floor. Thus, new mechanisms have to be devised to protect producers against price risk.

We feel that some arrangement like MSP must continue but there is strong need and scope to reform the basis and coverage of MSP. Though CACP is required to take several factors into consideration while recommending MSPs, in actual practice MSPs are based on projected cost of production of concerned crop.[6] When cost of production is the basis for MSP, inefficiency gets in-built into the production. Farmers do not have to bother if growing a particular crop on the land unsuitable for its cultivation would raise cost of production. This is exactly what has happened in the case of extension of rice cultivation to semi-arid regions and sandy soils in the states like Punjab and Haryana, which is creating a host of environmental and natural resources problems in addition. Second, fixing MSPs based on cost of production totally neglects changes in society's preference

6. This is also acknowledged by Abhijit Sen Committee Report on Long Term Grain Policy (2002) para 3.3.

for a commodity. This way, incentive through MSPs can result in serious imbalances in what is being produced and what is required or demanded. Third, during the years of shortage and scarcity, more emphasis is needed on augmenting supply which gives some justification to give farmers a price higher than the cost of production. When there is no scarcity of the produce, then it becomes more important to ensure that what is produced gets sold. In such a situation, price based on demand side factors become more relevant and it becomes prudent to give an equally strong weight to demand side factors[7] as to cost of production or supply side factors in the determination of MSP.

Further, scientific basis should be used to arrive at imputed value of costs like rent on own land, and interest and depreciation on fixed investments. In no case, MSP should be beyond market clearing price as that drives out private trade, put excessive burden for procurement by official agencies and hurts consumers.

Under the new dispensation, CACP should suggest two types of prices, namely, Minimum Support Prices (MSP) and Market Insured Price (MIP) to provide price guarantee. The MSP should be restricted only to basic staples like paddy and wheat due to their importance in national food security. Other major crops should be covered my MIP.

The MSP in the basic staples should be made effective in all the districts which have the surplus. The coverage should be changed with new districts becoming surplus or old districts becoming deficit due to various reasons like diversification away from cereals. In some of these districts, MSP should be ensured through procurement, restricted to buffer stock norms and PDS requirement. In the remaining districts any negative deviation from MSP should be met by the system of deficiency price payment (DPP) in regulated markets. This option is often rejected on the ground that sellers and traders would connive to manipulate market and sales. This can be checked in two ways. One, this problem should not be there in the districts

7. This can be done by computing market clearing level of price that would result in absorbing net availability of projected production in domestic market. This price can then be used to compute corresponding level of MSP relevant to demand side factors. Here, it is pertinent to point out that for the year 2000-01, which was not a good agricultural year as cereal production was 7 million tonne below trend, equilibrium between demand and supply implies that cereal prices should have been 27 per cent lower than actual market price (see Chand, 2003, for details).

where markets are relatively more developed and competitive. Two, magnitude of DPP should be restricted to the level of sum of market taxes and market charges.

In low productivity regions having large potential like states of Bihar, East Uttar Pradesh, Orissa, Assam, Chhattisgarh and West Bengal, MSP should be ensured through procurement. These states have poor marketing infrastructure and underdeveloped and exploitative private trade. Thus, focus of procurement should gradually shift from traditional Green Revolution belt to the untapped region. This would help in boosting deceleration in growth of cereal output and in reaping technological gains. Agriculturally developed region has relatively well-developed marketing infrastructure and private trade is keen to undertake marketing of grains in this region. If government restrictions on trade are removed then private trade would take active part in agriculture marketing and reduce the need for government procurement and supply.

The other important crops should be covered by MIP. CACP should declare MIP based on paid out cost (A2) and emerging domestic and international demand and supply situation before commencement of sowing season. MIP should work on the similar lines as income insurance scheme prepared by the Ministry of PDS and Consumers Affairs and Ministry of Agriculture, Government of India. Any farmer having marketable surplus of the crops selected for MIP should be offered attractive terms for going for price insurance for expected quantity of crop surplus. A part of the price insurance premium should be paid by the state and central governments. This way, MIP should provide the guarantee against the prices going below the floor level and cover the risk against price fluctuations.

Price Stabilisation and Food Security

Given the volatility in international prices India should continue to maintain reasonable level of buffer stock. Some researchers found trade to be a much better option than buffer stock for inter-year price stabilisation, resulting from fluctuations in domestic production (Jha and Srinivasan, 1999). These findings were based on a very narrow time base. Comparison of domestic and international prices for the longer time series indicate that buffer stock is a better option than trade for safeguarding the interests of consumers as well as for producers (Chand, 2003). Therefore, India should continue to maintain the buffer stock for maintaining inter-year price stability. The level of buffer stock on this count should be around million tonne.

India continues to have large population living below poverty line. This section does not have purchasing power to buy required foodgrains at market price to meet minimum nutrition requirement. Therefore, PDS must continue for those living below the poverty line. Moreover, it needs to be streamlined and better targeted so that it covers those who need it most and does not become another avenue to swindle the public resources.

Total requirement for PDS is estimated to be 21 million tonne per annum (Economic Survey, 2000-01: 50). Procurement for PDS would be a continuous exercise requiring purchase of rice and wheat each year. For price stability, procurement would be needed when anticipated output is above the trend or normal level of output. Thus, total procurement of grain in a given year should be around the sum of quantity needed for PDS and excess of estimated output from normal production. Similarly, maximum level of buffer stock should be 18.13 million tonne which is the sum of stock needed for PDS for six months (21 divided by 2) and highest shortfall observed in grain production during the recent 10 years (which is found to be 7.63 million tonne except a very abnormal year like severe drought of the year 2002-03). The amount of foodgrains needed for PDS supply and inter-year price stabilisation could be partly met from the procurements undertaken to enforce MSPs and remaining quantity should be purchased through competitive bid from the markets where prices are ruling lowest.

References

Chand, Ramesh (2002). *Trade Liberalisation, WTO and Indian Agriculture: Experience and Prospects*, Mittal Publications, New Delhi.

———. (2003). "Government Intervention in Foodgrain Markets in India in the Changing Context", *Policy Paper* 19, National Centre for Agricultural Economics and Policy Research, New Delhi.

Chand, Ramesh, P. Kumar and Sapna Sinha (2004). Impact of Agricultural Trade and Related Reforms on Domestic Food Security in India, Report of the study done for FAO Rome, Institute of Economic Growth, Delhi, November.

Government of India (2002). *Report of the High Level Committee on Long Term Grain Policy*, Department of Food and Public Distribution, Ministry of Consumer Affairs, Food and Public Distribution, New Delhi, July.

Jha, Raghbendra, K.V. Bhanu Murthy, Hari K. Nagarajan and Ashok K. Seth (1997). "Market Integration in Indian Agriculture", *Economic Systems*, Vol. 21(3), pp.217-234.

Jha, Shikha and P.V. Srinivasan (1999). "Grain Price Stabilisation in India: Evaluation of Policy Alternatives", *Agricultural Economics*, Vol. 21(1), pp.93-108.

Wilson, E.J. (2001). "Testing Integration of Agricultural Markets in India: Conceptual and Empirical Considerations using Wholesale Prices", in D.P. Chaudhri and S.S. Acharya (eds.), *Indian Agricultural Policy at the Crossroads*, Rawat Publications, Jaipur and New Delhi.

World Bank (1999). *India Foodgrain Marketing Policies: Reforming to Meet Food Security Needs*, Vol. I and II, Report No. 18329-IN, April 17.

———. (2002). *World Development Indicators 2002*, Washington DC.

Part III

Research, Technology and Extension

6

Public-Private Partnership in Agricultural R&D

Challenges and Prospects

SURESH PAL and DAYANATHA JHA

Introduction

The national agricultural research system (NARS) in India has successfully ushered the 'green, white, yellow and blue revolutions'. The country is not only self-sufficient in food production but also in a position of strength in the world market in some commodities. The accumulating body of evidence indicates significant contribution of agricultural research and development (R&D) to the growth in agricultural total factor productivity, generating impressive rates of returns (more than 50 per cent) to the investments (Rosegrant and Evenson, 1992). However, recent changes in agricultural, economic and scientific environments have impacted the national agricultural R&D policy in many ways. Commercialisation of agriculture, diversification towards high-value crops, conservation of natural resources, development of marginal areas, increasing consumers' preference for quality products, intellectual property rights (IPR)-related constraints in technology transfer, etc. are some of the new challenges, besides continuing priority for household food and nutrition security and poverty alleviation. Economic liberalisation and globalisation provide new opportunities for export-led growth in agriculture by achieving and exploiting export competitiveness. On the scientific front, advancements in biotechnology provide new opportunities for enhancing growth potential and economic efficiency in agriculture, and also attract multiple stakeholders in funding, provision and commercialisation of R&D services. In order to respond to these new, complex R&D needs and to avail emerging growth opportunities, R&D system has to be more strong and vibrant.

A number of reforms are necessary for enhancing ability of the agricultural R&D system to respond to the new challenges. The most important among these reforms is modernisation of the public R&D system through organisation and management reforms, so that it addresses R&D needs of multiple stakeholders in a cost-effective manner. Dependence on the public system may not be sufficient to attain desired level of R&D intensity, and therefore, alternate sources of funding should supplement the public funds. These funds should be utilised to target high impact priority areas by developing appropriate institutional arrangements (Pal and Byerlee, 2003). As argued in this chapter, private sector can play an important role in this direction. The public and private sectors can interact in several ways for providing R&D services, depending upon their comparative advantage and national research needs. The public and private sectors can come together to articulate R&D needs and pool their resources to address them in a partnership mode. The sharing of prioritised demand-driven R&D agenda on the principle of comparative advantage in funding and delivery of R&D services can improve overall efficiency of the system manifold.

Such partnerships are quite common in the developed NARSs having a significant presence of private R&D organisations with formal regulations in place for commercialisation of technologies. The Indian NARS is developing on these lines and appropriate policy and regulatory measures will be useful in accelerating this process. This chapter outlines some of the issues to enhance the role of private R&D in India and to generate synergies by fostering its partnership with the public sector. The chapter first presents level of public and private investments in agricultural R&D in India. This is followed by a discussion on the rationale for and current status of the public-private partnership. The measures taken to strengthen the public-private partnership in the Indian context are discussed in the next section. Finally, the chapter raises some issues for further action.

Agricultural R&D in India

Intensity of Investments

The Indian NARS is dominated by the public funded and administered institutions, namely, Indian Council of Agricultural

Research (ICAR) and the state agricultural universities (SAUs). The participation of private sector both in research and extension is at the margin. The country spent 0.42 per cent of her agricultural gross domestic product (AgGDP) on agricultural research and education (R&E) during the triennium ending 2001, which was slightly higher than that in TE ending 1983 (Table 6.1). In absolute terms, the R&E expenditure increased from Rs. 7,808 million at 2001 prices in 1981-1983 to Rs. 17,695 million in TE 1999-2001. Initially, the share of state government funds was higher, but rapid expansion of the ICAR system raised the central government share, and now both the sources of funds contribute equally to the national kitty. Contrary to the R&E funding, most of the extension expenditure (more than 95 per cent) was contributed and spent by the state governments through their line departments. Although the extension expenditure in real terms increased from Rs. 2,169 million in TE 1981-83 to Rs. 6,548 million in TE 1999-2001—a more than threefold increase, the investment intensity as per cent of AgGDP remained low (0.17 per cent) (Table 6.1). Even if we consider the fact that ICAR/SAU system spends on frontline extension, i.e. on-farm testing, refinement and transfer of new technologies, training etc., overall extension intensity remained still low, as compared to the R&E intensity in the country. These levels of research and extension intensities are inadequate to modernise the infrastructural facilities and address expanded R&D agenda. It may be noted here that the corresponding levels of research and extension investment intensities are more than 2 per cent and 1 per cent of AgGDP for developed countries and 0.6 per cent and 0.3 per cent for the developing countries. Therefore, in order to raise the intensity equal to the developing countries' average, allocations of public funds to agricultural R&D should be doubled over a period of time. At the same time, efforts should be made to encourage the R&D system to generate resources by commercialisation of technologies and services. The private sector can also help bridge this gap in research and extension intensity. As seen subsequently, the private sector is currently investing in those technologies which can be embedded in inputs (embodied technologies), *viz.*, chemicals (pesticides and fertilisers), mechanical and biological (mainly hybrids) technologies. Most of these private investments are supporting in-house private research efforts and not much interest is shown to support research in the public or other institutions.

Table 6.1

Public Investment in Agricultural Research, Extension and Education in India

	1981-1983	*1999-2001*
Agricultural Research and Education		
Annual Public Expenditure (Rs. Million at 2001 Prices)	7808	17695
Public Expenditure as Percentage of AgGDP	0.36	0.42
Share of the Central Government in the Total Funding (%)	47.6	49.5
Share of the State Governments in the Total Funding (%)	52.4	50.5
Agricultural Extension		
Annual Public Expenditure (Rs. Million at 2001 Prices)	2169	6548
Public Expenditure as Percentage of AgGDP	0.10	0.17
Share of the Central Government in the Total Funding (%)	4.6	7.6
Share of the State Governments in the Total Funding (%)	95.4	92.4

Source: Based on data in Pal and Byerlee (2003) and Pal (2003).

Besides increasing agricultural R&D intensity, there are several other issues which require immediate attention. First is that the contribution of some states, particularly in the rainfed and eastern region, to agricultural R&D is low. In these states, most of the funds are utilised for salary and pension and the share of operating expenses is very low. This problem appears more acute when we compare ICAR with SAUs—expenditure per scientist is very low in the SAUs, which barely meets salary and other overhead expenses. Research infrastructure and scientific manpower is affected adversely in SAUs, and as a result, ICAR has taken greater role for applied research. Thus, there is a need for correcting this imbalance in funding by higher allocation of state funds to agricultural R&D. This requires sensitisation of policy makers at the state level to the payoffs of investing in agricultural R&D. The other concerns relate to the need for improvement of efficiency of public R&D organisation and human capital development. Public R&D organisations should work closely with stakeholders to align R&D agenda with immediate felt needs and balance multiple research objectives like efficiency, sustainability of production systems and equitable development. This may require greater decentralisation of the systems and institutionalisation of objectives and transparent management tools (Pal and Byerlee, 2003).

The Role and Determinants of Private R&D[1]

Private sector can efficiently provide those goods and services which generate profits. Therefore, private sector's participation in R&D would depend upon the scope for appropriability of technologies. The rate of appropriability would be high in those goods and services which have high excludability (exclusion of non-authorised users) and high subtractability or rivalry (extent to use of a product affect its use by others). If we look at the characteristics of R&D products, embodied technologies developed through applied research are classified as toll or private goods as these have moderate to high degree of excludability and subtractability. Therefore, embodied technologies can be provided efficiently by the private sector (Table 6.2). But new knowledge generated through basic research is classified as public good having low excludability and subtractability and therefore, can be provided by the public sector. Since agricultural research by definition is applied research, participation of private sector is justified on economic grounds. Some applied research like crop and resource management research, generating information-based disembodied technologies has low appropriability in the short run, and therefore, may not attract private investment. Therefore, presence of the public sector is essential to provide disembodied technologies.[2] In the Indian context, effective demand for technologies is also constrained by preponderance of small and marginal farmers and it has tremendous implications for R&D (Jha, 2001). The public sector has a special obligation in this regard. Furthermore, efficiency of applied research is contingent upon basic research support and therefore, close interactions between the public and private sectors is inevitable.

As noted above, the main driver of private R&D investment is the ability of private firms to appropriate R&D benefits which, in turn, is affected by a number of factors. Important among these are demand for new technologies by farmers, supply-side factors determining R&D cost, nature of technology and government regulatory policies (Pray and Echeverria, 1991; Umali, 1992). These factors in the Indian context are discussed below.

---

1. This section is largely drawn from Jha and Pal (1999).
2. For detailed discussion on these issues, see Umali (1992).

Table 6.2

Nature of Public-Private Partnerships in Agricultural R&D

Activity	*Funding of R&D Services*	*Provision of R&D Services*	*Example*
1. Research	Basic Public, some private funding for strategic research	Public	New knowledge
Applied			
Embodied	Largely private, public for 'orphan crops'	Private for profit	Hybrids
Disembodied	Public	Private for non-profit, private input agencies	Crop and resource management
Adaptive			
Embodied	Private	Small private companies	Seed management
Disembodied	Public	Private non-profit with public support	Crop and resource management
2. Manpower training	Public, cost recovery	Public	Education and training in frontier areas
3. Regulations	Public, cost recovery	Public with private contracting	Varietal testing and release
4. Extension	Public, cost recovery	Public and private	Imparting skills, information on new technology

Demand for new technologies: The demand for new technologies is determined by size of the market and price and income levels. Given the size of agricultural sector, and increasing trend in commercialisation of agriculture and demand for high-value agricultural products, there is continuous expansion in the demand for new technologies in the country. Product prices, including research products, are influenced by sectoral (input and output prices) and macroeconomic policies (fiscal policy, trade policy, exchange rate, etc.). Greater reliance on market forces and integration of the national economy with rest of the world would encourage competition and efficient functioning of the markets. Relative market prices would decide direction of research by allocating more resources to those commodities which are in high demand. The new economic policies aimed to accelerate the pace of economic development would further increase the demand for new technologies. Higher demand for quality agricultural products will increase agricultural income, which in turn increases the demand for new technologies. Thus, assured, expanding market for new technologies is conducive to attract private research investment in the country.

Supply-side factors: Private R&D investment is significantly influenced by the supply-side factors like cost of R&D, scientific opportunities and basic research support. Research cost consists of cost of inputs (capital, stock of knowledge, manpower) and technical efficiency of the R&D system (Umali, 1992). Since public research system is strong in India, it will continue to provide basic research support and trained scientific manpower to private R&D institutions. Furthermore, quality of scientific manpower, developments in molecular biology, and accumulating stock of knowledge can improve the technical efficiency and reduce the lag and cost of R&D for the private sector. Thus, there are strong reasons for increasing the pace of private R&D investment in the country. Apart from these supply-side factors, nature of technology also affects private investment. For example, development of double-cross hybrids attracts more investment as these hybrids inherently exclude non-authorised commercialisation of technology through protection of inbred lines.

Public policies: Private R&D investment is also affected by macroeconomic, agricultural and R&D regulatory policies. Macroeconomic and agricultural policies affect private R&D investment as these policies have significant effect on input and output prices and R&D cost. The economy-wide reforms initiated in 1991, are expected to attract greater private-sector activities in the economy, including agricultural R&D. Similarly, R&D regulatory policies are reformed to attract the private investment. These reforms include lifting restrictions on the entry of foreign-owned companies, liberalising import of seed/germplasm under the New Policy for Seed Development and increasing access of private R&D programmes to public research material. ICAR is also encouraging contract research with the private sector and other organisations. Exemption of R&D expenditure and revenue from sale of certified seed from corporate tax, and provision of 'truthful labelled' seed sale under the Seed Act of 1966, are strong stimulating factors for private investment.

Private research investment has responded well to favourable regulatory policies and research support of the public institutions. For example, implementation of the New Policy for Seed Development in 1988 and free access to public research materials (inbred lines) have induced private investment in hybrid seed research (Pal and Tripp, 2003). Private research investment more than doubled between 1985 and 1995 (Pray and Fuglie, 2001). This indicates that further efforts to strengthen the linkages between public and private sectors and to provide level-playing field would ensure healthy growth of the NARS and efficient delivery of improved technologies to end users.

Another important regulatory policy encouraging private R&D investment is the protection of proprietary material. The Protection of Plant Varieties and Farmers' Rights Act (2001) and the amendment of the Patent Act to include product patents also will be major deviation from the past. In order to comply with the agreement on the trade-related aspects of intellectual property rights of the World Trade Organization, these provisions to protect intellectual property is effective from January 2005 and are expected to provide tremendous boost to private R&D. But the success of these new laws in terms of mobilising private investment would depend upon their smooth and effective enforcement.

Private Agricultural R&D Investment

Private R&D Investment in India

Rapid growth in private agricultural R&D investment spending in India has outpaced the capacity to track its capacity, orientation and impact. The broad estimates available, indicate that the business funding (largely private) for agricultural R&D constituted about 11 per cent of the total R&D funding. Most of these funds were utilised for in-house R&D. In real terms (1995 prices), private R&D expenditure increased from Rs. 800 million in 1985 to Rs. 1,695 million in 1995, registering an annual growth rate of 7.5 per cent which is higher than that for public funds (about 5 per cent) during the corresponding period.

As seen from Figure 6.1, the largest private investment occurred in chemicals (pesticides and fertilisers) and food processing, followed by seed and machinery. More recently, growth has been in plant breeding and biotechnology, animal health and poultry. A significant growth in these sectors is contributed by the transnational companies. A similar trend has been echoed by other Asian countries, except Malaysia and Philippines where the share of private R&D is more than twice of India. In the case of developed countries, the share of private sector is more than half, excepting Australia where it is less than in India (Table 6.3). However, the composition of private spending is quite similar to that in India. For example, in USA, spending by chemical and food processing companies dominates the private R&D, followed by plant breeding and biotechnology (Figure 6.1). Here it may be noted that in India private funding is mostly for in-house private R&D, whereas private funding accounts for a significant proportion (13 per cent) of funding in USDA and the state agricultural universities.

Figure 6.1

Composition of Private Research Investment in India and USA

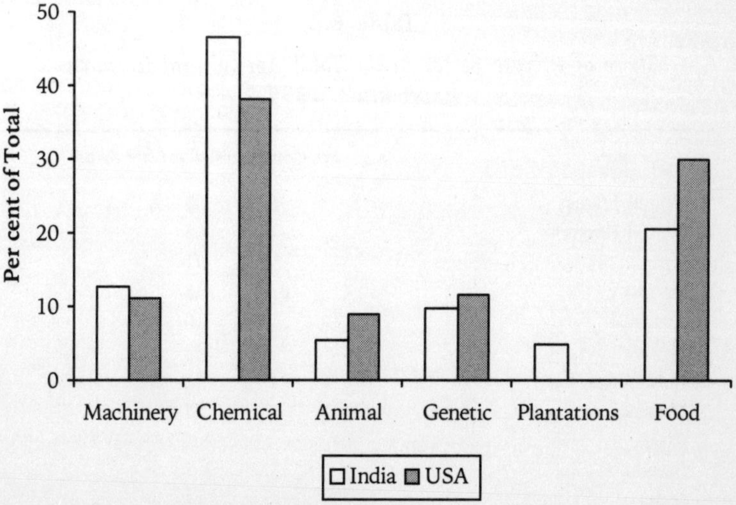

Source: Pray and Basant (2001) and Fuglie *et al.* (1997).

International Scenario

Table 6.3, shows the share of private sector in the total research expenditure. In the developed countries, like USA and UK which have large market, well-developed science infrastructure and strong intellectual property rights, private sector, mainly input industries, contribute more than half of the national agricultural research expenditure. On the other hand, in the developing countries like India and Brazil, the share of private investment is low in spite of well-developed science infrastructure and markets. Lack of IPRs, strong presence of public sector in inputs industry and restrictive domestic policies in the past, have restricted the growth of private R&D investment in these developing countries. With economic liberalisation, trade reforms and strengthening of IPR regime under the WTO regime, the growth of private sector has showed impressive growth. Food and post-harvest research account for lion's share of private research in Australia, Japan, New Zealand, USA and Netherlands. But chemical research including agricultural related pharmaceuticals research is major focus of the private sector in USA, UK and Germany (Alston *et al.*, 1998). Plant breeding research is of moderate priority for private investment in developed as well as in developing countries.

Table 6.3

Share of Private Sector in the Total Agricultural Research Expenditure, 1995

Country	*Per Cent Share of Private Sector*
United States	53
United Kingdom	63
Japan	51
Germany	58
Australia	10
Mexico	28
Philippines	22
Malaysia	21
China	3.2
Brazil	8
India	14

Source: Based on data in Alston *et al.* (1998), Pray (2002), Pray and Umali-Deininger (1998), Pray and Fuglie (2001) and Pal and Byerlee (2003).

Public-Private Partnerships

Conceptual Framework

A number of theoretical concepts are applied to study the public-private partnerships. The new institutional economics literature see the partnership as a strategy to minimise transaction costs associated with developing and enforcing contractual relations in provision of a good or service. The transaction costs are mainly determined by the frequency and uncertainty of a transaction, limit to rational behaviour of economic agents, and asset specificity of the transaction (Williamson, 1975). For example, a private seed company has to transact with public plant breeding programmes for new varieties and source seed. A high transaction cost with high asset specificity of establishing a plant breeding programme may help develop partnership with public-private plant breeding programmes (see ICRISAT model, Table 6.4). On the other hand, a low transaction cost will favour market-based transactions, while high low asset specificity can lead to vertical integration bringing seed production and plant breeding under a hierarchical structure. The second important conceptual framework used is the recent developments in the theory of organisational behaviour. The analysis blurs the classical difference between public and private sectors, and underlines the need for partnerships for efficient provision of a good or service with equitable social benefits, whilst maintaining higher flexibility, accountability of private sector and social interest of public sector (O'Looney, 1992). Other approaches focus on traditional welfare analysis in use of scarce resources, development of networks of innovations for given social and economic institutions, and incentives and relationships that shape the flow of knowledge and information (for a detailed discussion, see Spielman and Grebmer, 2004).

One may infer that incentives, problems and risks associated with incentives, contextual realities and nature of goods or services are important for developing and enforcing the partnerships. Since R&D is a risky activity with high asset specificity, contractual relations that shape the flow of knowledge are critical for establishing research partnerships. Macroeconomic policies and social and economic institutions further influence the attitudes and pace of research partnerships. For example, greater reliance on market forces and enabling institutions like IPRs may facilitate research partnerships, while public and private sector will continue to maintain a negative perception in an inward-looking economic environment.

Table 6.4
Some Examples of Public-Private Partnerships in India

R&D Area	*Institutions Involved*	*Nature of Partnership*	*Synergy Achieved*
1. Hybrid rice programme of ICAR	ICAR, SAUs, IRRI, Mahyco	Co-financing of upscaling research	Technology refinement and upscaling
2. Pearlmillet and sorghum consortium of ICRISAT	ICRISAT and private seed companies	Private funding of ICRISAT breeding programme	Focused priorities for plant breeding
3. Zero-tillage for the rice-wheat system	Rice-Wheat Consortium, ICAR, SAUs, private manufacturers	Training and further technical support to drill manufacturers	Technology refinement and transfer
4. Commercialisation of technologies, NATP	Public R&D organisations and private industry	Competitive public funding for pilot testing and commercialisation of technologies	Refinement and commercialisation of technologies
5. Seed industry	Public plant breeding and biotech programmes and private seed companies	Private delivery of public material	Improved efficiency of the system
6. Integrated pest management	ICAR, SAUs, NGOs	Refinement and upscaling of IPM packages for different crops	Cost-effectiveness and acceleration of adoption
7. Extension	ICAR, NGOs	Public funding for private delivery of extension services and farmers training	Improved research-extension-farmer linkages

Source: Compiled by authors.

infrastructure facilities, and market for inputs and new technologies is expanding rapidly. ICAR, as an apex agricultural R&D organisation of the country, has initiated a process of reforms to respond to new R&D challenges and to actively involve private sector in the national R&D efforts. It initiated dialogues with private R&D organisations, NGOs and other stakeholders. A number of policy decisions were taken through a consultative process (Box 6.1). These decisions underscored continuity of dialogue, sharing for resources, expertise and cost and benefits of technologies in a transparent manner, capacity building, and developing a culture of mutual confidence and trust. Although these initiatives are quite comprehensive and path breaking in several ways, there are a few examples of successful partnerships (Table 6.4). In the case of hybrid rice, ICAR, SAUs, IRRI and national private seed companies collaborated for development of male sterile lines, development of hybrids and refinement of seed multiplication technologies. The partnership upscaled hybrid rice technology and intensified plant breeding and seed multiplication activities in private sector. The technology is now commercialised and being adopted even in marginal areas of Eastern India because of significant yield advantage. A similar example of upscaling and popularisation of technology is the resource conservation technologies like zero-tillage for the rice-wheat system. In this partnership, zero-tillage technology was refined and popularised in a partnership of an international organisation (i.e. CIMMYT), ICAR institutes, SAUs and private drill manufacturers. The technology led to significant cost and water saving, and is spreading rapidly in the rice-wheat system. The public research system from other South Asian countries, particularly Pakistan, and Nepal also participated in this partnership and benefited from the technology. Partnership with non-profit private organisations, or NGOs was established for the *krishi vighyan kendras* (KVK) for demonstration of new technologies and farmers' trainings. In this experiment, NGOs managed a KVK which was funded by ICAR. NGOs were also involved in farmers' participatory research like validation and local adaptation of the module for integrated pest management and farmers' training in use of IPM package. In order to encourage public-private partnerships for pilot testing and commercialisation of new technologies, ICAR also established a competitive grant programme under the National Agricultural Technology Project.

Box 6.1

Initiatives Taken by ICAR to Foster Public-Private Partnerships

1. Characterise and target the potential domain for different R&D services providers based on comparative advantage.
2. Formation of functional groups for guidance for research planning, sharing and conservation of genetic resources, achieving global competitiveness.
3. Procedures for accreditation of private R&D organisations, guidelines for functional relationships, IPRs, etc.
4. Active role of private sector in policy planning and research evaluation in public R&D organisations.
5. Need assessment for capacity building, including HRD, in frontier areas of science like biotechnology.
6. Enhancing technological options of farmers matching their resource, production, market and institutional environment through strategic dissemination of complementing technologies from public and private sectors.
7. Utilisation of ICAR revolving fund and competitive grants for strategic technological interventions.
8. Promotion of contract research and consultancy services of ICAR for private R&D.
9. Documentation of resources, technologies and services of the public sector available for the private sector.
10. Develop mutual confidence and trust.

Source: Pal and Joshi (1999).

In spite of these successes, there are certain constraints and rigidities which need to be addressed. First and foremost is inordinate delay in response to a private sector's request for a partnership. Private sector would appreciate and value a timely response from the public organisations which is possible in a decentralised system. Delay and uncertainty in establishing a partnership may enhance transaction cost. In order to avoid this, private sector would prefer to enter into some kind of agreement with other private companies, or with an international organisation. Perhaps the ICRISAT's consortium of private seed companies reflects this concern. A group of private seed companies, both national and international, have formed a consortium to fund plant breeding programme of ICRISAT for pearlmillet and sorghum (Table 6.4). The member companies pay annual fee and have access to advanced breeding material. The material is available to the public plant-breeding programmes, but not to non-member seed companies. Private seed companies benefit from advanced breeding material and with a minimise research cost, while ICRISAT is able to generate substantial resources to fund its breeding programmes for the crops. A similar partnership can be established by the national plant-breeding programmes with the national and state seed companies. The National Botanical Research Institute has taken a lead in this direction for Bt cotton, but their initiative is constrained by the lack of freedom to operate. In addition to addressing technical issues like freedom to operate in an era of IPRs, development of mutual confidence and trust among the partners is a major issue which shall build over a period of time. However, this requires transparent procedures and commitment to honour the contract and confidentiality of information. While all these issues are important for working in a partnership mode, there are other modes of partnerships which are largely governed by markets. The markets for technologies provide ample opportunities to work independently to complement each other's activities through market-based contracts. For example, public sector can develop inbred lines or semi-finished breeding material, which can be taken by private seed companies on agreed conditions for development of a finished product. This can be further licenced to another private seed company for multiplication and distribution of seed. The government should play a facilitating role in such cases.

The Case of Seed Industry

This section highlights the degree of and facilitating conditions for public-private partnerships in the provision of seed, and also examines their sustainability. Table 6.5, indicates the existence of a number of conditions pertaining to incentives, comparative advantage and regulatory framework reinforcing the public-private partnership. All the elements or functions of seed provision involve some degree of interface between the public and private sectors. This is particularly noteworthy in the provision of source seed, where the main facilitating factors are open access to public varieties and a transparent mechanism for acquiring the seed. The ICAR has taken further initiatives to foster the partnership by developing mechanisms for sharing resources, improving private sector access to the products of public research institutions, encouraging public-private joint programmes and involving the private sector's participation in policy-making (Pal and Joshi, 1999). Since both the sectors have incentives (the public sector to make a wider research impact and the private sector to commercialise public varieties), such a partnership is likely to be sustainable.

Table 6.5
Public-Private Partnership in the Provision of Seed

Elements	*Nature of Interface*	*Sustainability*
Acquisition of Source Seed	• Open access to public varieties • Supply of source seed by the public sector • Commercial sale of foundation seed by public seed agencies	• The public sector has the incentive of wider technology impact • Resource generation by the public sector • Provision under seed law • Transparent mechanism to acquire source seed
Seed Multiplication	Training of private sector personnel in seed production techniques by public research institutions	Increasing understanding of private sector as potential client of public research products
Quality Control	Extending public seed certification and testing services to private seed agencies	• Provision under seed law, but seed agencies argue for liberal procedure • Incentive of subsidy on certified seed of 'new' variety
Conditioning and Storage	Private processing of public agency's seed on contract basis and *vice versa*	• Incentive of increasing market share in seed sale • Utilise excess seed-processing capacity
Marketing	• Private sale (by seed dealers) of public agency's seed • Trade in commercial seed between public and private seed agencies	• Commercial incentive for the private sector • Public sector to bridge seed demand-supply gap
Seed Information	Private delivery of information of varieties through television and farm magazine	• Private media to cover programmes/information of public (including farmers) interest • Private sector unlikely to promote new varieties

Source: Pal *et al.* (2000).

The interface is also seen in seed conditioning and quality control. The contract sharing of processing facilities is certainly an encouraging feature. But the seed agencies argue for some liberalised form of seed certification. Seed companies have the incentive to maintain seed quality and improve brand reputation, although they still have much work to do. The government has the responsibility of enforcing seed quality standards. It is important that these elements of quality control are embedded in a regulatory framework without affecting the system's efficiency adversely.

A major weakness in the partnership is the inadequate attention paid by private seed companies to promote new public varieties. For example, in the case of rice, the formal seed system is less effective in delivering the seed of new varieties and information about them (Pal *et al.*, 2000). As of now, private seed companies do not have commercial incentives to invest in the promotion of new rice varieties. As and when hybrid rice is widely adopted, there will be an increasing participation on the part of private seed companies in the delivery of seed and information on hybrids because of the higher incentives in proprietary hybrids. In the case of non-hybrid rice, there could be two options. First, effective enforcement of the Plant Variety Protection Act, may provide some incentives to the private sector, leading to private investment in variety development. This will be largely influenced by the companies' perception of the potential seed demand, even if farmers use farm-saved seed and exchange seed with fellow farmers. The second possibility could be to assign exclusive marketing rights of public varieties to private seed companies, which would then presumably invest more in variety promotion. But the second option could lead to some kind of monopoly situation in the seed market, and therefore, may not be a reality in the near future. Irrespective of how events unfold, the public sector has to assume greater responsibility for the dissemination of seed information by strengthening its ongoing programmes, such as seed minikits. Another possibility could be to involve private seed companies, NGOs, farmers and extension agencies in variety testing.

This example demonstrates that even forms of public-private partnerships can be of mutual benefit to both the sectors and can serve farming community in a more effective manner. There is a need for promoting such partnerships in provision of R&D services to marginal and isolated agricultural production environment. One successful example of this has been, public delivery of private seed, mostly of vegetables, in inaccessible regions of Himachal Pradesh, where the government procures seeds from private seed companies through open tender and the line department distributes seeds to farmers.

Concluding Remarks

It is clear from the foregoing discussion that the Indian agricultural R&D is still dominated by public organisations, and private R&D is now expanding rapidly. It is quite unlikely that increasing private participation will bridge the gap in the intensity of agricultural R&D in near future. Nevertheless, both the sectors can complement each other's role, and useful synergies could be obtained by developing partnerships in development and dissemination of technologies. The experience gained so far echoed the trend observed in developed countries. It is quite likely that majority of the partnerships could be developed through market-based transactions and the public and private sectors can complement each other's role. However, there are certain factors which necessitate the need for the collaborative partnerships. Most of the national R&D companies may not compete with the multinationals in the new regime of IPR and therefore, would look forward to the public system for R&D support, even on benefit-cost-sharing basis. This type of arrangements can work better if there is a timely response from the public system, and the mechanisms, particularly for cost-benefit sharing are transparent and simple. Both the sectors should develop mutual trust and confidence and learn from the experience. In particular, the public sector should take lead in transfer of technologies, and wherever necessary provide incentives and funding support for delivery of sustainability-enhancing agricultural technologies, and capacity building at the grassroots level for technology adaptation. Finally, although it is necessary to honour secrecy of the agreements, it is important that benefits and experiences of the public-private partnerships are adequately documented and widely disseminated for encouraging others to learn and participate.

References

Alston, J.M., P.G. Pardey and J. Roseboom (1998). "Financing Agricultural Research: International Investment Patterns and Policy Perspectives", *World Development*, Vol. 26(6), pp.1057-1071.

Fuglie, K., N. Ballenger, K. Day, C. Klotz, M. Ollinger, J. Reilly, U. Vasavada and J. Yee (1997). *Agricultural Research and Development: Public and Private Investment Under Alternative Markets and Institutions*, AER 735, Economic Research Service, USDA, Washington, DC.

Jha, D. (2001). "Agricultural Research and Small Farms", Presidential address delivered at the 60th Annual Conference of the Indian Society of Agricultural Economics, *Indian Journal of Agriculture Economics*, Vol. 56(1), pp.1-23.

Jha, D. and Suresh Pal (1999). "Strengthening ICAR-Private Sector Interface in Agricultural Research", in Suresh Pal and P.K. Joshi (eds.), *New Paradigms for Agricultural Research Management*, workshop proceedings, National Centre for Agricultural Economics and Policy Research, New Delhi.

O'Looney, J. (1992). "Public-Private Partnerships in Economic Development: Negotiating the Trade-off between Flexibility and Accountability", *Economic Development Review*, Vol. 10(4), pp.14-22.

Pal, Suresh (2003). "Evaluation of Initial Experiences with Agricultural Extension Reforms in India", Paper presented at the 25th International Conference of Agricultural Economists, 16-22 August 2004, Durban, South Africa.

Pal, Suresh and D. Byerlee (2003). "The Funding and Evolution of Agricultural Research in India: Evolution and Emerging Policy Issue", *Policy Paper* 16, NCAP, New Delhi.

Pal, Suresh and P.K. Joshi (eds.) (1999). *New Paradigms for Agricultural Research Management*, Proceedings of the workshops, National Centre for Agricultural Economics and *Policy Research*, New Delhi.

Pal, Suresh and Robert Tripp (2003). "India's Seed Industry Reforms: Prospects and Issues", *Indian Journal of Agricultural Economics*, Vol. 57(3), pp.443-458.

Pal, Suresh, R. Tripp and A. Janaiah (2000). "Public-Private Interface and Information Flow in the Rice Seed System in Andhra Pradesh (India)", *Policy Paper* 12, NCAP/DRR/ODI, New Delhi, xi+41 p.

Pray, C. and K. Fuglie (2001). *Private Investment in Agricultural Research and International Technology Transfer in Asia*, AER 805, Economics Research Service, USDA, Washington, DC.

Pray, C. and R. Basant (2001). "India", in C. Pary and K. Fuglie (eds.), *Private Investment in Agricultural Research and International Technology Transfer in Asia*, AER 805, Economics Research Service, USDA, Washington, DC.

Pray, C.E. (2002). "The Growing Role of the Private Sector in Agricultural Research", in D. Byerlee and R.G. Echeverria (eds.), *Agricultural Research Policy in an Era of Privatization*, CABI Pub., Wallingford, UK.

Pray, C.E. and R.G. Echeverria (1991). "Private Sector Agricultural Research in Less-developed Countries", in P.G. Pardey, J. Roseboom and J.R. Anderson (eds.), *Agricultural Research Policy: International Quantitative Perspectives*, Cambridge University Press.

Pray, C.E. and D. Umali-Deininger (1998). "The Private Sector in Agricultural Research System: Will it Fill the Gap?", *World Development*, Vol. 26(6), pp.1127-1148.

Rosegrant, M.W. and R.E. Evenson (1992). "Agricultural Productivity and Sources of Growth in South Asia", *American Journal of Agricultural Economics*, Vol. 74(3), pp.757-761.

Spielman, D.J. and K. von Grebmer (2004). "Public-Private Partnership in Agricultural Research: An Analysis of Challenges facing Industry and the Consultative Group on International Agricultural Research", *EPTD Discussion Paper No.* 113, IFPRI, Washington, DC.

Umali, D.L. (1992). "Public and Private Sector Roles in Agricultural Research: Theory and Experience", *World Bank Discussion Paper* 176, Washington, DC.

Williamson, O.E. (1975). *Markets and Hierarchies*, Free Press, Collier Macmillan, London.

7

From Technology Development and Dissemination to Learning Approaches: Institutional Change for Rural Development

RAJESWARI S. RAINA and RASHEED SULAIMAN V.

Introduction

This chapter explores how linear knowledge flows and technological determinism work as the institutions/norms that govern public, private and civil society organisations involved in agricultural technology generation and dissemination. Based on an institutional analysis of successful technologies and the actors/organisations involved in these processes, this chapter argues for, (i) a shift from dissemination approaches to learning approaches; (ii) increasing partnerships among appropriate stakeholder groups along with modifications or changes in rules/norms that enable working in partnership; (iii) a change in perspective whereby the ultimate user is not the only beneficiary, but all the actors/organisations are beneficiaries—as learners—with their expectations/gains stated explicitly, and (iv) increasing and enabling more and appropriate platforms for learning (say, facilitated capacity development exercises/experiments) in different contexts with location-specific partnerships to enable hands on learning, innovation and development.

The past decade has been witness to a change in the ethos of Indian agricultural policy. Increasingly, the trend is to give up on the public sector and its role in agricultural development. The relative ineffectiveness of public sector is touted as the main reason for encouraging private and voluntary sector involvement in agricultural research and extension. Paradoxically, State patronage of public sector agricultural research and extension for technology generation, development and diffusion continues. Little has been done to change the way public sector agricultural research and extension is organised and governed.

In the agriculture sector there is increasing demand to change or improve the performance of the public sector organisations, increase the social accountability of the private sector, enhance the presence/ power of voluntary/civil society organisations and build more effective partnerships among all of them. The governance of agriculture to ensure agricultural development and livelihood security, involves the management of technologies as well as the ways and means that make technologies work—i.e., the institutions, rules/ norms. Like the AMUL innovation and development cluster, there are several other clusters *albeit* smaller, that teach us that these ways of working or rules that govern the way these actors/organisations function, have been crucial in enabling their partnerships with other organisations/actors including farmers, mutual learning and sharing of technology and knowledge, flexibility and ability to evolve, etc.

Yet there are strong norms that persist in mainstream agricultural research and extension organisations, their donors and policy makers. The two important ones are

(a) Linear knowledge flows: The linear models of R&D, where the explicit organisation of distinct functions—technology generation, dissemination, and adoption, are conducted in different organisations, arranged in a rigid linear top-down hierarchy,

(b) Technological determinism: The unwritten and accepted habit of thinking about solutions to rural/agricultural development problems as technical solutions that originate from science, and therefore (by default) of science as the single and most important source of knowledge for development.

This chapter will analyse how these norms/institutions shape the generation and application of knowledge in the agricultural/rural development sector. We explore these norms that govern the distinct compartments of research, extension and adoption, and govern the way each compartment deals with the rural realities and complexities of the development process. This understanding is essential to help us see how these norms/institutions can be changed/modified/

broken. This chapter focuses on the extension component, and the ways of working that are evident in our technology diffusion mechanisms; but the chapter discusses agricultural research and extension as being part of a larger system of agricultural innovation, where there are several learning processes evident in the technology development-diffusion continuum.

The Organisation of Agricultural Research and Extension in India

The consolidation and reorganisation of the ICAR (Indian Council of Agricultural Research) in 1966 took place with active inputs from a wide range of actors, including public and private sector agencies of the local economy and international public and private donor agencies like the USAID, and the Rockefeller, Ford and Kellogg Foundations (see Rajeswari, 1992). The reorganisation process involved technological and institutional inputs including funding, scientific personnel, equipment or strategic technical assistance in planning and implementing research programmes like the All India Co-ordinated Research Project and the 'package approach' to agricultural development. The actors also brought new norms and organisational formats for agricultural education. They engaged in negotiations and generated support for establishment of extension services at the State level.

In the 1950s and 1960s, the public sector agricultural research organisation was live with contending coalitions committed to professional excellence and social relevance in seeking to determine the direction, pace and significance of change in agriculture (Rajeswari, 1992; Biggs and Smith, 1998). In its involvement with other organisations or actors, the agricultural research organisation was learning from and with them, and changing. The public sector R&D approach to rural development and the application of technologies to this end, is evident in the massive compendiums of rural technologies produced by the public sector research organisations. That these archaic modes of knowledge production and utilisation continue in mainstream agricultural science/rural technology generation, development/diffusion organisations is a matter of serious concern.

The extension organisation has in similar fashion gone through several organisational changes since its origin in a broad-based Community Development Programme in the 1960s. The Training and Visit (T&V) system is the extension methodology, introduced as a structural change for greater technology impact in Departments of Agriculture in Indian states since the late 1970s. The T&V system rests on, "the assumption that an outside agency can accurately assess what is good for rural people and that the solution to rural under-development and poverty is the provision of science-based technical knowledge" (Nitsch, 1994: 21). This institution of hierarchy defines the functional basis of the technology-society interface in agriculture. Critiques have, however, come up with alternatives that are considered to be more relevant to and consistent with conditions for dynamic changes in agriculture (see, for example, Chambers, Pacey and Thrup, 1989; Scoones and Thompson, 1994; Roling, 1988; Nitsch, 1994; Biggs and Smith, 1998).

Some of these criticisms and suggestions for extension reform were taken up by the Government and other private and voluntary sector agencies. For instance, a wider approach to delivery of knowledge inputs in rural areas, also known as 'extension plus' approach, has been tried in a few donor funded agricultural development programmes such as KHDP (Kerala Horticulture Development Programme) and DASP. Extension plus involves improved access to markets, research, advice, credit, infrastructure, farmer organisation development and business development services, etc. (Sulaiman and Hall, 2002; 2004). But in the mainstream extension services—in the Departments of Agriculture in every State, technology dissemination as given in the 'package of practices' (mainly for crop/commodity production) supplied from the State Agricultural Universities (SAUs) continues to be the only role of and expectation from extension. In the private sector, agri-business firms such as Rallis and Mahindra and financial institutions like BASIX have innovated mechanisms to provide integrated technical support to farmers (*ibid.*, and Sulaiman, 2003). But public sector extension has been largely unable to learn lessons from these experiences, or interact fruitfully with these private endeavours. It is argued that public sector extension has a legacy of working in isolation, while working in partnership is essential to play the expanded role (Sulaiman *et al.*, 2005).

The recent growth in private and NGO activities in technology development and dissemination has brought new questions to public sector extension. First and foremost, it is clear that there is no 'either or' question here—both private and public sector extension are necessary and have their respective roles to play (Ekbior and Parallada, 2001; Sulaiman *et al.*, 2005). Private sector or NGO led extension efforts are not enough and there is a dire need for public sector extension. This is because the former focuses almost exclusively on favourable and well endowed areas, medium and large farmers, and crops with commercial potential where they are assured a reasonably good profit (Sulaiman *et al.*, 2005). The latter being largely un-organised does need a consistent interaction and support from public sector knowledge components—especially in the emerging intellectual property rights scenario. Secondly, the commodity focused private extension though very useful, is highly limited because it does not engage with any of the key issues that confront rural development today; these range from gender impacts/relationships to degradation of natural resources and/or market development in itself to enable entry to a wider range of products and services (Sulaiman, 2003). Third and more process oriented is the concern that private (and even voluntary/NGO led) extension survives by keeping certain core competencies with itself. In other words, though immediate short term gains in production/productivity and cost reduction or even resource conservation and empowerment of the local people with technical/organisational skills may be visible, few private agencies enable capacity development for technological and institutional changes in a rural population. The 'means of development' are always retained in the hands of the private sector—the poor can access it at a price, again dictated by the private owner of the technology/knowledge. Finally, the need for reform in public sector extension and in the civil society role in developing these capacities for rural development rings urgent. All (public/private/civil society) initiatives in technology dissemination need to learn how technology dissemination can be nested into the broader livelihoods needs/problems of the poor and small/marginal producers. The linear knowledge flows from public and private sector research organisations/firms seem to have worked for those who have access to the basic amenities or advantages in life. The privileged are those who can find the ways and means to access the knowledge/technologies they need, adapt them and adopt them, with the help of other institutional arrangements like appropriate credit, price policies, service and maintenance facilities, and the communication channels that the poor cannot access on their own.

There is an increasing awareness of the limited capacity within public sector agricultural research and extension organisations to address the increasing concerns over poverty, ecological degradation, rural employment, and overall development. Suggestions have been made for institutional and organisational change in agricultural research and extension to meet these challenges.[1] Much of what has been prescribed by social scientists for institutional reform in R&D and extension organisations can be summarized into:

(a) increased investments (1-2 per cent of Agricultural GDP) in R&D,

(b) better and more sophisticated research priority setting,

(c) improved technology transfer and dissemination mechanisms,

(d) organisation and management (O&M) reforms including delegation of decision-making capacity down the line to Principal Investigators especially financial decentralisation, incentives for scientists, training for extension workers, etc.,

(e) re-defining the national, regional and location-specific goals and R&D actors (the upstream research, advocacy and facilitation role of the national level ICAR and the regionally differentiated, strategic and applied, location specific, and locally accountable research and teaching for SAUs the two central components of public R&D), and

(f) creation of new autonomous bodies to integrate field extension activities at the district level and privatisation of extension services.

But these recommendations do not unfortunately change the way knowledge is produced or utilised in society.

---

1. The National Agriculture Policy (GoI, 2000), the NATP–Main Document (ICAR, 1998), and several articles including Jha (2001), Paroda and Mruthyunjaya (1999), Mruthyunjaya (2002), Raina (2003a).

Institutions and the Governance of Agricultural Research and Extension

Increasing evidence of several actors/organisations playing active and varied roles in agricultural/rural innovations has puzzled conventional wisdom about knowledge/technology generation and its utilisation. For one, the agricultural knowledge system now confronts a rapidly evolving social, economic, scientific and ecological context. These contexts are more complex because with increasing concerns about poverty and ecological degradation we witness an overall disillusionment with the application of science to rural development problems and an increasing concentration of scientific prowess in the hands of a few experts and their massive enterprises—whether multinational/private, public or voluntary. That in frontier areas like information technology and biotechnology the borders between these sectors are being re-drawn with quasi public-quasi private R&D programmes and technology incubation initiatives makes the context more complex.

Knowledge production is moving steadily from Mode 1 (generated within a disciplinary context, governed by linear rules, in distinct organisations) to Mode 2 (created in broader transdisciplinary contexts, in a non-linear fashion, in networks/groups of actors who take on different roles in the generation, modification, utilisation etc. of knowledge/technology) (Gibbons *et al.*, 1994). Cases of Mode 2 knowledge production and utilisation reveal that (i) the means of development are many—technology is but one among them, and (ii) several actors/organisations have access to (and the capacity to modify) these knowledge/technology inputs, processes and outputs. In the next section we explore how and why the sciences/knowledge for agricultural and rural development continues to exist in narrow linear formats offering exclusive access to a select few, and unable to reach out to and involve wider networks of organisations and individuals. The governance of knowledge seems to decide how and why the poor have/do not have access to the means of development—including knowledge.

A Prologue to Governance and Institutions

The greatest lessons we learn from AMUL is that technology is but one among several 'means of development'. Agriculture in India bears testimony to our inability to disseminate the ways and means by which "the means of development" can be put "into the hands of small producers" (to quote from a title—Kurien, 1997).

While agricultural research is obsessed with technological solutions, AMUL teaches us that technological innovations and institutional innovations always go together. One does not work without the other, though the causal sequences may change from case to case. While technology dissemination is part of a linear hierarchy of knowledge flowing from top to bottom, AMUL is live with non-linear hands on learning, adaptations, and generation of new technologies/knowledge. While agricultural science takes for granted the long time lags between technology generation, dissemination and adoption and conceptualises the three as activities taking place within different organisations, the dairy cooperatives in AMUL combine simultaneously, active innovations in the field, research activities and development communication—where extension effort in fodder cultivation, animal nutrition/pest control, milk processing technologies, etc, are at the forefront offering and learning lessons from the field, with the farmers. While the institutional history of the ICAR is riddled with attempts to seek legitimacy and approval from the bureaucracy, the AMUL institutional history is studded with dynamic changes (technological and institutional) to legitimise itself and prove its worth to the farming/dairying community (Kurien, 1997; Raina, 2003a).

Theoretically, the lessons from the AMUL experience validate the basic tenets of evolutionary (Veblenian) economics where the crucial difference in operationalising development is in the institutions or rules and norms that govern the organisations/actors involved in the development process. These institutions or rules, norms and values, some that are explicit and some not so clear, govern the growth and evolution of the structures (cooperatives and related organisations) transforming themselves (the rules and norms) in the process and gradually abetting the evolution of the entire system.

The AMUL case teaches us that the way technology is governed depends on the institutional arrangements that go with or enable the technology. Exploring these institutions then will help us understand how these institutions/rules govern agricultural research and extension. The dissemination (as we know and practice it from linear technology transfer models) of technology, is handled predominantly by three sectors in the agricultural knowledge system—the public extension services, the private product/service extension agencies, and the outreach divisions of NGOs. These organisations being governed by different types of capital, and different sets of institutions (rules/ norms) and therefore with different ways of working, have different technology dissemination approaches. (Yet, they all believe in technological solutions, and in the 'delivery' or dissemination of these technological solutions.) Let us briefly review what we mean by these ways of working, or rules and norms, or institutions that govern the way organisations work.

In the realm of innovations, broadly including technology generation and its impacts, institutions have been characterised as necessary to cope with uncertainty, to manage conflicts and ensure cooperation among different research/development actors, and to provide appropriate incentives for these actors (Edquist and Johnson, 1997). Institutions may also be used to encourage or hamper certain lines of inquiry, and in yet another form can become entities that bring rigidity, allegations of 'institutional sclerosis', and the demand for progressive institutional reform (Edquist and Johnson, 1997). Institutional economics classifies 'institutions' into hard and soft, formal and informal, mature and evolving; and 'institutional change' as driven by or preceding technological change, designed or self-grown, exogenous or endogenous, radical or incremental, moving towards a market equilibrium, a series of punctuated equilibria, or a perpetual non-consummatory evolution. In analysing and recommending strategies for institutional reform it is important to note that institutions are "sets of common habits, routines, established practices, rules or laws that regulate the relations and interactions between individuals and groups" (Edquist and Johnson, 1997: 46). Institutions are the "working rules for going concerns"; institutions define organisations. (Bromley, 1985). "(O)rganizations are formal structures with an explicit purpose and they are consciously created. They are players or actors." (Edquist and Johnson, 1997: 47).

With reference to the agricultural R&D establishment, the distinction between organisations and institutions has been reiterated mainly using the case of organisational changes in the ICAR. Institutions or the way we govern research and extension organisations are a major determinant of how research effort is measured (Rajeswari, 1995), how professionalism is constructed, expertise understood and research evaluated (Raina, 1999a, b), how legitimisation of research is sought and impact assessment done (Hall *et al.*, 2000 and 2001; Raina, 2003a, b) and how extension is constrained and forced to under-perform (Sulaiman and Hall, 2004). The ICAR reveals a case of several organisational changes over time, with little institutional change[2]. Since its re-organisation in the 1960s, in a context marked by dynamic partnerships, the agricultural research and extension organisations have witnessed a perpetuation of the same linear R&D hierarchies of knowledge generation-dissemination-adoption, the same publications oriented discipline-based assessments and incentives for research, the same administrative norms reinforcing administrative accountabilities and hindering partnerships with other stakeholders, rigid professional hierarchies and patterns of control, a tradition of reporting and rewarding only successes, a strong mistrust of other agencies, a tradition of upward accountability for resource utilisation rather than client satisfaction, and increasingly limited opportunities for scientists and extension officers to learn from others in the field and from each other (Raina, 2003a, and Sulaiman and Hall, 2004).

Institutions Governing Technology Generation, Development and Diffusion

The Norms of Linear R&D

The prescriptions for reform in Indian agricultural research and extension organisations continue to be informed by a linear understanding of the science-technology-society continuum and an organisational and functional segregation between research and extension. The recommendations for institutional reform in research and extension reveal a partial understanding of the real processes of

---

2. Two points worth noting here, for our discussion about technology dissemination and learning, are that:

 (i) the green revolution in India arrived in a context of wide ranging dynamic partnerships fostered by several organisations (national and international); and

 (ii) the green revolution is a classic innovation case where technological changes (HYV-chemicals-irrigation) were accompanied by institutional changes (with new price policies, PDS, infrastructure development—roads, credit, rural markets, input supply, targeted agro-industry (fertilisers) subsidies and policies).

innovation—knowledge generation and utilisation—in the agriculture sector, a selective instrumental use of the social sciences, as well as a misinterpretation of the concepts of institutions and organisations (Hall *et al.*, 2002a; 2004; Biggs *et al.*, 2001; Raina, 2003a, b).

The diffusion of technologies in a linear fashion, from the science that generates it to the extension effort that disseminates it down to the farmer who uses it, is the institution or rule that defines the organisation of public sector research and extension. This linear flow of knowledge and technologies is a myth, and has been widely discredited in the literature (Biggs, 1990; Roling, 1988; Roling and Wagemaker, 1998). Yet in the agricultural research and development administration, the structural and functional bifurcation of research and extension as two distinct organisations continues. This demarcation of functional boundaries for research and extension enables compartmentalised accountabilities, limited to, say, release of varieties or identification of pathogens in research, and number of farm visits or hours of training conducted for extension. It ensures that the world of agricultural science does not face or acknowledge the complex processes of technology generation and use, and can continue to legitimately ignore the technological contexts (see, Hall and Clark, 1995).

Many failures of agricultural research are passed on to the inefficient and inadequate extension services. Extension can in turn blame research for producing irrelevant knowledge or technologies inappropriate for small and marginal farmers. Both research and extension can together blame the policies that distort domestic or international commodity prices, input subsidies, or the political clout of the sugar or cotton lobbies. The linear model also ensures that policy, research and extension can together reproach the ignorant and illiterate farmer for failing to appreciate the fruits of technological change whenever adoption rates are negligible.

The social sciences play a major role in legitimising this compartmentalisation of the science-technology-society continuum, and the linear model of agricultural R&D. The assumptions are that: (a) there is a direct causal relationship between science and agricultural development, and (b) institutions do not matter or (at best) they are a direct function of relative factor scarcities. The social sciences, agricultural economics in particular, are used to legitimise the organisation of agricultural research and extension (Raina, 2003b). Econometric estimation of their respective impacts using proxy variables (research expenditure, publications, personnel, adoption rates, farmers education, income increases, etc.) are necessary in the political and economic legitimisation of the linear model and increased funding for agricultural research (little of the credit and funds go to extension).

Despite being invalidated in reality and discredited academically, the linear model survives because of two attractive advantages. These are: (a) the enhanced funding and legitimisation through econometric estimation of returns to investment in (commodity-wise) research and (separately) extension, and (b) the hierarchically justifiable scope for selective attribution of failures (not counted in the quantitatively measured successes). The linear model and the social sciences that sustain it seem to have outlived their utility. Donors in the R&D scene now demand plausibility instead of precise internal rates of return, causal linkages, processes and negotiations that lead to successful innovation instead of lists of publications or varieties released (Herdt and Lynam, 1992; Baur *et al.*, 2001; Hall, 2002; Matlon, 2003).

Given the continuing institutional sclerosis within public sector agricultural research and extension and the increasing role of private and civil society/voluntary sectors in crucial technology generation, development and delivery functions (that were expected exclusively from the public sector earlier), it is imperative that reforms or new rules/norms take root in the public sector. We behold now, a future marked by an unquestioning surrender of public sector extension, at best with some internationally funded organisational tinkering. Will this ensure technology development and access to the means of development (besides technology) for the rural poor?

Technological Determinism

As a norm, institution or rule that governs agricultural research and extension, technological determinism dictates that technology solves social and economic problems. This well entrenched and accepted norm drawing from reductionist assumptions closes the options for exploring social and/or institutional mechanisms to address development problems (Rolings and Wagemakers, 1998).

The history of extension effort has witnessed two major phases—the dissemination approach and the needs assessment approach. Both are based on the firm belief that knowledge flows from the research arena down to the knowledge diffusion stage. Unlike the dissemination approach that still is dominant in Indian SAUs and the KVKs of the ICAR, the needs assessment approach followed largely by the NGOs (some of them who do take relevant public sector research results to rural users) and some private enterprises, sees extension as an "encounter between the advisor and the farmer" (Nitsch, 1994). The idea is that the advise—technology or information given has to meet perceived needs of the end user (the farmer). The needs assessment approach is a definite improvement over the dissemination approach, and by virtue of having taken on the assignment of finding out what the farmers need (for a crop/pest/any farm problem), accessing and delivering that advise (input), the extension agent here is endowed with a lesser sense of superiority. The extension agent here learns about the need, understands that she/he has certain stakes in the needs assessment and technology delivery, and does not therefore perceive the farmer as the only beneficiary. Needs assessment conducted by many private firms (the Monsanto Corp. and Hindustan Lever Ltd included) and many NGOs (especially the ones specialising in the development and delivery of one particular technology or group of technologies say, drying equipment/farm implements/pest management) does see and carefully addresses their own stakes in the enterprise of technology/advise delivery.

But needs assessment is a tricky business—as some NGOs have learnt rather painfully. While it increases the confidence of the extension advisor and can even prove (in the short term) uptake of technology, like the dissemination approach, it fails to see the farming system and its contexts. Governed by the institution of linear knowledge flows, it fails to understand that farming represents a complex system of many interacting factors, and is in itself a repository of several knowledge forms (experiences, local ecological knowledge, social relationships, narratives, folklore, myths, etc.) in which the technical knowledge that is advised as a solution to one need may actually conflict with other experiences/knowledge forms. In such complex systems, one need or problem is part of several other deficiencies and problems that are embedded in the total system. The assumption is that this one (or a few) need/problem often can be separated, described and analysed in isolation, and technological solutions prescribed for this one, discrete well-defined need (Nitsch, 1994). Even with participatory needs assessment that has become a norm with most NGOs involved in technology delivery, the key assumption is that 'technical solutions' work—and work on their own, once the needs/problems are identified.

We find that despite several organisational changes and new approaches, the linear knowledge flows and an obsessive technological determinism are two dominant institutions or norms that govern agricultural research and extension. It is these rules/norms that govern the methods and conduct of research—whether it is a crop breeding programme or soil conservation research programme, and extension—whether it is advice on recommended doses of fertilisers or demonstration of new weeding equipment. The evolution of public sector research and extension reveal how the rules/norms that govern an organisation are important. If public sector extension is to engage fruitfully in providing an expanded portfolio of services, we need to engage with questions about how to change the rules, institutions, or the organisational cultures. "If organizations are the players and institutions the rules, then how are the rules changed?" (Edquist and Johnson, 1997: 57). For instance, the organisational culture prevailing in the public sector extension includes: rigid hierarchy and centralised modes of planning; a tradition of assessing performance in terms of technology adoption; a history of rewarding only success and thus a reluctance to report and analyse reasons of failure; a history of working independently and a mistrust of other agencies; and a tradition of upward accountability for resource utilisation rather than output achievement and client satisfaction (Sulaiman, 2003). A number of issues related to governance of public sector plague the functioning of public extension services, just as there are norms governing private sector and NGO organisations marketing or delivering their technologies—in effect reducing their ability to learn how to deliver the 'means of development' to poor farmers.

The changing role of extension from technology transfer to mutual learning demands a complete breakdown of the conventional 'extensionist' with reference to the farmer (Nitsch, 1994). In India, extension practices have changed over time; but the role of extension and its relationship with research has remained "stuck in the institutional design of technology dissemination" (Sulaiman and Hall, 2002: 229). Mutual learning as the approach to extension needs a higher level of flexibility and wide range of expertise, the moral and social conviction to ensure that collective learning takes place in the innovation system (*ibid*). Extension has to break out of its habits/ rules/institutions of defining problems and needs, which direct it to seek technical and science-based solutions that come from above—the scientific realm. Mutual learning approaches can help extension agents to seek and learn from farmers—thereby reversing existing linear hierarchies and evidently expanding the sources of knowledge (and its context specific variations) Once these rules or institutions are changed extension can see itself involved in the complexities of local farming systems and the extension agent/advisor along with the farmer and other involved in the local complexities can engage in a joint learning process, in which all of them learn more about the problems in the complex situations and do not try to bring in specific solutions for (reductionist) isolated problems/needs within this complexity (Nitsch, 1994; Roling and Wagemaker, 1998).

Without mutual learning as the key approach, an external agent (like the public sector extension officer, private/voluntary sector agent) can not get to know the technological institutional arrangements that operate in farming systems and also govern the relationships of the farming system with its space-time context. Mutual learning approaches are essential for extension, farmers and all other stakeholders to see that technologies and institutional arrangements are inseparable—they go together as the means of development. How can mutual learning be encouraged as the norm governing knowledge exchange in extension?

Learning to Deliver as Part of Wider Innovation Systems

Agricultural and rural innovations have taught us that complex situations have no clear-cut one point solutions (Nitsch, 1994; Hall *et al.*, 2004). Ideally, what can be done and has been done in several successful innovation clusters is to get partners to engage in an active learning process, "a continuous and never-ending knowledge generating enterprise" (Nitsch, 1994: 34). This learning process that contains 'critical observation, reflection and experimentation in a dialogue' and series of interactions/decisions/actions/results/ processes among relevant actors in the complex farming systems context, then helps us see that research, extension and farming are no longer confined to their conventional knowledge generating, disseminating and adopting roles. They are all part of an evolving learning process—part of wider innovation system of continuous learning and improvement. This, the process of 'continual innovation' is the key criterion for success and sustainability in all rural development efforts (Krishna *et al.*, 1997; Hall *et al.*, 2004). Continual innovation involves "utilizing learning process and problem-solving strategies, with maturing institutional relationships, both internally and externally, that enable rural people to have more control over their situations and futures" (Krishna *et al.*, 1997: 198). For reform in extension organisations and methods, it is essential to understand how innovation takes place, and explore how learning processes and institutional arrangements are central to successful innovation systems.

The innovation systems framework gives us a broad set of principles or operational guidelines to understand and enable learning processes. A successful innovation system in its simplest form reveals the following features:

- Interaction of diverse research and non-research actors.
- Combinations of technical and institutional innovations.
- Continuous evolutionary cycles of learning and innovation.
- Shifting roles for information producers, information users and a need based exchange of knowledge, and
- An institutional context that supports interactions and knowledge flows between actors.

The innovation systems approach helps us understand and distill the principles or lessons from such development clusters (like AMUL). These then can then be applied to or (to use a more conventional/mainstream word) disseminated to several other development situations to create their own context specific development clusters. But the process of dissemination (again, used as a mainstream construct) here involves more than mere extension visits/trainings of beneficiaries. It involves active learning processes and capacity development—of the extensionists, researchers, farmers/ end users, related input suppliers or processors, financial and other service organisations. In other words, in complex contexts like agriculture and dairying, there are no models or given technologies that can be picked, packed and transferred. There are principles that can be understood, modified, and re-applied to different context specificities. It is important to facilitate learning processes to understand and operationalise these principles in different contexts; it is not advisable to transfer the 'model' to other contexts.

Encouraging learning processes and creating the right platforms (institutional and organisational arrangements) for learning are obviously emerging as answers to rural development problems. We need to ask how these learning processes can be facilitated and, how and what role can extension play in such learning platforms? The general principles or thumb-rules of learning show that it involves:

(i) partners and partnerships to learn from and with; and

(ii) the right internal working arrangements that help such partnerships and learning approaches.

To take these principles further—into the operationalisation of learning processes in real rural/agrarian contexts we need to ask why the linear model and technological determinism (with a single authoritative scientific source of knowledge) continue to dominate as the rules of the game or institutions that govern rural innovations? What is it that ensures the perpetuation of such redundant rules/ norms?

We shall here briefly explore a few cases where innovations take place—along with changes in the technology itself (technological innovations–adaptations) and in the ways or rules/norms of working (institutional innovations—including partnerships with other stakeholders and norms that facilitate these linkages). Constant learning is the hallmark of these cases. What are the lessons for extension? What are the changing expectations from public, private and civil society actors in such an innovation system with scope for continuous learning and change?

Learning Approaches and Innovation Systems—Some Cases and Lessons

Learning approaches are central to any innovation system. The past two decades have highlighted the many drawbacks of the linear model of agricultural R&D, and brought a deeper understanding of innovation as a dynamic non-linear process. The evolutionary economics perspectives of Nelson and Winter (1982), and the empirical evidence of non-linear technology development and diffusion processes from Freeman (1987) were landmarks in this paradigm shift in innovation studies. Drawing from the institutional economics theory,[3] an innovation systems perspective emphasises the historical and evolutionary patterns of events. Further, the innovation systems concept grew with its application to analysis of policies and institutions that support innovation.

An innovation systems perspective helps us see that innovations emerge from systems of actors. Innovations are both technological and institutional. Lundvall (1992) places learning and the role of institutions as the critical components of these systems. All major technological changes in the modern world have come with appropriate institutional changes. The Green Revolution would have been a non-starter, if all we had was the imported Norin-10 genetic material and the wheat varieties bred from this parent material. If it were not for the drastic changes in price policy, investments in rural infrastructure, credit arrangements, private investment in key agro-chemical industries, subsidies, major overhaul and reorganisation of the agricultural research, extension and education organisations, vibrant public distribution systems and such institutional innovations, India might not have had a Green Revolution at all.

Involving wide networks of actors in society, institutional innovations are always slow, more complex and painful to arrive at, compared to the technological innovations. The major breakthroughs in the adaptation and utilisation of a technology (be it electricity or railways) takes place only after the institutional innovations have picked up, and gained momentum (Lundvall, 2004). The social sciences highlight how these institutional innovations are brought

---

3. For different versions of institutional economics see Field (1984), Hodgson *et al.* (1994).

about as a process, with gradual and sometimes drastic changes in society—more specifically in the social organisation of activities.

Learning Approaches in Some Cases of Innovation

An innovation systems conceptual framework builds on the actors (and potential actors) and the competencies and patterns of relationships among the actors in the system. The analysis focuses on the nature and dynamics of these relationships and the way these systems of actors and institutions evolve and learn. Here we discuss a few cases of active innovation systems where learning approaches are evidently crucial to the success of the innovation system and its evolution.

In each case here we highlight the extension role and the learning approaches that have replaced or evolved from conventional extension roles because of the changes in the rules/norms that govern the innovation system. It is these modified or new rules/norms that we need to pay attention to; how do we facilitate these transformations in the rules that govern rural/agricultural innovations? What are the lessons that these cases offer?

(a) Micro-irrigation Technologies in India

The Business Development Services (BDS) approach used by major private development organisations like IDE (India) to enable increased adoption of drip irrigation, is imbued with several learning features (Raina, 2004). IDE(I) has used a 'market creation' approach to development (IDE(I), 2003; Steenbergen, 2003). Drip irrigation equipment is seen as part of the answer to a rural livelihoods question; the major problem being severe seasonal stress and migration *en masse* to avoid the stress period when no cultivation or consumption is possible in these villages in Solapur (a district in the semi-arid parts of the Deccan plateau). But this technology is nested within options for cultivation of pomegranate, a hardy horticultural tree crop that can survive in marginal soils and major water stress. The drip irrigation equipment and pomegranate innovations promoted by IDE(I) is part of the wider livelihoods innovation systems in the region. Prosperity and substantial reduction of migration from pomegranate growing villages is proof of this successful, evolving innovation system.

Here, in the BDS approach, every actor involved in learning, training, cultivating, harvesting and marketing—in the entire gamut of pomegranate innovations, is an enterprise, with its own interests in the development issues concerned. In the IDE(I) market creation approach, the farmer, resource-poor or otherwise, is a micro and small enterprise (MSE). As an entrepreneur, the farmer or farm family is not a passive beneficiary located at the tail end of the R&D chain, but an active participant in the market, and its innovation processes and related institutions. IDE(I)'s market creation approach essentially focuses on the incentives that each actor has to participate in the process. In this market creation or BDS approach, each of the actors, including the passive beneficiary small-scale farmer in the conventional (linear) R&D approach, has an active and profit-based, business-oriented role in innovating and improving the system. Wherever possible IDE(I) helps people develop their entrepreneurial skills—particularlv in the poor, arid/semi-arid regions, where conventional R&D and other development efforts have not focused on market skills.

Despite aggressive promotion of the subsidised ISI mark[4] drip irrigation systems by other private/public extension efforts, the low cost AMIT kits have found their way to the small-scale and marginal farmers, especially in the resource-poor regions. By locating horticultural production and irrigation technologies within this market creation approach, the BDS approach challenges the central assumptions of the linear technology generation, diffusion and adoption model. Table 7.1 here summarises the key assumptions made in the linear R&D model, which the BDS approach has challenged. In three discussions, with two of the IDE(I) personnel in the State, two drip-irrigation kit dealers, and some pomegranate farmers, it was clear how and why linear technology dissemination could not reach these poor farmers cultivating marginal soils in semi-arid regions.

4. The ISI mark is issued to all products approved by the Bureau of Indian Standards, as per the BIS Act of 1986.

Table 7.1

Assumptions of Linear R&D Models Challenged by the Business Development Services (BDS) Approach

Linear R&D-Assumptions	*BDS–Gaps Identified/Changes Made*
Science leads to relevant solutions	R&D does not understand social constraints;
Establish R&D organisations	Isolated organisations with no local linkages;
Technological solutions work	Appropriate institutional actors/ relationships are needed;
Technologies are ready for adoption	Special efforts at adaptive improvements;
Diffusion of technology	Disbursement mode is inadequate;
One technological solution-identified, assessed, delivered	Technologies and institutional arrangements identified, accessed/modified, and utilised;
Subsidies–orchards/drip systems-facilitate access to the poor	Access limited to rich farmers who possess appropriate social/other capabilities;
Access to input/output markets exist	Existing markets/market mechanisms are beyond the risk bearing profile of small-scale or marginal farmers;
Public services are available	To a few with credit worthiness–biases/social relationships operate;
Target small-scale farmer beneficiaries	Families forced to migrate–survival at stake-special effort at learning why and how?
Specific roles for specific organisations	Each organisation/actor plays several roles & with scope to learn and change to other roles;
Farmers are the beneficiaries	All stakeholders benefit/therefore must learn about each other; and
Science knows best	Each stakeholder has special knowledge/experience.

Source: Adapted from Raina (2004).

The learning approach evident here evolved within the network of actors in this innovation cluster—the learning community. By iteratively discussing and exploring the local technological, ecological and social conditions/opportunities the development and adaptation of drip irrigation was embedded in a wider more holistic system of poor/marginal natural resources, drought, seasonal stress, migration, economic and social exploitation, caste/regional politics, etc. It is through a well articulated mutual learning process that the technological and institutional innovations (drip irrigation equipment & collective ownership of wells and new water allocation norms) were identified and promoted. There was no linear flow of knowledge—scientists collaborating in this innovation system were learning from local contexts, farmers were experimenting and designing new drip irrigation microtubes, laterals, layouts, pomegranate pruning and plant protection methods, etc., researchers were helping and learning with farmers, dealers were documenting lessons, modifying services that went with the equipment.

(b) Technology Informatics and Design Endeavours (TIDE)

Rural energy innovations provide another striking example of a learning approach. The fuel-efficient dryers and stoves designed and promoted by TIDE in Bangalore, are utilised for a wide range of post-harvest processing operations in the States of Karnataka, Kerala and Tamil Nadu. The organisation has won accolades for its work on fuel efficient dryers and stoves for processing arecanut, coconut, cardamom, fish, vulcanizing rubber, etc. These are not technologies designed and left in shelves or in compendiums. These are active innovations alive and evolving in the field. This is an organisation with a clear strategy for learning, with a conscious and sometimes natural habit of discussing openly and critiquing amongst each other in the organisation and its extended networks of public sector, private, and NGO partners. The organisation has a policy to discuss and analyse the way things work in each sub-sector or equipment piece disseminated.

TIDE uses an approach of 'entrepreneurship development'. The organisation does this with active learning in the field as well as among scientific circles and services/locally relevant sub-sectors. The approach of entrepreneurship development draws from the need for local presence, ownership and capabilities to handle the technology. TIDE's version of technology assessment is an iterative process of learning from the field and placing the right partnerships—with local NGOs, Government Departments, CBOs, and other civic actors (with some visibility and influence in the local arena)—in place. For entrepreneurship development, the organisation takes young aspiring workers from the villages and trains them to (apprentice with) work with TIDE on the development and dissemination of these energy efficient devices. The apprenticeship lasts at least for an year or year and a half. TIDE firmly believes that technology dissemination needs adaptation to local conditions (fuel, labour use patterns, drying/stove demands, access to markets, availability of other services like credit, transportation etc.), and that concentrating on the technical efficiency alone of the fuel may not deliver the goods to the people. It has learnt from field experiences that the poor have a variety of demands from each device and tailor the energy-efficient equipments to suit these demands and fuel types, labour constraints, gender requirements, etc.

Technology dissemination—even if it is seen without any of these local and scientifically relevant conditions—involves an entire range of skills and managerial techniques. These new skills acquired often see an organisation like TIDE, (which is actually an intermediary organisation—or an NGO designed to promote fuel efficient technologies in the rural areas) developing and indulging in new roles and new ways of working. Both TIDE and IDE(India) reveal the importance of adequate organisational flexibility in shaping these actors and agencies in the system. This movement of actors beyond conventional roles is characteristic of innovation systems. It is enabled by the learning processes these organizations indulge in. Both TIDE and IDE ensure that the means of development are developed and utilised in the local context; i.e., the technologies and the social skills and systems to make these technologies work are locally owned and operated. These organisations operate by institutions or rules of non-linear and evolutionary knowledge generation and utilisation systems, where there are both technological and institutional innovations.

Conventional agricultural research and extension organisations in the public sector have not been able to encourage such institutional innovations though do generate a fair share of technologies. Table 7.2 presents the differences and similarities between an agricultural research system and an agricultural innovation system. This distinction of the different ways of working is essential to draw attention to the sorts of institutional changes that are needed for agricultural research and extension organisations to better locate themselves in wider innovation systems in which they seek to participate.

Table 7.2

Similarities and Differences between Agricultural Research Organisations and Agricultural Innovation Systems

Institutional Features	*Agricultural Research and Extension Organisations*	*Agricultural Innovation Systems*
Guiding agenda	Scientific	Developmental
Relationships involved	Narrow, hierarchical	Diverse, consultative
Partners	Scientists in other public agencies	Various combinations of scientist, entrepreneurs, farmer and development workers from the public and private sectors and civil society organisations
Selection of partners	Predetermined by institutional roles defined by the arrangement of the research system	Coalitions of interest. Determined by the nature of task, national institutional context and skills, and resources available
Role of partners	Fixed. Predetermined by institutional roles defined by the organisation of research and extension effort	Flexible. Determined by the changes in/evolution of tasks, institutional contexts and the skills, and resources available
Prioritising tasks	Fixed. By researchers for research, and by extension managers for dissemination.	Consensual. By stakeholders and through discussions of needs and system complexities. Employs systems concepts, technology foresight and technology/socioeconomic assessment techniques
Work plans and activities	Fixed at beginning of project	Flexible and iterative
Mandate for research/task approach adopted	Fixed by institutional norms of the research system	Negotiated through coalitions of interest
Knowledge produced	Technical/scientific	Technical/scientific and institutional
Knowledge	Technology dissemination/ needs assessment approaches	Mutual learning and sharing
Knowledge communication	Delegated linearly to extension services	All actors/components in the system communicate with each other
Indicators of performance	In scientific terms to other scientists, in number of	In development terms to donors. In terms of fulfilling

contd. ...

...contd. ...

Institutional Features	Agricultural Research and Extension Organisations	Agricultural Innovation Systems
	trainings or meetings conducted, or number of seedlings delivered/	role in task network to other partners
Responsibility for achieving impact	Other agencies dedicated to extension and technology promotion	All stakeholders including scientists and their partners in specific networks
Capacity building	Trained scientists and research infrastructure	Collective capacity of task networks, social capital, partnership skills

Note: This table polarises the differences between these two paradigms and has been exaggerated for illustrative purpose.

Source: Adapted from Hall *et al.*, 2004: 10.

The IDE, TIDE and AMUL cases, demonstrate the need for institutional and organisational arrangements appropriate to a particular context and task. They reveal the networks linking the diversity of research and non-research actors involved in technology development, diffusion and use. An important feature of successful innovation systems is the blurred identity among different actors—researchers and extensionists, researchers and clients, governing bodies (policy makers) and researchers, policy makers and service providers (say, market contractors, nursery growers, drip irrigation dealers, etc.), when all are involved in the innovation process (Sulaiman and Hall, 2002). There are no compartments of origins and endpoints of innovations, no strictly defined phases of generation, dissemination and adoption. The make up of the group of partners, the role they play and the institutional arrangements that govern their collective action, will always be specific to the task and context, and can only be explored incrementally through continuous learning processes.

In our analysis of governance of agricultural research and extension it is important to recognise the lessons presented by the innovation systems approach. Some of the central principles of innovation, such as the emergence of partnerships, context specific changes/flexibilities expected and different and evolving capacities among the actors/organisations involved, tell us that it is insufficient to 'train' actors/organisations in the innovation systems approach. The conventional training approach does not enable mutual learning and therefore it is important to enable 'facilitated capacity development' exercises/experiments among various actors/organisations (Sulaiman and Hall, 2004; MacKay and Horton, 2002) enabling hands-on learning and evolution of technologies and rules/norms/institutions.

Planning and management of knowledge in innovation systems focus on learning approaches. There is a need to establish and formalise learning and reflection on processes and institutional arrangements, to recognise that rules/norms and ways of working—i.e., institutional knowledge is complementary to new technical knowledge. We must create opportunities, platforms for learning and learn to supplement monitoring and impact assessment procedures with incentives that encourage an organisation to learn and to evolve (Chambers, 2002; Mac Kay and Horton, 2002; Hall *et al.*, 2002b; Raina, 2002; Hall *et al.*, 2001). Widespread acceptance of these principles of innovation systems is a necessity in India; our innovation systems must be able to change and reform themselves to meet contemporary development needs and opportunities.

Enabling and Operationalising Learning Approaches

A platform for learning is a necessary condition for successful technological and institutional innovations. Here the decentralised public and private sector partnerships mediated through/by civil society organisations are the basic structures needed. These learning platforms extend beyond the immediate public-private partnerships, transforming the basic rules/norms of technology generation, development, dissemination and utilisation.

In a learning community the focus is on operationalising systems thinking, building true collaborations and effective partnerships between actors in a complex innovation system (Fisk *et al.*, 1998). Extension in such innovation systems has to play a crucial role in facilitating learning at different levels and parts of the system. It has to become a learning organisation in itself. A learning organisation is "an organization that is continually expanding its capacity to create its future." (*ibid*, quoting Senge, 1990). From its current existence as 'technology dissemination' units in large public sector Departments of Agriculture, private business enterprises, or NGOs, how can extension become an active learning organisation enabling learning processes in wider innovation systems? A brief recap of the analysis in this chapter is called for.

The chapter brings out the different ways of governing technology generation and dissemination. Using AMUL, TIDE and IDE as counterpoints against the conventional agricultural research and extension, it shows how technology is but one component in an entire system. Innovation systems actively combine technological and institutional innovations. Real development demands that people, especially the poor farmers have access to and control over the 'means of development'—technology being only one among these means.

Despite several organisational formats of technology generation and dissemination, the institutions/rules that govern these organisations are linear knowledge flows and technological determinism. The shift in approach from pure technological dissemination to needs assessment approaches may not help very much because the assumption again, is that technological needs can be identified/assessed by external agents (with participation of local people) and delivery of technological solutions is the answer to the particular rural problem targeted. Unless these local contexts and systems are understood, and a diverse range of stakeholders involved in innovation, technologies and the institutional arrangements necessary for development cannot be identified and enabled. The rules/norms governing extension have to shift from linear knowledge flows and technological determinism to the norms/institutions of a learning community.

The chapter then introduced the innovation system framework which emphasises that the learning processes and learning communities are central to innovation. Theoretically the innovation systems framework highlights the way technological and institutional innovations (like a co-operative/new incentive structures) go together, and emphasises that innovations do not arise from one single source (such as scientific research) but are the creation of several actors/organisations. These technological and institutional innovations evolve in a non-linear fashion from several (non-scientific and scientific) actors. It is therefore, important to understand how these different actors come together in each innovation system, as partners or collaborators, each one bringing one special skill, knowledge, improvement to the system, continuously learning from each other and from the technologies, institutions and systems/contexts they change. Unlike the research and extension organisations in the linear model which are easy to govern (with just one specific function), the actors in the innovation system have multiple capabilities, and blurred identities with changing roles—from being an information supplier (typical of extension) to adaptive researcher (enabling modification of a cultivation practice or drip irrigation layout) to marketing manager (helping farmers negotiate a better deal with the truck transport agents) to facilitator (filling up the loan forms, bringing four-five families together to agree on water allocation rules from shared wells, establishing a local SHG or NGO), etc. The chapter presented the difference between institutions and organisations, and highlighted the institutions of 'linear flow of knowledge' and 'technological determinism' that govern public sector R&D actors, private and voluntary technological dissemination and marketing endeavours. What then are the norms/institutions that govern organisations that have enabled these two-partnerships and mutual learning-features? If linear knowledge flows and technological determinism are the norms/institutions that govern conventional extension activities in public/private/NGO sectors, how can these norms/institutions be changed?

Enabling Learning

Some important lessons come out of the learning processes in successful innovation systems and the technological and institutional innovations that have been key to these successes. First and foremost, learning took place in successful cases of rural development because of 'initiatives that came from different sources–a range of outsiders and insiders' (villagers). These people had 'deep respect for the capabilities of the people whose lives they hoped to help improve' and they sought and found some kind of 'key constituency/agency/ research organisation/development department/NGO to spearhead the innovation system—the new technologies, new organisational formats and new opportunities.' There were 'certain hybrid organisational formats'—quasi-public-private, quasi NGO-public sector movement, that enabled these innovations. Finally the common denominator was 'the process of institution building from below,' where institutional innovations were crucial at initial stages and became accepted operating procedures later (See Krishna *et al.*, 1997).

How did partners get together? How did thcy learn together? We need to explore these questions to understand how we can facilitate the transition from current 'technology dissemination' approaches to 'mutual learning' approaches in innovation systems. Essential steps (though not in the same order) to facilitate learning approaches (Fisk *et al.*, 1998), create a learning platform and enable meaningful rural innovations through learning (Hall *et al.*, 2004) are:.

(i) Identify people who can build partnerships: There are several people in conventional/mainstream organisations and in alternative organisations/groups, who are creating alternatives to currently accepted ways of doing or thinking. The lesson that we drawn upon here is that innovation systems involve the right people—who bring in their organisations too at a later stage. They begin as a small group of individuals and become a learning community where experiences are shared, learning and change catalysed and accelerated.

(ii) Help them build the relationships: The message here is to build linkages between/among complementary pools of knowledge/expertise/experience/views/rituals/etc. Building relationships across a diverse spectrum gives the group a greater chance to 'leverage change'.

(iii) Encourage systems thinking: Here, the actors/organisations who are party to the learning experiment have to see themselves as part of the system of rural problems and try to learn from local components/actors in the system. Multiple perspectives in a diverse group of actors often forces the group to maintain a systems perspective.

(iv) Build strong and organic relationship with the main constituency(ies): If the learning group/community has a broad collaborative base representing a diversity of ideas and cultures, the constituency most attentive will naturally be involved. But the learning community has to make an effort to articulate its purpose and methods to the key constituency—in agricultural R&D it might be ICAR institutes, SAUs or NGOs.

(v) Facilitate partnerships: Find means for farmers, agricultural scientists and extension workers to partner with existing community-based organisations with a similar/common purpose or mission.

(vi) Explore and expand the relationship with the donors and policy makers: Ensuring that management will buy into the lessons learnt. Funding agencies in a learning community experiment as part of a wider innovation system addressing (technological and institutional innovations for) rural livelihoods, are part of the learning community.

(vii) Document and cultivate all outcomes (new rules, new projects, new funding mechanisms/incentives etc.) facilitated by the learning community. This will enable the learning community explain 'how' the innovations made were actually achieved.

(viii) Develop an evaluation culture: In order to document the project while it is ongoing and also to use this self-reflexive evaluation to correct or guide the project process.

Successful innovation systems and the learning approaches central to these systems often started off as a small project—a pilot effort. These pilot projects 'free of preconceptions and formalism, led to new formulations for structure and process that became the core innovation and capability of the programme' (Krishna *et al.*, 1997: 294). It is this openness and lack of preconceived notions and ideas about what the rural problems are, that forms the ground rule for all learning approaches. To be involved in this dynamic learning approach public/private and civil society organisations should re-design their personnel policy, monitoring and evaluation mechanisms, and internal mandates to enable the emergence of learning communities appropriate to each context.

Increasing private sector presence in Indian agricultural research and extension has caused much apprehension about how the poor will access technologies and gain from agricultural knowledge generated by research. Civil society initiatives can play a major role in ensuring that the poor have access to and control over the technologies with the capacity for informed decisionmaking. But these civil society initiatives are few. Most NGOs or other civil society engagements with agricultural technology seems to be directly in technology dissemination or needs based technology transfer, which as we have discussed above, forecloses some important learning opportunities. The real cost then with such private (for profit) technology dissemination and NGO (not for profit) technology transfer is that the means of development, the capacity for accessing and controlling knowledge, is not vested with the rural small/ marginal farmers. While the technology reaches the farmer, all knowledge of how the adaptations were made, where other forms of the technology have been developed or adapted and utilised, the institutional arrangements that enabled this technology dissemination, etc. remain as intangible knowledge vested with the private or NGO actors. Since equal non-hierarchical participation of the farmers/all stakeholders is not a condition for technology dissemination, the other components of the knowledge system always remain alien to the rural population/farmers.

In the dynamic successful innovation clusters, one of the important features has been "the way the local people utilise various organisational capabilities, once these have been created and command confidence to solve a wide range of problems and meet a variety of needs" (Krishna *et al.*, 1997: 295). The trick obviously lies in the delivery of the means of development—and not mere technology transfer. These successful innovation clusters have created 'multi-faceted and evolving capabilities at the local level' and among donor or policy maker levels (Krishna *et al.*, 1997: 295). One of the key principles is to enable peoples' access to and control over their means of development.

In the current context of policy makers and politicians selling off public sector services to private sector, and seeking blueprints of alternatives that work, we must point out that: (a) private extension is not answer or a substitute for public extension. It is important for public sector research and extension to pro-actively seek partnerships and work on location specific complexities using learning approaches to guide them in their capacity developments; and (b) the agricultural innovation systems framework is not an administrative and bureaucratic model for governing agricultural technology. It is a system that has implications for transforming the way existing bureaucracies function. It is a set of principles or ways of working that can used as a policy tool, i.e. as a way of organising thinking about the analysis and understanding of how innovation can be nurtured and how socioeconomic change can be accelerated.

All the actors/organisations involved in learning approaches must understand that building a learning community is not easy—it takes time. Since conventionally we are used to producing tangible outcomes—say a production technology, a new marketing strategy, or validating the economic performance of the technology, we may not see immediately that in a learning community both the tangible outcome and the process of learning and creating change are important. A one point, one visit, technology dissemination by one extension officer is not enough. "Time is spent on forming relationships, learning to collaborate, and teaching ourselves and others" (Fisk *et al.*, 1998). In an innovation system that has imbibed the learning approach, we will find conventional extension organisations, but with new rules/ways of working, organisational formats, expectations and renewed commitment to the delivery of capacity to all components of the innovation system.

This chapter argues that it is the norms/institutions of, (i) linear flows of knowledge and (ii) technological determinism (compartmentalised technological solutions) that determine the effectiveness or otherwise of research and extension organisations. A transfer of extension functions from public to private/voluntary agencies may not lead to technology adoption and better rural livelihoods as long as these are the norms governing extension. When it comes to using knowledge to transform rural livelihoods, it is these rules/norms, the approach to technology/knowledge and people that matters more than the organisations that deliver technology and the nature of capital investment in those organisations. An indifferent and complacent public sector research and extension is more detrimental to rural development than a profiteering multinational.

References

Baur, Henning, Michael Bosch, Stephan Krall, ThomasKuby, Alison Lobb-Rabe, Paul-Theodor Schutz and Andreas Springer-Heinze (2001). (mimeo) "Establishing Plausibility in Impact Assessment", by the *Workgroup on Assessing the Impact of Agricultural Research in Development*, GTZ, Eschborn.

Biggs, S.D. (1990). "A Multiple Source of Innovation Model of Agricultural Research and Technology Promotion", *World Development*, Vol. 18(11), pp.1481-1499.

Biggs, Stephen D. and E.J. Clay (1981). "Sources of Innovation in Agricultural Technology", *World Development*, Vol. 9(4), pp.321-336.

Biggs, S.D. and G. Smith (1998). "Beyond Methodologies: Coalition-Building for Participatory Technology Development", *World Development*, Vol. 26(2), pp.239-248.

Biggs, S.D. and Harriet Matsaert (1999). "An Actor-oriented Approach for Strengthening Research and Development Capabilities in Natural Resource Systems", *Public Administration and Development*, Vol. 19, pp.231-262.

Biggs, S., H. Matsaert and A. Martin (2001). "Changing Natural Resource Research and Development Capability: Whither Social Capital?", in R. Jeffery and B. Vira (eds.), *Conflict and Cooperation in Participatory Natural Resource Management*, Palgrave, London, pp.204-225.

Bromley, D.W. (1985). "Resources and Economic Development: An Institutionalist Perspective", *Journal of Economic Issues*, Vol. 19(3), pp.779-796.

Chambers, R. (2002). "Professional Error, Critical Awareness and Good Science", paper presented at International Conference on *Why has Impact Assessment Research not made more of a Difference?*, San Jose, 4-7 February, 2002.

Chambers, R., A. Pacey and L-A Thrupp (eds.) (1989). *Farmer First: Farmer Innovation and Agricultural Research*, Intermediate Technology Publications, London.

Edquist, C. and B. Johnson (1997). "Insitutions and Organizations in Systems of Innovation", in C. Edquist (ed.) *Systems of Innovation, Technologies, Institutions and Organizations*, Pinter, London, pp.41-63.

Ekbior, Javier and G. Parallada (2001). "Continuous Innovation Process: Public-Private Interactions and Technology Policy", in D. Byerlee and R.G. Echeverria (eds.) *Agricultural Research Policy in an Era of Privatisation: Experiences from the Developing World*, CABI, Wallingford, UK.

Field, A.J. (1984). "Microeconomics, Norms and Rationality", *Economic Development and Cultural Change*, Vol. 32(4), pp.683-711.

Fisk, J.W., Oran B. Hesterman and T.L. Thorburn (1998). "Integrated Farming Systems: A Sustainable Agriculture Learning Community in the USA", in Roling and Wagemaker (eds.) *Facilitating Sustainable Agriculture*, Cambridge University Press, Cambridge, pp.217-231.

Freeman, Christopher (1987). *Technology and Economic Performance: Lessons from Japan*, Pinter, London.

Gibbons, M.C. Limoges, H. Novotny, M. Troww, P. Scott and E. Schartzman (1994). *The New Production of Knowledge*, Sage, London.

Government of India (2000). *National Agriculture Policy*, Ministry of Agriculture, New Delhi.

Hall, A.J. (2002). "The Development and Use of the Innovation Systems Framework in India: Northern Perspective", in *North South Cooperation: International Conference, 3 December 2001, Amsterdam*, Royal Netherlands Academy of Arts and Science, Amsterdam.

Hall, A. and N. Clark (1995). "Coping with Change, Complexity and Diversity in Agriculture—The Case of Rhizobium Innoculants in Thailand", *World Development*, Vol. 23(9), pp.1601-1614.

Hall, Andrew, N. Clark, R. Sulaiman V., M.V.K. Sivamohan, and B. Yoganand (2000). "New Agendas for Agricultural Research in Developing Countries: Policy Analysis and Institutional Implications", *Knowledge, Technology and Policy*, Vol. 13(1), pp.70-91.

Hall, Andrew, Geoffrey Bockett, Sarah Taylor, M.V.K. Sivamohan and Normal Clark (2001). "Why Research Partnerships Really Matter: Innovation Theory, Institutional Arrangements and Implications for Developing New Technology for the Poor", *World Development*, Vol. 29(5), pp.783-797.

Hall, Andy, Rasheed Sulaiman V., B. Yoganand and Norman Clark (2002a). "Partnerships in the Indian Agricultural Innovation System: Lessons and Ways Forward", Workshop on *Agricultural Policy: Redesigning R&D to Achieve the Objectives*, held at the Indian National Science Academy, 10-11 April 2002, New Delhi.

——. (2002b). "From Measuring Impact to Learning Institutional Lessons: An Innovation Systems Perspective on Improving the Management of International Agricultural Research", paper presented at International Conference on *Why has Impact Assessment Research not made more of a Difference?*, San Jose, 4-7 February, 2002.

Hall, A.J., B. Yoganand, R.V. Sulaiman, Rajeswari S. Raina, C. Shambu Prasad, Guru C. Naik and N.G. Clark (eds.) (2004). *Innovations in Innovation: Reflections on Partnership, Institutions and Learning*, CPHP, South Asia, ICRISAT, and NCAP, Patancheru and New Delhi.

Herdt, R.W. and J.K. Lynam (1992). "Sustainable Development and the Changing needs of International Agricultural Research", in D.R. Lee, S. Kearl and N. Uphoff (eds.) *Assessing the Importance of International Agricultural Research for Sustainable Development*, Cornell University Press, Ithaca, pp.1-14.

Hodgson, G.M., W.J. Samuels and M.R. Tool (eds.) (1994). *The Edgar Companion to Institutional and Evolutionary Economics*. Edward Elgar, Aldershot.

ICAR (1998). *National Agricultural Technology Project—Main Document*, ICAR, New Delhi.

IDE (2003). (mimeo) Annual Report—Project title "Capacity Building to Achieve Sustainable Water Technology Markets in Africa and Asia", IDE, New Delhi.

Jha, Dayanatha (2001). "Agricultural Research and Small Farms", *IJAE*, Vol. 56(1), pp.1-23.

Krishna, A., N. Uphoff and M.J. Esman (eds.) (1997). *Reasons for Hope: Instructive Experiences in Rural Development*, Kumarian Press, West Hartford, Connecticut.

Kurien, V. (1997). "The AMUL Dairy Cooperatives: Putting the Means of Development into the Hands of Small Producers in India", in A. Krishna, N. Uphoff and M.J. Esman (eds.), *Reasons for Hope: Instructive Experiences in Rural Development*, Kumarian Press, West Hartford, Connecticut.

Lundvall, B.A. (1992). *National Systems of Innovation and Interactive Learning*, Pinter, London.

——. (2004). "Why the New Economy is a Learning Economy", *DRUID Working Paper* No. 04-01, Danish Research Unit for Industrial Dynamics.

MacKay, Ronald and D. Horton (2002). "Expanding the Use of Impact Assessment and Evaluation in Agricultural Research and Development", paper presented at International Conference on *Why has Impact Assessment Research not made more of a Difference?*, San Jose, 4-7 February, 2002.

Matlon, Peter (2003). "Foreword", *Agricultural Systems*, Vol. 78(2), pp.123-125.

Mruthyunjaya (2002). "Crafting Research Institutions into New Age Institutions—The Case of ICAR", Workshop on *Agricultural Policy: Redesigning R&D to Achieve the Objectives*, held at the Indian National Science Academy, 10-11 April 2002, New Delhi.

Nelson, R.R. and S.G. Winter (1982). *An Evolutionary Theory of Economic Change*, Harvard University Press, Cambridge.

Nitsch, Ulrich (1994). *From Diffusion of Innovations to Mutual Learning—The Changing Role of Agricultural Advisory Services*, Swedish University of Agricultural Sciences, Uppsala.

Paroda, R.S. and Mruthyunjaya (1999). *NARS in the Asia Pacific Region—A Perspective*, FAO-RAPA, Bangkok.

Raina, Rajeswari S. (1999a). "Professionalisation and Evaluation: The Case of Indian Agricultural Research", *Knowledge, Technology and Policy*, Vol. 11(4), pp.69-96.

——. (1999b). "Patronage and Evaluation in the Indian Council of Agricultural Research", *Evaluation*, Vol. 5(3), pp.278-302.

———. (2002). "Disciplines, Institutions and Organizations: Impact Assessments in Context", paper presented at International Conference on *Why has Impact Assessment Research not made more of a Difference?*, San Jose, 4-7 February, 2002.

———. (2003a). "Institutions and Organizations: Enabling Reforms in Indian Agricultural Research and Policy", *International Journal of Technology Management and Sustainable Development*, Vol 2(2), pp.97-116.

———. (2003b). "Disciplines, Institutions and Organizations: Impact Assessments in Context", *Agricultural Systems*, Vol. 78(2), pp.185-212.

———. (2004). "Technological and Institutional Innovations: The Pomegranate Innovation System in Maharashtra", in A.J. Hall, B. Yoganand, R.V. Sulaiman, Rajeswari S. Raina, C. Shambu Prasad, Guru C. Naik and N.G. Clark (eds.), *Innovations in Innovation: Reflections on Partnership, Institutions and Learning*, CPHP, South Asia, ICRISAT, and NCAP: Patancheru and New Delhi.

Rajeswari, S. (1992). Unpublished Ph. D. dissertation, The Organization of Agricultural Research in India: An Economic Analysis of Technology Generation, 1860-1990. Centre for Development Studies, Thiruvananthapuram, Kerala.

Rajeswari, S. (1995). "Agricultural Research Effort: Conceptual Clarity and Measurement", *World Development*, Vol. 23(4), pp.617-635.

Roling, Niels (1988). *Extension Science - Information Systems in Agricultural Science*, Cambridge University Press, Cambridge.

Roling, Neils and Wagemaker (eds.) (1998). *Facilitating Sustainable Agriculture*, Cambridge University Press, Cambridge.

Scoones, I. and J. Thompson (eds.) (1994). *Beyond Farmer First: Rural People's Knowledge, Agricultural Research and Extension Practice*, Intermediate Technology Publications, London.

Steenbergen, Frank van (2003). "Creating Markets with the Poor: Selling Treadle Pumps in India", *Gatekeep Series, No. 107*, IIED, London.

Sulaiman, Rasheed V. (2003). Innovations in Agricultural Extension in India, SD Dimensions-Knowledge, June 2003, FAO, Rome.

Sulaiman, Rasheed V. and A. Hall (2002). "Beyond Technology Dissemination–Can Indian Agriculgural Extension Re-invent Itself?", *Policy Brief, 16*, NCAP/ICAR, New Delhi.

Sulaiman, Rasheed V. and A.J. Hall (2004). "Towards Extension Plus: Opportunities and Challenges", *NCAP Policy Brief* No 17, National Centre for Agricultural Economics and Policy Research India, New Delhi, India.

Sulaiman, Rasheed V., Andy Hall and N. Suresh (2005). "Effectiveness of Private Sector Extension in India and Lessons for the New Extension Policy Agenda", *AgREN Network Paper* No.141, ODI, London.

8

Rice Technologies for Rainfed Environments of Asia

SUSHIL PANDEY, B.C. BARAH and L. VELASCO

Introduction

It is now well-established that the Green Revolution in Asia has had a major impact on food production growth during the past three decades. The production of the major cereal of Asia, rice, increased rapidly in the wake of Green Revolution. The package of agricultural technology that included improved seeds and fertilisers spread rapidly throughout the irrigated areas of Asia. Government support in the form of increased investment in irrigation, fertiliser subsidies and the provision of rural credits played critical roles in the rapid diffusion of this technology. The rapid increases in productivity lowered the real price of rice and generated positive impacts on the welfare of the poor (Osmani, 1998; Evenson and Gollin, 2003).

The productivity impact of these technologies in rainfed areas has been somewhat modest despite some positive spill-over effects. Some improved rice varieties developed for irrigated environments have found ways in rainfed environments also, but the productivity gains in these heterogeneous and risky environments have been modest. Farmers often continue to rely on landraces which tend to have stable performance despite their lower average yields. Where farmers have adopted improved varieties, high-levels of risk discourage them from investing in fertilisers and other inputs necessary to obtain significant yield gains.

This chapter draws heavily from the paper on the project "Socio-economic Dynamics of Rice Production Systems of Eastern India". The project is funded jointly by the Indian Council of Agricultural Research and the International Rice Research Institute. A number of ICAR institutes and State Agricultural Universities participated in this collaborative research without naming, we thank our collaborators in the project.

Although the initial responses of agricultural research systems and public policies have been to follow the approaches that were found to be successful in irrigated areas, there has now been an increasing realisation that rainfed areas require a different approach to agricultural R&D. Such an approach would need to recognise the specificities of rainfed systems and farmers' adaptive strategies that have evolved over centuries of rice farming.

The main objective in this chapter is to provide an overview of constraints facing rice productivity growth in rainfed areas and their implications for agricultural research, with special emphasis on eastern India where rainfed rice predominates. The chapter is organised as follows. The first section consists of an overview of the rice productivity growth patterns in rainfed and irrigated areas of Asia. In the second section, an analysis of growth patterns in rice productivity in eastern India is presented. This includes both the state and district-level analyses. The third section highlights the major issues related to rice productivity growth in eastern India. The penultimate section provides a discussion of some technological and policy options for raising rice productivity in eastern India. The concluding comments are included in the final section.

Growth Patterns in Rice Productivity in Asia

The trends in area, yield and production of rice in Asia are shown in Figure 8.1. The yield of rice at the beginning of the Green Revolution was around 2t/ha for Asia. This has now doubled to around 4t/ha. Yield growth resulting from technological change has been the main source of production growth of rice in Asia.

During the period 1960-2001, the yield of irrigated rice grew at the rate of 2.15 per cent per annum. The growth rate of rainfed rice was lower at 1.64 per cent per annum only. As a result, the current yield of irrigated rice is 4.9t/ha, whereas yield has reached only 2.7t/ha in rainfed areas. This difference in both the growth and the yield levels across the rainfed and irrigated area represent differential diffusion of improved rice technologies in these two environments. Overall, Green Revolution technologies were more successful in raising yields in irrigated areas than in the riskier and heterogeneous rainfed environments.

Figure 8.1

Trends in Rice Area, Yield and Production in Asia

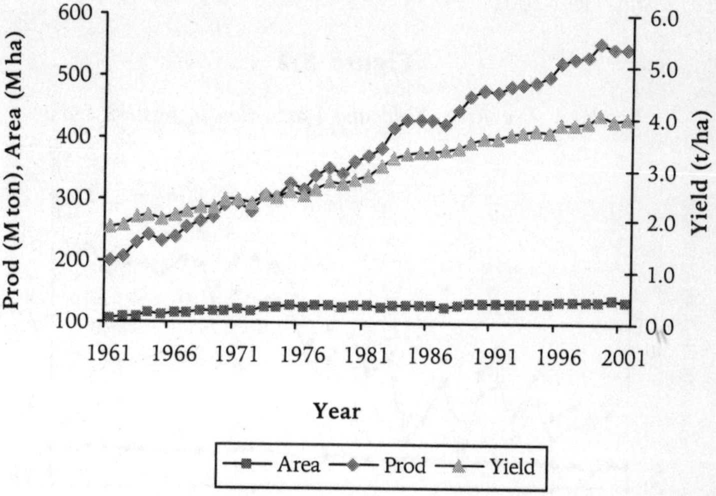

Rice Productivity in Eastern India

Eastern India covers a vast geographical area, that includes the states of Assam, Bihar, Chhattisgarh, Jharkhand, West Bengal and eastern Uttar Pradesh. Rice production is the single most dominant agricultural activity in these states. In 2001, eastern India grew 25.6 million ha of rice. This accounted for 57 per cent of the total rice area in India. Of this, a total of 19 million ha was grown under rainfed conditions. This includes approximately 4 million ha of upland rice and 1 million ha of deepwater rice, with the balance being rainfed lowland. The technological requirements in these environments that vary widely in hydrological conditions are naturally different.

Up until 1981, the modest growth in output in eastern India was driven mainly by an expansion in area with the yield remaining more or less constant. However, yield growth picked up after 1981 and is now clearly the major source of growth in output in eastern India (Figure 8.2). Among the states of eastern India, West Bengal has achieved the highest level of average yield with eastern Uttar Pradesh having the second highest (Table 8.1).[1] Chhattisgarh and Orissa had the lowest average yield of rice in the late nineties. Overall, the average yield of rice in eastern India almost doubled between 1970-1972 and 1999-2001.

Figure 8.2

Trends in Rice Area, Yield and Production in Eastern India

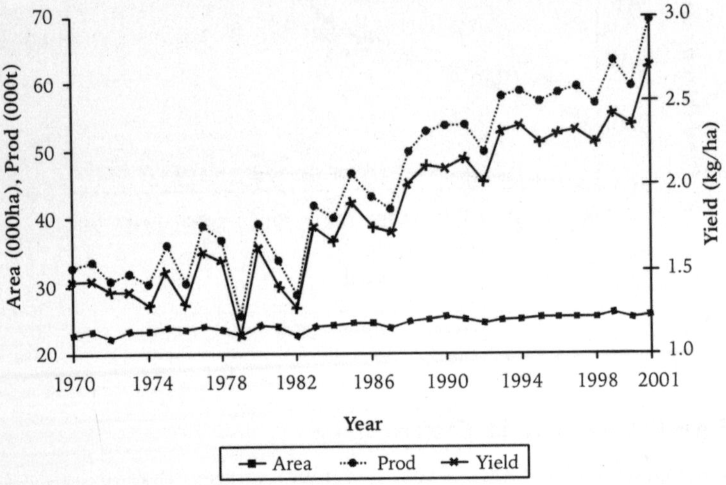

Note: Rice yield and production are expressed in terms of rough rice (i.e., unhusked paddy) using the conversion factor of 1kg of unhusked paddy = 0.66kg of milled rice.

The analysis of growth rates in rice yield, area and output indicates that eastern India underwent a sustained growth during 1970-2001 (Table 8.2). The growth in productivity and output in every state was positive and statistically significant. Eastern Uttar Pradesh and West Bengal performed particularly well, with the annual compound growth rate in production of 5.02 per cent and 3.25 per cent, respectively. This growth rate in rice output was well in excess of the annual population growth rate in these states. Assam and Chhattisgarh also sustained an annual growth rate in output of over 2 per cent per year. Except for Orissa, which experienced a slight increase in production per capita due to its lower population growth rate, the other two

1. India statistical systems report rice yields and production in terms of milled rice. In this report, these variables are expressed in terms of rough rice (i.e., unhusked paddy) using the conversion factor of 1 kg of unhusked paddy = 0.66 kg of milled rice.

states barely managed to keep the per capita rice production at a constant level. Combined Bihar and Jharkhand performed relatively poorly with the annual growth rate in rice output of 1.72 per cent—well below its population growth rate.

Table 8.1

Average Rice Yields (t/ha)

	1970-1972	*1980-1982*	*1990-1992*	*1999-2001*	*Yield Gain Between 1970-1972 and 1999-2001 (kg/yr)*
Assam	1.51	1.61	1.94	2.24	25
Bihar & Jharkhand	1.35	1.24	1.48	2.37	35
Chhattisgarh[a]	1.23	1.23	1.67	1.64	14
E. Uttar Pradesh	1.06	1.41	2.46	3.18	73
Orissa	1.32	1.34	1.94	1.88	19
West Bengal	1.84	1.79	2.95	3.51	58
E. India	1.41	1.44	2.10	2.50	38
All India	**1.67**	**1.94**	**2.62**	**2.99**	**46**

Note: Rice yield and production are expressed in terms of rough rice (i.e., unhusked paddy) using the conversion factor of 1 kg of unhusked paddy = 0.66 kg of milled rice.

[a]: Also include five eastern districts of Madhya Pradesh that have a relatively large area of rice and belong to same agroclimatic region. These districts are Balaghat, Jabalpur, Mandla, Seoni and Shahdol.

Table 8.2

Growth Rates (Per cent) of Rice Area, Yield and Production, 1970-2001

	Area	*Yield*	*Prod*
Assam	0.79***	1.49***	2.28***
Bihar & Jharkhand	-0.20*	1.93***	1.72***
Chhattisgarh[a]	0.71***	1.39***	2.10***
E. Uttar Pradesh	0.76***	4.27***	5.02***
Orissa	0.02	1.72***	1.75***
West Bengal	0.60***	2.65***	3.25***
E. India	**0.38*** **	**2.32*** **	**2.70*** **

Note: ***, ** and * indicate statistical significance at 1 per cent level, respectively.

[a]: Also includes five eastern districts of Madhya Pradesh that have a relatively large area of rice and belong to same agroclimatic region. These districts are Balaghat, Jabalpur, Mandla, Seoni and Shahdol.

Dividing the period 1970-2001 into three time segments, the changes in performance of growth in rice productivity for these time segments are presented in Table 8.3. The results show that eastern India underwent a faster rate of change in rice productivity after 1980. During 1970-1979, the output growth, driven mainly by area expansion, was positive but statistically insignificant. The growth in yield became the main source of production growth after 1980. The impressive growth in productivity experienced during 1980-89, however, was not maintained during 1990-2001. The growth rate in rice output dropped from 4.74 per cent per annum during 1980-89 to 1.86 per cent per annum during 1990-2001.

Green Revolution had just begun in the late sixties with the development of semi-dwarf and fertiliser-responsive improved varieties. In 1970, the area under modern varieties in Assam, Bihar, Orissa and Madhya Pradesh was below 10 per cent. Only Uttar Pradesh and West Bengal had a higher ratio at 15 per cent and 11 per cent, respectively. The adoption of improved varieties steadily increased over time, and during the triennium 1996, the adoption rate for eastern India was 69 per cent (Figure 8.3). In Uttar Pradesh, over 85 per cent of the rice area was planted to modern varieties (MV) during the triennium 1994-96.[2] West Bengal is close behind at 72 per cent and Bihar, Madhya Pradesh and Orissa have the adoption rate approaching 70 per cent. Even in Assam, which has the lowest rate of adoption, the estimates are above 50 per cent. Thus, modern varieties have spread quite well in eastern India, although opportunities for further expansion remain mainly in Assam, Bihar, Orissa and Chhattisgarh. In the case of eastern Uttar Pradesh and West Bengal, the spread of available modern varieties is approaching the ceiling level.

Expansion of irrigation, especially that of the private tubewell irrigation, has been a major phenomenon that played an important role in the rapid growth in rice production in eastern Uttar Pradesh and West Bengal. During the early 1980s, central and state governments initiated programmes for subsidising the expansion of groundwater irrigation in the Indo-Gangetic plains.

2. Even if we assume that modern varieties cover 100 per cent of the rice area in western Uttar Pradesh, the level of adoption in eastern Uttar Pradesh will be around 78 per cent.

Table 8.3

Growth Rates (Per cent) of Rice Area, Yield and Production Over Time

	1970-1979			*1980-1989*			*1990-2001*		
	Area	*Yield*	*Production*	*Area*	*Yield*	*Production*	*Area*	*Yield*	*Production*
Assam	1.47***	-0.87	0.59	0.51	0.57	1.08	0.29	1.39***	1.68***
Bihar & Jharkhand	0.51	-0.21	0.29	0.25	3.80*	4.05	0.38	4.24**	4.63**
Chhattisgarh[a]	0.66***	-3.72	-3.06	0.72***	2.02	2.73	0.11	-1.69	-1.58
E. Uttar Pradesh	0.90*	-1.03	-0.13	1.43*	6.08***	7.50***	0.30	2.63***	2.93***
Orissa	-0.91*	-0.53	-1.44	0.40	3.50	3.90	0.05	-0.63	-0.58
West Bengal	-0.05	0.83	0.78	1.11**	5.49***	6.60***	0.22	2.08***	2.29***
E. India	**0.27**	**-0.55**	**-0.27**	**0.72****	**4.03*****	**4.74*****	**0.22***	**1.64*****	**1.86*****

Note: ***, ** and * indicate statistical significance at 1 per cent level, respectively.

[a]: Also includes five eastern districts of Madhya Pradesh that have a relatively large area of rice and belong to same agroclimatic regions. These districts are Balaghat, Jabalpur, Mandla, Seoni and Shahdol.

Figure 8.3

Percentage Area Under MV Rice

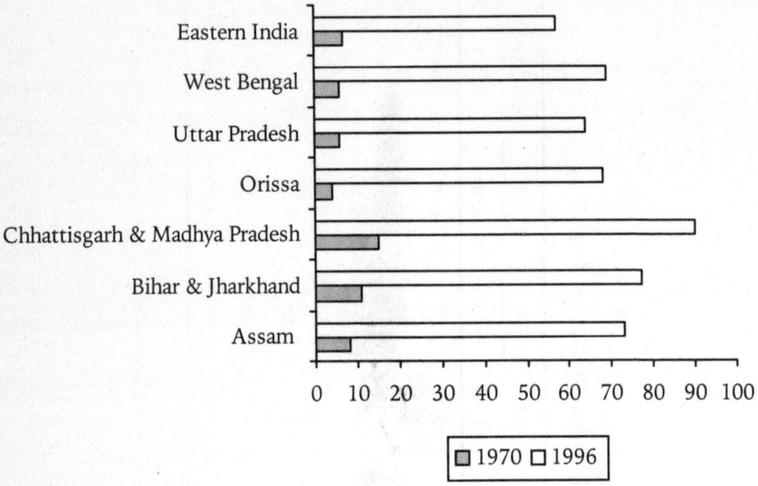

An important characteristic of groundwater utilisation in Uttar Pradesh and West Bengal is the existence of an active groundwater market. Farmers who lack adequate capital for investing in pumps or those with a very small irrigable area purchase water from neighbours who have installed pumps. As a result of the evolution of groundwater market, even small and marginal farmers are able to acquire groundwater in small divisible quantities as needed (Pant, 1992; Shah and Ballabh, 1997). Notwithstanding the problems associated with irregular power supply and the high cost of diesel-operated pumps, irrigation has now become widely accessible in these two states and, to a limited extent, in other states of eastern India. The reduction in risk due to ability to provide supplemental water as and when needed for the winter rice crop has then encouraged rapid adoption of modern varieties and the increased use of fertilisers in eastern India. In the case of West Bengal, groundwater irrigation was also instrumental in the expansion of summer rice cultivation.

The spatial pattern of changes in rice productivity in eastern India is summarised in Table 8.4. The average rice yield during 1970-1979 was in the range 1-2t/ha in 90 per cent of the rice area of eastern India. During 1990-1999, only 47 per cent of the rice area was in this

Table 8.4

Percentage Rice Area under Different Yield Categories

	Yield Group				
	< 1 t/ha	*1-2 t/ha*	*2-3 t/ha*	*3-4 t/ha*	*> 4 t/ha*
Assam					
1970-1979		100			
1980-1989		88	12		
1990-1999		55	45		
Bihar & Jharkhand					
1970-1979	2	98			
1980-1989		86	14		
1990-1999		69	31		
Chhattisgarh[a]					
1970-1979	19	81			
1980-1989	6	94			
1990-1998	12	69	19		
E. Uttar Pradesh					
1970-1979	29	71			
1980-1989		70	30		
1990-1999			80	20	
Orissa					
1970-1979		100			
1980-1989		93	7		
1990-1999		72	28		
West Bengal					
1970-1979		79	21		
1980-1989		20	70	10	
1990-1999		10	46	33	11
Eastern India					
1970-1979	7	89	4	0	0
1980-1989	1	73	24	2	0
1990-1999	2	47	39	10	2

Note: Area and yield estimates based on district-level averages.

[a]: Also includes five eastern districts of Madhya Pradesh that have a relatively large area of rice and belong to same agroclimatic region. These districts are Balaghat, Jabalpur, Mandla, Seoni and Shahdol.

yield range, with 51 per cent of the rice area having the yield greater than 2t/ha.

Despite this achievement at the aggregate level, the growth has been non-uniform across the states. During 1990-1999, almost all of the area having yield in the range of 1-2t/ha was concentrated in Bihar, Chhattisgarh and Orissa. In these states, the proportionate area with yield in this range was above 60 per cent. On the other hand, eastern Uttar Pradesh had no district in this yield range and West Bengal had only three hilly districts in this yield range, accounting for only 10 per cent of rice area of the state. A large proportion of rice area in these latter two states, has rice yield exceeding 2t/ha. Given that Bihar, Jharkhand, Chhattisgarh and Orissa account for over 50 per cent of the total rice area in eastern India, growth in productivity in these states is critical to the overall productivity performance of eastern India.

The performance across districts over time suggests that the yield growth has been widespread in eastern Uttar Pradesh and West Bengal. In West Bengal, yield has remained in the 1-2t/ha interval in the hilly districts of Coochbehar, Darjeeling and Jalpaiguri only. In Assam, Darrang, Goalpara, Kamrup and Lakhimpur are the four districts where yield has continued to stagnate within the 1-2t/ha range. These districts represent North Bank Plains zone and the Lower Brahmaputra Valley zone. Chronic incidence of flood may be a major cause of low productivity in these zones. In Bihar, only three districts Gaya, Patna and Shahabad moved from 1-2t/ha yield interval during 1970-1979 to 2-3t/ha yield interval during 1990-1997. These districts belong to South Bihar Plains zone. Rice productivity growth in other districts of Bihar has remained too low for them to move to the 2-3t/ha yield category. The coastal districts of Ganjam and Puri and the inland districts of Sambalpur and Bolangir are the only four districts that have made this transition in Orissa. In the case of Chhattisgarh, Raipur is the only district that has made this transition.

The overall picture that emerges from this analysis is that of a fairly broad-based yield growth in West Bengal and eastern Uttar Pradesh. In other states of eastern India, growth is limited to some pockets only. While favourable conditions have led to growth in some districts, productivity growth in other districts has been modest. This differential performance could have resulted from the variations in biophysical conditions (e.g., soil type, rainfall patterns), investments in irrigation and other infrastructures, and institutional setup across districts and states.

Issues for Rice Productivity Growth in Eastern India

Although India has made tremendous progress in reducing poverty at the national level from 37 per cent in 1991 to 26 per cent in 2000, the level of poverty in eastern India is still higher than the national average. Bihar and Orissa still have the poverty ratio exceeding 40 per cent. Except for West Bengal, the poverty ratio in all other states of eastern India exceeds 30 per cent. Given that more than half of the poor people of India now live in eastern India, a further reduction in the national poverty level is dependent largely on the success in eastern India.

Despite an impressive performance during the 1980s, the growth in rice production in eastern India has slackened considerably, during the 1990s. The growth process of 1980s that is based mainly on the expansion of groundwater irrigation and the active promotion of technologies available at that time, seems to have run out of steam. It appears that easier gains have already been made and further productivity growth will require a concerted effort in several directions. A new wave of technology and investments in increasing rice productivity is needed to keep the rate of output growth in this important region of India above the rate of population growth. Further, agricultural growth in eastern India is as important now as it was during the 1980s. However, the research and development strategies for eastern India must be cognizant of the evolving characteristics and new challenges that have arisen during the 1990s. We now turn our attention to these factors.

Increasing Number of Small and Marginal Farmers

As further research and development efforts are made to improve the agricultural productivity in eastern India, a factor that needs to be taken into account is the preponderance of small and marginal farmers. Except for Madhya Pradesh, more than 70 per cent of the farm households owned less than one ha of land in 1991 (Table 8.5). This percentage has increased over time historically and is expected to increase further with population growth. The implication for agricultural research is that the technology developed should be suitable to the growing number of these small farmers. These small and marginal farmers are unlikely to be able to apply large quantities of cash inputs (such as fertilisers) or make lumpy investments in farm machinery. Thus, rice technologies for these farmers should not be dependent on heavy use of cash inputs but should rely mostly on the use of labour.

Table 8.5

Percentage of Households Owning Less than One Hectare

	1961	*1971*	*1981*	*1991*
Assam	–[a]	–	–	74
Bihar & Jharkhand	68	72	76	80
Chhattisgarh & Madhya Pradesh[b]	40	40	46	47
Orissa	63	69	66	72
Uttar Pradesh[c]	57	65	68	73
West Bengal	69	78	82	84
All India	**60**	**62**	**67**	**69**

Note: a: Not available.
b: Separate data for Chhattisgarh not available.
c: Whole of Earstwhile Uttar Pradesh

Source: *India Rural Development Report* (1999).

A small farm size also means that rice production will constitute a small proportion of the gross income earned by the farmer. The livelihood of farmers who have a small endowment of land depends on multiple activities not just on the production of a single crop. In addition to rice, they also grow many other crops, produce livestock and also engage in non-farm activities where possible. Farm-level data from eastern India indicate that the share of rice in the total household income can be less than 15 per cent for small and marginal farmers (Pandey *et al.*, 2000). Such farmers may value other economic activities more than the additional production of rice, especially if there are clear trade-offs. Thus, only those rice technologies that mesh well with other components of the livelihood systems are likely to be adopted. For example, a long-duration rice variety is unlikely to be adopted if farmers use the land for high-value post-rice crops or for grazing soon after the harvest of short-duration rice varieties. Similarly, farmers who migrate seasonally for work after planting rice are unlikely to practice an intensive crop care that requires a regular monitoring of crop and soil conditions. By the same reasoning, crop establishment methods that require precise and careful planting are likely to be rejected in favour of simpler but robust methods.

An important area of policy intervention in eastern India is to foster markets for the services produced by lumpy capital investments. It may be uneconomic for small farmers to make such investments due to small farm size. However, such investments can be made divisible through the development of rental markets. The development of rental market for water pumps in eastern India is a case in point. However, these markets are not yet fully competitive with the suppliers extracting some degree of monopoly rents from the buyers (Shah and Ballabh, 1997). A more reliable supply of electricity, subsidies for more efficient water conveyance systems, changes in the free-boring schemes to increase the participation of small farmers and the removal of subsidy-induced distortion in the choice of pumping devices, would encourage the development of more efficient water markets in eastern India.

While adoption of improved technologies by small rice farmers will increase their production and food intake, it will not necessarily lead to a proportionate increase in the marketed surplus. In addition, marketing costs would tend to rise as small quantities of outputs are collected from large number of small producers and processed by the marketing channel. The technologies suitable for small farmers alone, may not be able to provide the marketed surplus needed for the growing urban population in an efficient manner. The implication is that technology development should occur in two fronts simultaneously: for small as well as for large-scale producers. The seed-fertiliser technology is generally divisible and hence, is suitable for all categories of farmers, irrespective of the farm size. However, the relative abundance of labour in densely-populated areas of eastern India implies that technologies for large farms should not be labour-substituting but labour-absorbing. Mechanical technologies that are purely labour-replacing are, hence, less appropriate in eastern India. Some mechanical technologies that may appear to be labour-saving in the first instance, actually may increase the total labour use by facilitating more intensive cropping (double or triple cropping). A good example of this is irrigation pumps. Naturally, such technologies are very suitable for the resource endowment of eastern India. The implication is that the potential for labour absorption of a new technology should be assessed at the system level, not at the level of individual crops and that there may be a clear role for mechanical technologies in some instances.

Rice Varieties Released and Adoption Levels

By 2000, improved varieties of rice released in India reached 632. This number includes both the state and the national release. The number of rice varieties released per million ha is highest for the irrigated environment (Table 8.6). Despite the fact that the area under rainfed lowland is almost similar to that for the irrigated environment, the number of varieties released for the former is half of those released for the latter. In terms of the number of varieties released per million ha of area, the rainfed upland ecosystems fare better. Within the rainfed lowland, the number of varieties released for the less favourable sub-ecosystems such as the semi-deep and deep water conditions is much lower (Prasada Rao *et al.*, 2000).

Table 8.6

Rice Varieties Released in India

	*No. of Varieties**	*Area (M ha)*	*No. of Varieties/ Area (M ha)*
Irrigated	378	17.8	21
Rainfed Low Land and Deep Water	164	17.5	9
Rainfed Upland	90	7.0	13

Note: * Source of data on the total number of varieties released by rice ecosystem: Prasada Rao *et al.* (2000).

Using the number of varieties released for each ecosystem as an indicator of the level of research investments made for that ecosystem, the rainfed lowlands which dominate in eastern India fare poorly, relative to the irrigated environment. It is often argued that even if the number of varieties targeted to the rainfed lowland environment is low, there has been a tremendous spill-over benefit in the form of adoption of varieties bred for irrigated environments in rainfed environments. The level of adoption of MVs in eastern India is above 60 per cent and quite a substantial proportion of these varieties were originally released for irrigated areas (Janaiah and Hossain, 2002).

While rainfed areas have definitely benefited from this spill-over effect (especially where farmers have access to supplemental irrigation), the average yield level in large parts of eastern India still remains very low. These varieties bred for irrigated conditions may not be well-adapted to the highly variable growing conditions of rainfed lowlands in eastern India and/or farmers are not able to manage these varieties well. Thus, while adoption has occurred as farmers saw an opportunity to obtain a modest increase in yield compared to their own traditional varieties, improved varieties that are adapted specifically to rainfed environments are needed to fully exploit the potential that exist in these systems. To this end, important progress is being made through the ICAR/IRRI shuttle breeding programme that has now developed several lines with good yields even at a modest level of fertiliser input. Such programmes need further strengthening and support. In addition, participatory varietal selection and breeding programmes for rainfed environments hold much promise of developing and delivering suitable varieties for these rainfed ecosystems (Courtois *et al.*, 2001; Witcombe *et al.*, 1996).

As compared to the Green Revolution strategy of developing a few elite lines widely adapted to large geographic areas, improved varieties for highly variable rainfed environments need to be adapted to the specific conditions of the target domain. Diversity of environmental conditions, even within a single farm, also implies that breeding should be aimed at developing several varieties with different characteristics rather than a few elite lines. In traditional systems, farmers have managed the heterogeneous rainfed environments by maintaining a diversity of rice varieties, each suitable to their specific niches. In addition, farmers value varying attributes of rice, such as maturity period, grain quality and straw yields, not just the grain yield, and grow different varieties to obtain these different output attributes (Kshirsagar *et al.*, 2002). A modern breeding programme that builds upon farmer needs and their knowledge systems is needed for rapid progress in these rainfed environments. This represents a major change in mindset compared to the more traditional centralised breeding approach which has been successful in the irrigated areas. This decentralised approach to breeding naturally calls for a closer partnership with farmer organisations and NGOs in the conduct of research and technology testing.

Varietal Replacement

Eastern India is characterised by a low rate of replacement of rice varieties (Table 8.7). As compared with the all-India average of 14 per cent, Bihar, Madhya Pradesh and West Bengal have a much lower rate of seed replacement. Farmers basically keep their own seeds and use them from year to year. Low rate of seed replacement basically means that (a) old seeds that may be of lower quality are not replaced with better quality seeds of the same variety, and (b) seeds of newly released varieties do not enter the seed systems at a rapid rate. Both these factors contribute to a lower rate of growth in productivity. A low seed-replacement rate is symptomatic of a limited access to quality seeds which are distributed mostly by the public sector in eastern India. Limited access to seeds may result from (a) farmers' lack of purchasing power, (b) lack of information about new seeds, (c) poor quality control of seeds, and (d) institutional constraints related to public sector seed distribution.

Table 8.7

Seed Replacement Rate

	Replacement Rate (in Per Cent)
Eastern States	
Assam	-
Bihar & Jharkhand	1.5
Chhattisgarh & Madhya Pradesh[a]	3.0
Orissa	10.3
Uttar Pradesh[b]	9.0
West Bengal	5.4
Non-eastern States	
Andhra Pradesh	32.1
Haryana	8.5
Karnataka	1.2
Maharashtra	-
Punjab	4.6
Tamil Nadu	0.1
All India	**14.0**

Note: The data are for mid-nineties and are estimated assuming a seed rate of 50 kg/ha.

[a]: Separate data for Chhattisgarh not available.

[b]: Whole of Uttar Pradesh.

Source: Pal *et al.* (2000).

A full-scale discussion of the constraints related to public sector distribution of seeds in eastern India is beyond the scope of this chapter (Pal *et al.*, 2000). However, an important constraint seems to be the difficulty in efficiently multiplying and distributing seeds to a large number of subsistence-oriented farmers. Private sector has limited commercial interest in providing quality seeds to subsistence farmers who may be unwilling to pay a price premium for high quality seeds. Hence, seed production and distribution in eastern India has remained primarily in the public domain. Even after a variety is released, there are considerable delays in the various stages of seed multiplication which is done primarily by the National Seed Corporation, State Agricultural Universities and State Farm Corporations. The quality control of seeds during the multiplication stage is often inadequate. In addition, the formal seed distribution systems are poorly-linked with farmers' own informal seed systems. Although farmer demands for new seeds are assessed in some way, the whole process of seed multiplication and distribution is very much top-down. As a result of these constraints and limited funding available to seed corporations, the quantity of seeds made available through the public sector system is grossly inadequate to cover large areas. Fortunately, initiatives are being put in place to improve the efficacy of seed production systems through a greater participation of farmers. Large gains can be made through institutional reforms of seed production systems so that the time lag between the variety release and the seed availability to farmers is reduced (Pandey and Rajatasereekul, 1999).

Rural Infrastructure

Rural infrastructures include power, irrigation, transport, fertiliser distribution system, credit distribution system, rural health and agricultural marketing facilities. A clear positive correlation exists between the level of infrastructure and agricultural productivity (Bhatia, 1999). Thus, an increased investment in rural infrastructure is an effective way of raising the agricultural productivity. Unfortunately, the eastern Indian states rank the lowest in terms of infrastructure development. Without adequate public investment in irrigation, market development and transportation infrastructure, the rural economy of eastern India will fail to develop dynamic linkages with other sectors of the economy.

Closing the Yield Gap

The gap between experimental and farm-level yield is still wide in the eastern Indian states. Based on the average experimental yield of AICRIP trials and the state average yield, the yield gap has been estimated to be over 60 per cent in all states of eastern India except for West Bengal (Siddiq, 2000). At least, a part of this yield gap represents the difference between the environmental conditions of trial sites and farmers' average field condition. Yield gap due to such environmental variations cannot be generally removed. Nevertheless, the current magnitude of yield gap reflects the unexploited potential of eastern India in increasing rice productivity in the future.

Yield gaps can also be estimated by comparing the yield of 'best practice' farmers with that of the average farmer within a region. Such a measure of yield gap provides a more realistic estimate of yield gain that can be achieved through adoption of modern varieties and associated crop management practices. In this aggregated analysis, the district with the highest average yield in an agroclimatic zone is taken as the benchmark for comparing the average yield of all districts within the zone. The estimated district-level yield gaps by agroclimatic zones are shown in Table 8.8. Based on these results, the agroclimatic zones can be grouped into three categories. The zones with a 'low yield gap' are Barak and Central Brahmaputra valley zones and Hill zones of Assam, Chhattisgarh plains and coastal zone of Orissa. The yield gap in this group ranges between 4 per cent and 13 per cent. The zones with the medium yield gaps are Assam (Lower Brahmaputra Valley, North Bank Plains and Upper Brahmaputra Valley), eastern Uttar Pradesh Plains and West Bengal Plains. The yield gap in this group ranges between 23 per cent and 35 per cent. Finally, the plateau zone (Bihar, Chhattisgarh, Orissa and West Bengal) and Bihar plains have the highest yield gap ranging between 44 per cent and 61 per cent.

A low yield gap estimated as above, indicates that all districts within the zone have similar yields. This may arise if all districts have equally exploited the modern technology or if all districts are producing at a low-yield level due to lack of appropriate technology (or lack of access to such technologies). The average yield for this zone is low and ranges between 1.73 t/ha to 2.43t/ha. This suggests the need to develop suitable technologies for these environments and make them more accessible to farmers.

Table 8.8

Estimated Yield Gap

Agroecological Zone	*Average Yield (t/ha) 1995-1997*	*Highest Average Yield (t/ha) 1995-1997*	*Per Cent Yield Gap*	*Yield Gap Group*
Assam				
BVZ+CBVZ+Hill	2.43	2.73	13	Low
LBVZ+NBPZ+UBVZ	1.96	2.62	34	Moderate
Bihar & Jharkhand				
Plains	2.15	3.10	44	High
Chhattisgarh[a]				
Plains	1.73	1.95	12	Low
E. Uttar Pradesh				
Plains	2.98	4.04	35	Moderate
Orissa				
Coastal	1.95	2.02	4	Low
West Bengal				
Plains	3.42	4.22	23	Moderate
Chhattisgarh, Jharkhand, Orissa, West Bengal				
Plateau	1.57	2.53	61	High

Note: Yield gaps are estimated by comparing the mean of the triennium average yields of each group with the highest triennium average yield of a district in the same group. Rice yield and production are expressed in terms of rough rice (i.e., unhusked paddy) using the conversion factor of 1 kg of unhusked paddy = 0.66 kg of milled rice.

[a]: Also includes five eastern districts of Madhya Pradesh that have a relatively large area of rice and belong to same agroclimatic region. These districts are Balaghat, Jabalpur, Mandla, Seoni and Shahdol.

In the case of 'high-yield gap' group, appropriate technologies are apparently available but not being widely adopted. While farmers in some districts have adopted the technology, others are not able to make full use of such technologies. Obviously, a first step in developing a suitable strategy for this zone would be to assess the factors constraining technology diffusion. Such constraints may be socioeconomic or biophysical. Economists have emphasised the socio-economic constraints such as the farm size, security of tenure and access to credit in explaining variations in the level of technology adoption. These variables invariably play an important role. However, more recent evidence indicates that biophysical factors often play a more critical role in these rainfed environments (Hossain and Laborte 1996; Pandey *et al.*, 2000). A high degree of spatial heterogeneity means that a technology suitable in one location may not be suitable for another location. This suggests the need for more applied research and a greater role of on-farm testing of technologies to identify suitable domains.

For zones with a 'moderate' yield gap, a relatively high average yield (for West Bengal and eastern Uttar Pradesh) implies that the technology diffusion has been widespread but that some farmers are managing the technology better than others. The closure of yield gaps in this zone will require a greater provision of information for better management of crops such as crop establishment, pest control and fertilisation. These crop management technologies tend to be somewhat 'knowledge intensive' and the strategy for delivering such technologies would have to be quite different from the standard 'package' approach that promotes a package of technologies for a large area (Byerlee, 1994). Crop management advice for these environments needs to be more site-specific and specific to crop conditions. Obviously, this will require a major reorientation and strengthening of the extension system, and a greater recognition of the potential roles of adaptive research and farmers' knowledge systems.

Targeting Rice Technologies for Eastern India

Based on the patterns of productivity growth and the current average yield of rice, the states of eastern India can be divided into two groups. The first group includes, eastern Uttar Pradesh and West Bengal. The second group includes the other states. The productivity growth in the first group has been high during the 1980s. Adoption of modern varieties is high and farmers have benefited from the expansion of groundwater irrigation. Rice production system in this group is now becoming increasingly commercialised and diversified. The agricultural research and development strategy for this group, thus, will have to be somewhat different from the other group where rice yields are much lower. We now focus attention on research and policy interventions suitable to these two groups of states.

Due to increasing diversification and commercialisation of rice systems in the first group of states, the development of marketing systems for both inputs and outputs is of critical importance. Without an efficient marketing system, farmers in this zone will not be able to benefit from improved technology and the gains that have been made so far may be lost. For example, farmers who produce surplus for markets may lose if the price is depressed due to the inability of the marketing systems to siphon off excess local supplies. There is some evidence that this is already happening to a certain extent in West Bengal. In addition, farmers in West Bengal will increasingly look for opportunities for income gains through crop diversification. Rice technologies that facilitate crop diversification are needed so that food production is not compromised as agriculture becomes diversified.

One of the major sources of growth in the first group of states is the exploitation of groundwater. Both public and private irrigation schemes and water markets contributed to a rapid growth in rice productivity and crop diversification in these states. However, there are still opportunities for a more efficient extraction and use of groundwater.

Although the population density is quite high in West Bengal, the demand for labour-saving technologies for rice is likely to increase in the future, as farmers intensify land use and/or diversify to other crops and other income-generating activities. An important labour-saving technology for rice production is direct seeding as opposed to the traditional practice of transplanting. However, direct-seeded rice can suffer from poor and patchy establishment and difficulties of weed control (Pandey and Velasco, 1999). Development of rice technology is currently oriented mainly for transplanted culture and it would be desirable to shift this orientation towards direct seeding.

For the second group of states, the average yields are still low and the growth in productivity has been modest. These states still require technologies suitable to poorly-performing areas such as the Chotanagpur plateau. Drought is a major constraint that reduces productivity in the plateau and the plains of eastern Madhya Pradesh and Orissa (Pandey *et al.*, 2000). Although some scientific progress has been made, drought-tolerant varieties suitable to these environments are yet to be available to farmers. In addition, rice area in Chotanagpur plateau of Bihar has shrunk over time, as more land is being converted to agriculturally unsuitable wasteland. Research to increase the productivity of these drought-prone areas is strongly needed to generate the required impact in these areas. Drought management in these areas will also require interventions that go beyond a single crop and include the whole of the watershed. Approaches similar to those that have worked in the arid and semi-arid areas may have potential applicability in eastern India also (Rao, 2000).

One of the characteristics of rice systems in the second group of states is the low cropping intensity. In large tracts of Chotanagpur plateau and the Chhattisgarh plains, land is mostly left fallow after the harvest of rice. Low land use intensity is mainly due to lack of irrigation. While high cost may constrain the development of large scale surface irrigation schemes, watershed based approach complemented by traditional tanks and dugwells may provide some opportunities for intensification of land use. Some of these traditional tanks are poorly maintained and not managed efficiently. Similarly, there are no major programmes for promoting the use of dugwells for post-rice cropping. Increased public sector support for dugwells and institutional reforms to encourage community participation in the management of traditional tanks can play an important role.

There are still large areas in Bihar plains that can benefit from investments in drainage. Productivity in these areas is low due to excessive accumulation of water. The problem is caused partly by poorly designed road and railway networks that obstruct natural drainage as well as poor management of surface irrigation schemes. In addition to investment in drainage, the overall use of groundwater in the second group of states is very low. An aggressive campaign like those launched to support groundwater development in eastern Uttar Pradesh can help increase a better utilisation of groundwater in these areas.

The input use (such as fertilisers) in the second group of states is relatively low. A number of institutional constraints prevent farmers from having access to modern inputs. These include low level of infrastructure, limited credit availability and poor extension of technologies. Growth in these areas will remain sluggish without active involvement of the public sector in the provision of these public goods.

Concluding Remarks

To address the problems of low rice productivity and high poverty in eastern India, the Government of India initiated several programmes in support of agricultural development since the early 1980s. A comprehensive study of eastern India, popularly know as the Sen Report, developed a strategy for the agricultural sector of eastern India (RBI, 1984). A subsequent study conducted by the Planning Commission of India, identified factors that were important in determining the productivity growth of eastern India during the early 1980s (Rao, 1985). The implementation of development strategies outlined in these two documents played a major role in the productivity growth of eastern India during the late 1980s. Although the pace of growth has been variable spatially, agricultural sector of eastern India is now showing a considerable degree of dynamism.

Despite the achievements of the 1980s, a cause for concern is the slowdown in the growth rate of rice productivity in eastern India during the 1990s. It appears that the cumulative effect of the various interventions that led to the growth in the 1980s has spent itself and a new strategy is needed now to generate additional growth. Much of the growth in rice productivity in the1980s was driven by the expansion of irrigation (mainly groundwater) and the diffusion of modern varieties that were developed for irrigated environments. Public investments in irrigation and drainage and an active campaign to extend modern technologies were the critical elements of this growth process. These investments enabled utilisation of technologies that were suitable for the favourable rainfed environments. While opportunities still exist for yield growth through the continuation of the same strategy, it is increasingly clearer that yield growth in the more difficult rainfed environment requires a considerable strengthening of the agricultural research and extension systems. Modern technologies have made very little inroads in the large areas of Chhattisgarh plains and Chotanagpur plateau. These environments are much harsher with poor soils, higher frequency of drought and low level of infrastructure. The risk in production is high and the farmers are poorer than their counterparts in favourable rainfed environments. Very few rice varieties are currently available for these less favourable environments.

Developing suitable rice technologies for these environments requires a paradigm shift in research and development. As the possibility of using supplemental irrigation to stabilise the crop is limited, rice varieties and management practices that make efficient use of *in situ* moisture and nutrients are needed. A major goal of breeding programmes for such environments would be to stabilise the yield rather than to increase the yield potential. High variability also means that a specific technology is unlikely to be suitable over a large area and a much more 'tailor-made' approach to technology design is needed. Rice researchers would need to work much more closely with farmers in a partnership mode to be able to make an impact in these environments. Interventions for these systems may often be needed at the level of watershed than just at the farm level. A higher level of funding for a long period of time would be needed as the unit cost of such research and technology development will be higher than those conducted in the more homogeneous environments.

In addition to strengthening the rice research and development for rainfed environments, public sector can play an important role through investment in infrastructure and policy support. Poor infrastructure in eastern India is still a major constraint to productivity growth. Investments in irrigation development, drainage, and provision of credit and marketing facilities are important areas where public investment can have a high pay-off.

As globalisation of the Indian economy takes place, adequate policy support is needed to ensure that the eastern Indian farmers have sufficient incentives to increase rice productivity. Although the eastern Indian farmers have a comparative advantage in rice production within the country, the current rice policy provides a greater economic incentive to farmers in the irrigated areas of western and southern India. These rice farmers in the advanced areas are likely to benefit even more when India opens up its rice market. Removal of subsidies to rice producers in northern India and lowering of the procurement price will increase the profitability of rice production in eastern India and encourage farmers in this region to adopt improved technologies. Such a policy will make the costly transportation of rice from the surplus northern region to the deficit eastern region less important.

Policy support to encourage the diversification of agriculture in eastern India is also needed. Foodgrain production currently accounts for the overwhelming share of the gross cropped area of eastern India and very little diversification out of foodgrain production has taken place over the past several decades. While foodgrain production in this poverty-stricken region is an important way of addressing the problem of food insecurity, poverty reduction in the long run, requires diversification to other crops and other income-generating activities. Improvements in marketing infrastructures and institutions, establishment of agroprocessing industry, and support for rural industries are some of the policy interventions that enhance the structural transformation of agricultural sector in eastern India.

References

Bhatia, M.S. (1999). "Rural Infrastructure and Growth in Agriculture", *Economic and Political Weekly*, Vol. 34, pp.A43-A48.

Byerlee, D. (1994). "Technology Transfer Systems for Improve Crop Management: Lesson for the Future", in J.R. Anderson (ed.), *Agricultural Technology: Policy Issue for the International Community*, CAB International.

Courtois, B., B. Bartholome, D. Chaudhury, G. Maclaren, C.H. Misra, N.P. Mandal, S. Pandey, T. Paris, C. Piggin, K. Prasad, A.T. Roy, R.K. Sahu, V.N. Sahu, S. Sarkarung, S.K. Sharma, A. Singh, H.N. Singh, O.N. Singh, N.K. Singh, R.K. Singh, S. Singh, P.K. Sinha, B.V.S. Sisodia and R. Thakur (2001). "Comparing Farmers and Breeders Rankings in Varietal Selection for Low-input Environments: A Case Study of Rainfed Rice in Eastern India", *Euphytica*, Vol. 122, pp.537-550.

Evenson, R.E. and D. Gollin (2003). "Crop Variety Improvement and its Effect on Productivity: The Impact of International Agricultural Research", CABI Publishing.

Hossain, M. and A. Laborte (1996). "Differential Growth in Rice Production in Eastern India: Agroecological and Socio-economic Constraints", in V.P. Singh *et al.*, (eds.), *Proceedings of the International Conference on Stress Physiology of Rice*, 28 Feb.–5 Mar. 1994, Lucknow, UP, India, pp.221-239.

Janaiah, A. and M. Hossain (2002). "Impact of Coordinated Rice Improvement Program on Movement of the Improved Germplasm and Productivity Gains Across the Indian States", Paper presented at the International Conference on the Impacts of Research and Development, *Why Has Impacts Assessment Research Not Made More of a Difference?*, 4-8 Feb., Costa Rica.

Kshirsagar, K., S. Pandey, M.R. Bellon (2002). "Farmer Perceptions, Varietal Characteristics and Technology Adoption: A Rainfed Rice Village in Orissa", *Economic and Political Weekly*, Vol. 37(13), pp.1239-1246.

National Institute of Rural Development (1999). *India Rural Development Report*, Hyderabad, India.

Osmani, S.R. (1998). "Did the Green Revolution Hurt the Poor? A Re-examination of the Early Critique", in P.L. Pingali and M. Hossain (eds.), *Impact of Rice Research*, TDRI and International Rice Research Institute, pp.193-212.

Pal, S., S. Pandey and Abedullah (2000). "Growth and Variability in Agriculture Revisited: District-level Evidence of Rice Production in Eastern India", in S. Pandey, B.C. Barah, R.A. Villano and S. Pal (eds.), *Risk Analysis and Management in Rainfed Rice Systems*, Proceedings of the NCAP/IRRI Workshop, 21-23 September 1998, Los Baños, Manila, Philippines, International Rice Research Institute, pp.97-114.

Pandey, S. and L. Velasco (1999). "Economics of Direct Seeding in Asia: Patterns of Adoption of Adoption and Research Priorities", *International Rice Research Notes*, No. 24, pp.6-11.

Pandey, S. and S. Rajatasereekul (1999). "Economics of Plant Breeding; The Value of Shorter Breeding Cycles for Rice in Northeast Thailand", *Field Crops Research*, Vol. 64, pp.187-197.

Pandey, S., D.D. Behura, R.A. Villano, and D. Naik (2000). "Economic Cost of Drought and Farmers' Coping Mechanisms: A Study of Rainfed Rice Systems in Eastern India", *IRRI Discussion Paper Series*, No. 39, p.33.

Pant, N. (1992). *New Trend in Indian Irrigation: Commercialisation of Groundwater*, Ashish Publishing, New Delhi.

Prasada Rao V., V. Shobha Rani, L.V. Subba Rao, G.S.V. Prasad, K. Krishnaiah, K. Satayanarayana and B. Mishra (2000). "High Yielding Rice Varieties of India", *DRR Research Bulletin* 1.

Rao, C.H.H. (1985). *Report of Study Group on Agricultural Strategies for Eastern Region of India*, Government of India, Planning Commission, New Delhi, p.45.

——. (2000). "Watershed Development in India: Recent Experience and Emerging Issues", *Economic and Political Weekly*, Vol. 35, pp.3943-3947.

RBI (1984). *Agricultural Productivity in Eastern India*, Report of the Committee on Agricultural Productivity in Eastern India, Reserve Bank of India, Vols. I & II.

Shah, T. and V. Ballabh (1997). "Water Markets in North Bihar: Synthesis of Six Village Studies in Muzaffarpur District", *Economic and Political Weekly*, Vol. 32(52), December, pp.A183-A190.

Siddiq, E.A. (2000). "Yawning Productivity Gaps", *The Hindu Survey of Indian Agriculture*, Chennai, India, pp.39-44.

Witcombe, J.R., A. Joshi, K.D. Joshi and B.R. Sthapit (1996). "Farmer Participatory Crop Improvement, I. Varietal Selection and Breeding Methods and Their Impact on Biodiversity", *Expl Agriculture*, Vol. 32, pp.445-460.

Part IV

New Vistas: Vertical Coordination

9

Contract Farming and New Dimensions of Indian Agrarian Structure

P.K. JOSHI and PRATAP S. BIRTHAL

Introduction

The smallholders (< 2 ha) have dominated the Indian agriculture in the past and it is likely to continue in future as well, largely due to the imposition of Land Ceiling Act and lack of non-farm income opportunities. Their share in the total number of holdings increased from 70 per cent in 1971 to 80 per cent in 1995 (GoI, 2003). It is expected to reach 83 per cent by 2010 (Jha, 2001). The average size of landholding has reduced to 1.34 ha in 2001. For smallholders, the average size of landholding is as low as 0.63 ha. Obviously, the viability and sustainability of such tiny landholdings is a difficult preposition. It is because the smallholders are characterised as poor, usually undernourished and poverty stricken; and, by and large, practice subsistence agriculture with very limited marketable surplus.

In such a scenario, the fundamental issues that need to be looked into are: Does the existing dominance of subsistence farming have some opportunities to bring them out of the low-income trap? Do smallholders have better income augmenting opportunities in high-value agriculture emanating from the unfolding process of rising income levels and growing urbanisation, market liberalisation and globalisation?

Experiences gained from many developing countries suggest that agricultural diversification towards high-value commodities (such as fruits and vegetables, livestock and fisheries) have enormous opportunities for smallholders to augment their income (Ryan and Spencer, 2001; Barghouti *et al.*, 2003). Production of these

The authors are grateful to Ashok Gulati and Mruthyunjaya for providing all facilities to undertake this study.

commodities is labour-intensive and smallholders are efficient in production of these, compared to large farms because of low opportunity cost of labour.

Most of the high-value food commodities are perishable, and require effective transportation to the consumption centres, storage and value addition. These facilities are woefully lacking. The scale of production is small, and marketable surplus is low. Local markets are thin and transportation to urban centres is costly small marketed surplus of the individual producers. Open market prices of high-value commodities are highly fluctuating and often drop significantly even with small increase in their normal arrival. Value addition is low; hardly 2 per cent of the fruits and vegetables and 15 per cent of the milk enter into the commercial value-addition chain. In other words, lack of access to markets and information results into high transaction costs. Higher transaction costs are considered to be an important barrier to the development of high-value commodities, particularly on small farms. In order to expropriate the benefits of higher production efficiency, the transaction should be cost-efficient to both the sellers and buyers of the commodities. This would require institutions that add value to the farm produce by vertically coordinating the production, marketing, processing and distribution activities. Experiences gained in some developed countries as well as developing countries in Southeast Asia, Africa and Latin America have revealed, that contract farming have ample potential for benefiting the smallholders by assuring them markets and reducing their transaction costs (Runsten and Key, 1996; Warning and Key, 2000; FAO, 2001; Narayanan and Gulati, 2002; Martinez, 2002).

In this chapter, we examine the evolution and role of contract farming in the context of changing agrarian structure, and assesse their implications for smallholders. The chapter is organised into four sections. After the brief background, the following section gives the theoretical basis of contract farming for vertical coordination. The third section briefly documents the evolution of contract farming in India. The fourth section presents the empirical evidence from three case studies on impact of vertical coordination (through contract farming) on income, transaction cost and risk. The last section suggests policies to replicate successful models of contract farming for the benefit of smallholders.

Theoretical Basis of Contract Farming

As agriculture moves on the path of diversification and/or commercialisation, it becomes essential to enable farmers to reap benefits of market expansion through strengthening linkages between production and market. Institutions like cooperatives and contract farming are considered to be important means to achieve this.

These institutions lie on the continuum of two extremes of spot markets and full integration. In spot markets, goods are exchanged between buyers and sellers in the current time period. Producers are free to produce any commodity, and sell as much quantity and of any quality to any number of buyers depending on the market price. Buyers are also free to purchase any amount of quantity depending on their requirement. Prices are determined by the demand and supply situations. Spot markets are characterised by high uncertainty, as the production decisions are responsive to prices. On the other hand, in a situation of full integration, products move between the various stages of production-processing-distribution chain as a result of within-firm managerial orders rather than at the direction of the market prices. The firm has full control over quantity and quality of the products at different stages of supply chain. In between these two extremes lie a number of alternatives (cooperatives, producers' organisation and contract farming) of integrating the economic activity depending on the transaction costs, risks and returns associated with them.

Contract farming is an organisational arrangement in which farmers are contracted to produce the commodity desired by the firm. Contract farming emerge in response to market imperfections. Key and Runsten (1999), consider the following as the key market failures that discourage smallholders participate in the spot market.

Product markets: Spot markets particularly for high-value commodities are uncertain in quantity, quality and prices. The agribusiness firm contracts to get an assured supply of raw material of desired quality at predetermined prices or otherwise. The firm has a better control over operational as well as fixed costs, and can minimise the risk of underutilisation of its capacity and thereby, the cost of processing. Firms operating at their optimum capacity are able to utilise their fixed and operational resources gainfully. The firm thus, can have a competitive edge in the market and improves its market position.

From the farmer's perspective, markets for high-value food commodities are thin. Marketed surplus of smallholders is small, and selling in distant markets increases transaction costs. Institutional arrangements with guaranteed off-take of output, reduce market uncertainty, as well as the costs of information search.

Risks: Production and price risks are high for perishable commodities. Institutional mechanisms to guard against such risks are rare in developing countries, and therefore, farmers grow low-risk crops. Empirical evidences indicate, farmers are risk averse (Binswanger, 1980; Hazell, 1982) and are willing to pay a premium (lower product prices) for guaranteed income schemes. The firms that insure farmers against price risk can earn a premium in terms of having an assured supply of raw material. Compared to individual farmers, the firm is in better position to protect against income fluctuations by diversifying the production/supply sources geographically (Runsten and Key, 1996). The geographical dispersion of supply sources cancels the covariant variations in yields.

Information: The cost of information search and support services to an individual producer could be as high as to a single firm. The firm is in a superior position to acquire and disseminate information among a large number of producers at a much lower cost. The firm can utilise the production contracts to transfer inputs and information in a cost-effective manner. This is of considerable value to the producers, particularly to those who have no previous experience in undertaking production of the commodity in question.

Credit: High-value commodities are costly to produce. Smallholders are capital starved and need credit support. Credit markets are imperfect, fragmented and underdeveloped. Informal credit markets are exploitative, and institutional agencies are often biased against small farmers. Also, the transaction costs of institutional credit for small loans are quite high. The firm, on the other hand, by simultaneously effecting the farming and credit contracts is in position to lower the transaction costs to the producers. The firm too, faces lower transaction cost in terms of lower administrative and other costs. The product marketing arrangements reduce the risk of default.

Inputs and technology: Efficient production of high-value commodities requires a different set of inputs and technologies, which by and large, are not available to a common farmer. Transaction costs of acquisition of such technologies could be very high for an individual smallholder, while the firm has the advantage economies of scale. Additionally, farmers can utilise their labour more effectively in situations where land markets are rigid and labour is surplus.

Smallholders are often labour surplus. Rural labour markets are imperfect, and opportunity cost of labour is low. Production of high-value commodities is labour intensive, and the firm can take advantage of surplus and cheap labour by promoting production of high-value commodities at a low cost. If the firm produces itself, its dependence on hired labour increases the cost of production because of increase in the supervision cost of labour. By using contract farming option supervision costs become redundant for the firm as the family labour of the contract farmers does not require supervision.

Contract farming by overcoming the market imperfections can benefit the smallholders in terms of reduced transaction costs, higher profits and increased employment opportunities. Nevertheless, contract farming is not free from criticisms. It is often criticised on grounds of unequal bargaining power, high risks into new ventures, disruption in farming systems, farmers' indebtedness and over-reliance on advances and adverse effect on food security and income distribution (Glover and Kusterer, 1990; Little and Watts, 1994; Watts, 1994).

The main criticism however is against the firm's potential monopolistic tendency. If the market for a particular product is not competitive the firm may behave opportunistically forcing farmers to earn the net profits just above the one obtained from the alternative crop, particularly when the farmers have locked into sizeable investment into assets specific to the contract crop, which is difficult to transfer to other crops.

The terms, the contract, farming may have a negative impact on the welfare of smallholders. The agribusiness firm in order to reduce its transaction costs may effect contract with a few large producers rather contracting with a large number of small producers (Little and Watts, 1994). Since credit is an integral part of the contract of many firms, excessive dependence on the firm for credit may lead farmers, particularly smallholders into perpetual indebtedness.

Evolution of Contract Farming in India

Contract farming is not a new phenomenon for India (Singh, 2002; Singh and Asokan, 2004; Asokan and Singh, 2003). Even during the early 1970s, some models of contract farming had emerged for production of improved varieties of seeds (especially, of rice and wheat), sugarcane and milk. Subsequently, during late 1980s, a few private firms contracted farmers for some fast growing forest species, especially, poplar and eucalyptus (Saigal and Kashyap, 2002). During the early 1990s, vertical coordination (in the form of contract farming) started for vegetable production and processing (particularly, tomato). Mixed results were reported about the viability and sustainability of the various models of vertical coordination. Vertical coordination through cooperatives in the dairying sector, and seed production through contract farming were reported very successful models. On the other hand, cooperative and contract farming for sugar production are still continuing but their viability and sustainability is now questioned. Similarly, contract farming in afforestation could be expanded to a limited scale and was rated as a weak venture (Saigal and Kashyap, 2002). The same was reported for vegetable processing sector (Rangi and Sidhu, 2000).

Among the several reasons for the success or failures of the institutional arrangements in various commodities (Singh, 2002), the key factor was related to the government intervention. The successful models of milk and seed production had the least government intervention, while sugar had the maximum, particularly since late 1980s. In the case of forest, government policies favoured import of cheap timber than domestic production through contract farming. The failure of contract farming in vegetables was mainly due to opportunistic tendencies followed by the farmers as well as firms in the absence of a legal mechanism governing the contract. Besides, this model favoured large farmers; therefore, it received criticism in the context of equity, which encouraged the reverse tenancy (Haque, 2001).

Having learnt lessons from the past experiences, a number of industrial houses and bankers in India evolved innovative institutional arrangements for an assured supply of various commodities for domestic market, processing and export. A few state governments, namely, Tamil Nadu, Punjab, Haryana, Rajasthan, Madhya Pradesh and

Uttar Pradesh have amended their age-old legal marketing Acts to encourage contract farming in various commodities, particularly high-value commodities. Consequently, some well-known agroprocessing players like Hindustan Lever Limited, Nestle India Limited, Britannia Industries, Pepsi Co., Rallis India Limited, Escorts, Mahindra & Mahindra, Venkateshwara Hatcheries, Saguna Hatcheries, WIMCO, ITC BPL, JK Corp, Keventer Biotech Ltd., etc. have started adopting 'institutional structures' as a means of sourcing raw materials directly from the farmers. It was encouraging to note that such innovative institutions were gradually emerging in the niche areas and were coordinating successfully with the farmers in production, marketing, processing and export of high-value food commodities (Asokan and Singh, 2003). These institutions have attracted a lot of attention, and have been debated professionally on their role in distribution of benefits to farmers, particularly to the smallholders.

Empirical Assessment of Benefits from Contract Farming

We have undertaken three case studies, one each in milk, vegetable and broiler to assess the implications of contract farming. We have studied the Nestle India Limited—a multinational firm for milk and milk products, the Venkateshwara Hatcheries Limited (VHL)—a private sector domestic firm engaged in contract broiler farming, and the Mother Dairy Fruits and Vegetables Limited (MDFVL)—a wholly owned subsidiary of public sector entity (namely, National Dairy Development Board), which sources fruits and vegetables through producers' associations. For details on approach and methodology, refer NCAP-IFPRI study (Birthal *et al.*, 2004). In this section, we discuss salient findings related to impact of contract farming on (i) profit and transaction costs, (ii) scale of operation, and (iii) output prices and risk-sharing mechanism.

Profit and Transaction Costs

The key issue is to understand how the selected firms develop new institutional arrangements through contract farming and benefit farmers in promoting high-value food commodities? Profits obtained and costs incurred by the farmers are regarded as performance indicators of contract farming. The results reveal striking difference in the profits of contract and non-contract farmers for all the commodities under study (Figure 9.1). The contract farmers attained substantially higher net profit than the non-contract farmers. Milk contract farmers, for example, attained double the profit[1] than that of the non-contract milk farmers. The corresponding profit difference was 78 per cent for vegetable farmers and 13 per cent for broiler farmers. Such a high difference in profit was attracting farmers to supply their raw material to the firm and thus, was strengthening linkages in the evolving supply chain. It is evident that higher profit is one of the key motivations for the farmers to integrate with the firm(s) in supplying raw material(s).

Figure 9.1

Net Profit of Contract and Non-contract Milk, Broiler and Vegetable Producers

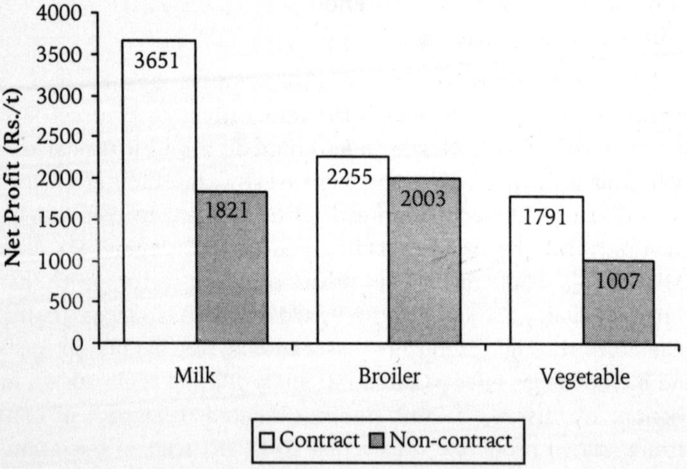

The advantage that contract farmers had over non-contract farmers was mainly due to savings in production and marketing costs. And to verify this observation, production and transaction costs of milk, vegetables and broilers were estimated for contract and non-contract

1. Dairy farmers supply cattle and buffalo milk that differs in fat content. The milk from both the sources was converted into 4 per cent fat corrected milk (FCM), following Hemme *et al.* (2003).

farmers. The results in Figure 9.2, clearly indicate that the total cost (production + transaction) of these commodities was much lower for contract than non-contract farmers. The costs of milk production of contract farmers were less by approximately 21 per cent in milk and 26 per cent in vegetable than those of non-contract farmers. The lower production costs can be mainly attributed to lower transaction costs (Table 9.1). The share of transaction cost in total cost for non-contract farmers was 20 per cent for milk and 21 per cent for vegetables; it was only 2 per cent for contract farmers. Such a comparison was, however, not possible in the case of broilers, as the firm provided free chicks, feed and veterinary services to the contract farmers. However, the transaction cost was comparable, which was 58 per cent less for contract farmers.

Figure 9.2

Production and Transaction Cost of Contract and Non-contract Farmers for Milk and Vegetables

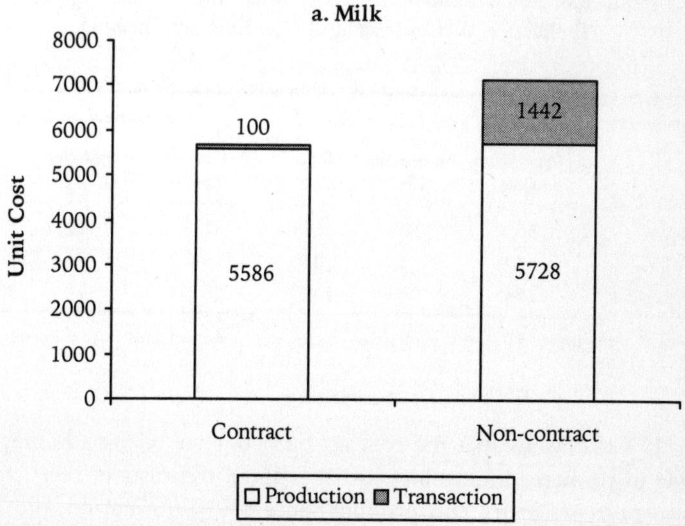

b. Vegetable

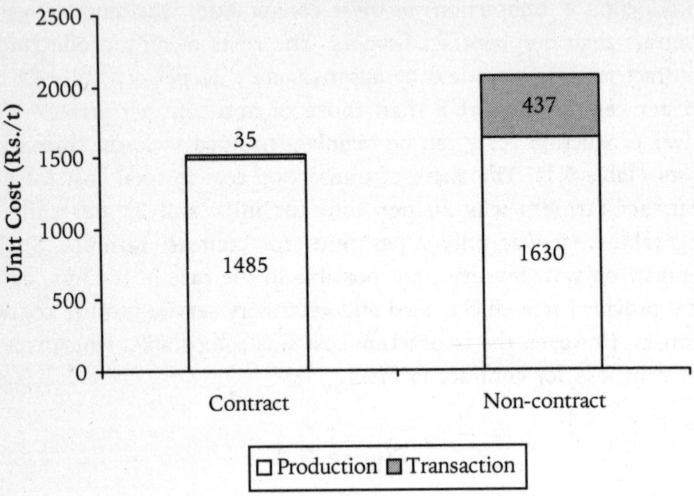

Table 9.1

Production and Transaction Cost of Milk, Broiler and Vegetable Production in Contract and Non-contract Farming

(Rs./Tonne)

Commodity	*Contract Farming*			*Non-contract Farming*		
	Production Cost	*Transaction Cost*	*Total Cost*	*Production Cost*	*Transaction Cost*	*Total Cost*
Milk	5586	100	5686	5728	1442	7170
Broiler*	808	38	846	27322	90	27412
Vegetable**	1485	35	1520	1630	437	2067

Note: * For broiler, the firm provides free chicks, feed and medicines to the contract farmers.
** Refers to spinach.

It was obvious that the contract farmers were taking advantage of new institutional arrangements that reduced the costs of their travel, transport of inputs and produce, access to information and new technology. In the case of milk and vegetables, the transaction costs were less on contract farms due to savings in time, transportation cost and labour cost for marketing of produce. These were mainly due to collection of these commodities by the firms from the producer's village. It may be concluded that access to market and information about new technology at negligible costs motivate farmers to participate in such evolving institutional arrangements.

In the case of broiler, hardly any cost was incurred by the contract farmers on extension, communication and transportation for acquiring inputs. These costs were as high as 80 per cent of the total transaction cost in broiler production. The principal attraction for the broiler farmers for participating in the contractual arrangement was the availability of chicks, medicines and feed without any direct financial liability on them. These inputs accounted for about 75 per cent in the total cost of broiler production and were the critical inputs for productivity and profitability. The firm bears mortality risk of 5 per cent, and remaining is to be borne by the producer. This means that broiler contract farmers were enjoying indirect credit for important inputs without any interest and, perhaps, that was the main attraction to the farmers, particularly smallholders, for establishing strong links with the broiler firm.

Reduction in transaction costs through vertical coordination is beneficial to the firm and the farmers, mutually. The firm gets an assured and timely supply of the desired raw material. It helps the firm in having a better control over its operational and fixed costs and minimising the risk on account of underutilisation of its capacity; thus, eventually minimising the cost of processing. It also enables the firm to improve its market reputation. On the other side, the farmers get assured market for their produce that is otherwise not possible on a regular basis. Greater access to market improves the farmers' capacity to withstand risks arising out of production and price fluctuations. Besides, they have a more reliable access to production inputs, capital, technology and information. Such a win-win situation was found to have remarkably increased farmers' participation in contract farming in niche areas and commodities; 76 per cent of vegetable farmers and 56 per cent of broiler farmers had expanded their scale of operation between 1990 and 2000. Non-contract vegetable and broiler farmers also expanded their scale of operation but only at a lower level, by 54 and 44 per cent farmers, respectively. Such a noticeable expansion by the contract farmers revealed that they were gaining from the innovative arrangements made for production and marketing.

Scale Effects

There have been apprehensions that smallholders would not be able to take full advantage of the new institutional arrangements (Glover, 1987; Watts, 1994; Key and Runsten, 1999). These arguments are based on the fears that firms in order to reduce their transaction costs (such as distribution of inputs, credit and extension services) may be inclined to have a tie-up with a few large farmers rather than dealing with a large number of scattered smallholders. Another factor that supports contracting with large landholders is their better capacity to invest in production-related inputs, technology information, and withstand risks. But, the large farmers have a better access to market information and strong bargaining power that might add to the firm's transaction costs.

To examine the state of affairs of smallholders[2] and their linkages with the firms, a disaggregated analysis was carried out based on the size of farms for vegetable production and scale of operations for milk and broilers. The distribution of smallholders in the sample, clearly showed that they were well represented in the contractual arrangements in the three case studies (Table 9.2). The doubt that the firm may ignore and discriminate against smallholders, did not have any ground. To take advantage of economies of scale, dairy and vegetable firms were contracting through producers' associations rather than dealing directly with individual farmers. The milk and vegetable firms had organised farmers into groups or cooperative associations for activities such as procurement of inputs, technical advice, facilitating credit needs, collecting output, etc. Such a mechanism has helped the firm in overcoming the difficulties faced in approaching too many scattered smallholders, individually. It eventually could help in controlling escalation in transaction costs.

It was well established that contract farmers, irrespective of size of the farms, were producing milk, broilers and vegetables at a lower cost

2. For milk, smallholders were considered as those who had milk animals up to 5; while farmers having milk animals between 6 and 10 were characterised as medium, and more than 10, as large farmers.

For broilers, those who had up to 5000 birds per cycle were defined as small farmers, and the ones with 5000-10,000 birds as medium, and with more than 10,000 birds as large farmers.

For vegetables, small farmers were those who had land less than 2 ha, and those having land between 2-4 ha as medium, and with more than 4 ha land, as large farmers.

Table 9.2

Distribution of Sample Farmers Associated with Contract Farming

(Per Cent)

Commodity	*Small*	*Medium*	*Large*
Dairy	56	27	17
Poultry	32	32	36
Vegetable	37	36	27

and were attaining higher profits than the non-contract farmers (Figure 9.3; Table 9.3). The smallholders could save approximately 28 per cent cost in vegetable production and 20 per cent in milk production as a result of contract farming. The corresponding savings in case of large farmers were 22 per cent and 14 per cent, respectively. This reduction in cost was mainly due to lower transaction costs (Tables 9.4 and 9.5). Large farmers have lower transaction costs. The pecuniary cost of production (that excluded family labour) of smallholders was however lower than that of large farmers. It was observed that by and large, the pecuniary costs increased with higher scale of business, while non-pecuniary costs (mainly family labour) showed a decline (Table 9.6). Smallholders are sufficiently endowed with own family labour, whereas large farmers generally depend on hired labour that needs to be effectively monitored, adding to their production cost. That was why large farmers preferred to select labour-saving production portfolio unless cheap and timely labour was available. It was corroborated clearly by the vegetable case study, wherein a marked difference was observed in area allocated to vegetables by small and large farmers. The smallholders allocated 57 per cent area to vegetables as compared to 34 per cent by the large farmers.

These facts revealed that smallholders were neither being deprived of their participation in contract farming nor were being exploited by the firms. The smallholders could minimise their transaction costs and increase their income by participating in contract farming. The savings in transaction cost were mainly on account of marketing their small produce through contract farming. As regard production, smallholders had the comparative advantage of utilising their own family labour, while for marketing their produce, they were taking advantage of the firm, which ensured procurement of perishable commodities at remunerative prices. Contrary to the argument favouring contracting of firms with large farmers, it was observed that the firms were finding it more convenient and beneficial to contract with smallholders and their associations. There were four obvious reasons for it: (i) less effect on overall supply in the event of crop failure of one or few farmers (idiosyncratic risk); (ii) more flexible production portfolio of smallholders, which would help in quickly responding to consumers' changing preferences; (iii) smallholders could ensure better quality as they strictly comply with the production practices advised by the firm; and (iv) low marketable surplus of smallholders increases their dependency on the firm for profit maximisation.

Table 9.3

Farm Size-wise Unit Cost of Production and Profit in Milk, Broilers and Vegetables of Contract and Non-contract Producers

(Rs./Tonne)

Farm Size	*Milk*		*Broiler**		*Vegetable***	
	Contract	*Non-contract*	*Contract*	*Non-contract*	*Contract*	*Non-contract*
			Unit Cost of Production (Rs./Tonne)			
Small	6266	7797	1022	27692	1522	2127
Medium	5489	6901	848	27854	1486	1985
Large	5475	6394	812	27052	1531	1958
All	**5686**	**7170**	**846**	**27412**	**1520**	**2067**
			Net Profit Over Total Cost (Rs./Tonne)			
Small	2446	866	2238	2087	1818	920
Medium	3745	2081	2273	2058	1809	1122
Large	4329	3604	2261	1934	1792	1167
All	**3651**	**1821**	**2255**	**2003**	**1791**	**1007**
			Net Profit Over Pecuniary Cost (Rs./Tonne)			
Small	4170	3229	2708	2328	2309	1532
Medium	4622	3881	2308	2136	2287	1659
Large	4892	4932	2266	1972	2215	1628
All	**4606**	**3720**	**2318**	**2107**	**2267**	**1585**
			Net Profit Over Total Cost (Per cent)			
Small	39.04	11.11	218.98	7.54	119.45	43.25
Medium	68.23	30.16	268.04	7.39	121.74	56.52
Large	79.07	56.37	278.45	7.15	117.05	59.60
All	**64.21**	**25.40**	**266.55**	**7.31**	**117.87**	**48.72**

Note: * In the case of broilers, the unit cost of production of contract producers is low because it does not include the cost of chick, feed and medicine, which are supplied by the firm free of cost.

** Refers to spinach.

Figure 9.3

Net Gain in Profit from Contract Farming Over Non-contract Farming (Per cent)

a) Over Pecuniary Cost

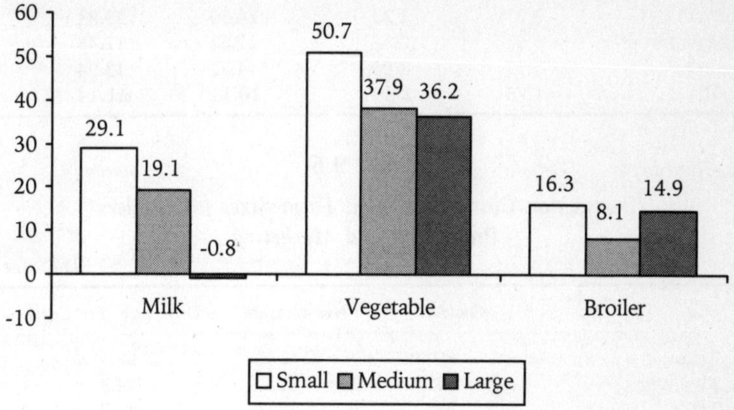

b) Over Total Cost

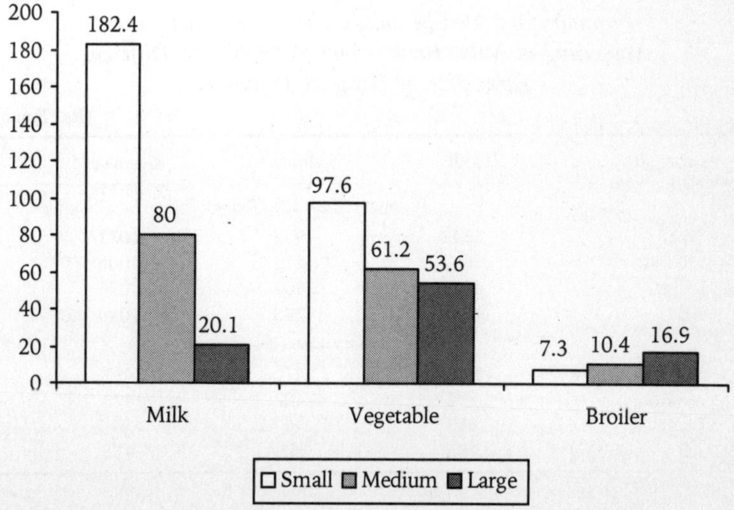

Table 9.4

Share of Transaction Cost in Total Cost of Milk and Vegetables Production and Marketing Under Different Farm Sizes

(Per cent)

Farm Size	*Contract Farmers*		*Non-contract Farmers*	
	Milk	*Vegetable*	*Milk*	*Vegetable*
Small	3.27	2.23	24.50	23.84
Medium	1.51	0.54	17.62	17.48
Large	1.17	3.00	14.72	13.94
All	**1.76**	**2.30**	**20.11**	**21.14**

Table 9.5

Transaction Cost of Different Farm Sizes for Broilers' Production and Marketing

(Rs./Tonne)

Size	*Contract*	*Non-contract*	*Difference (Per Cent)*
Small	59	142	58.5
Medium	37	81	54.3
Large	34	65	47.7
All Farmers	**38**	**90**	**57.8**

Table 9.6

Pecuniary and Non-pecuniary Cost of Production and Marketing of Milk, Broilers and Vegetables in Different Farm Size of Contract Producers

(Rs./Tonne)

Farm Size	*Milk*	*Broiler**	*Vegetable***
	Pecuniary Cost (Rs./Tonne)		
Small	4542	552	1031
Medium	4612	813	1008
Large	4912	807	1078
All	**4731**	**783**	**1044**
	Non-pecuniary Cost (Rs./Tonne)		
Small	1724	470	491
Medium	877	35	478
Large	563	5	501
All	**955**	**63**	**476**

Note: * Cost of chick, feed and medicines is not included as the firm supplies these inputs without any charges.

** Refers to spinach.

Price and Risk Sharing

There have been apprehensions that the contract farming would ultimately lead to monopsonic situation and could exploit farmers (Glover, 1987; Little and Watts, 1994). Such a situation arises when the market is not competitive and one of the trading partners acts opportunistically to exploit the farmers. To verify this phenomenon, we compared the prices offered to contract farmers with those in the prevailing market. We observed that the contract farmers were being offered relatively higher prices than the prevailing market prices. In case of vegetables, the contract farmers received 8 per cent higher prices, mainly for a better quality and as an incentive for ensuring a regular supply. In case of vegetables, the prices offered to the farmers were determined by the prevailing prices in the Delhi Fruit and Vegetable Market (one of the largest trading markets for fruits and vegetables in India) with a premium of 5-20 per cent above this benchmark price, depending upon commodity and quality. In case of milk, the prices were determined on the basis of SNF and fat content. Since the milk market is highly competitive, there was only a marginal price premium (4 per cent) for the contract farmers over the prevailing market prices. In the case of broilers, the prices were fixed by BROMARK.[3] Nevertheless, the firm shared additional profits due to rise in market prices with the farmers. Also, the firm offered an incentive of 25 per cent for a better feed-conversion ratio. In all these case studies, we did not observe any kind of monophonic behaviour to exploit farmers. Also, the existence of perfect competition in these markets did not allow any of these firms to trade in exceptionally large volumes and control the market.

Sharing of risk between the producer and firm is another advantage in the case of broiler industry. The firm bears full market risks. It is important because broiler prices are often faced with high price-volatility that affects profit considerably. Both the parties share the production risk depending on its nature and magnitude. The mortality risk up to 5 per cent of the chicks is considered to be natural and is borne by the firm. For mortality exceeding 5 per cent, the firm charges Rs. 0.10/kg of live body weight of the grown-up broiler for every one per cent increase in the mortality. Such a risk-

3. BROMARK is an apex organisation of the different stakeholders in broiler production.

sharing mechanism provides protection to the producers, particularly the smallholders, under volatile market conditions.

The implications of risk-sharing mechanism on profit and yield of contract and non-contract farmers were examined by computing the Coefficient of Variation (CV) in different cycles. The striking differences in CV of profits between contract and non-contract farmers are evident from Table 9.7. Whereas the CV of profit of contract farmers was almost stable over different cycles, it was very high with sharp fluctuations for non-contract farmers. Since there was not much difference in CV of yield between contract and non-contract farmers, the price volatility in case of broilers was the only reason for high variability in profits. It can also be seen that the CV of yield was higher for non-contract farmers during March-April and May-June periods. This was because of higher temperature during these periods, which had resulted in high mortality rate. Ramaswami *et al.* (2004), have estimated that contracting in broiler industry could shift about 88 per cent of risk from the farmer to the processor. Such a risk-sharing mechanism helps contract farmers, particularly the smallholders in improving their management strategies and minimising production and price risks. Experiences in the past have revealed that high risk in production and prices had led to the closure of several poultry farms. Alternatively, poultry farmers were gradually shifting to contract farming. No analogous risk-sharing mechanism was found in case of milk and vegetable production.

The study showed that the speculation of monophonic behaviour by the firm did not exist. On the contrary, farmers were enjoying benefits of assured procurement of their produce and higher prices. It was noted that assured prices and market access were encouraging farmers to diversify agriculture towards high-value and perishable commodities. Such a mechanism, which insures the farmer against price risk, benefits the firm also in terms of assured supply and better quality of raw material.

Table 9.7

Cycle-wise Coefficient of Variation (CV) in Yield and Profit of Broiler in Contract and Non-contract Farming

(Per cent)

*Production Cycle**	*CV*** *of Broiler Yield*		*CV*** *of Net Profit*	
	Contract Farmers	*Non-contract Farmers*	*Contract Farmers*	*Non-contract Farmers*
January-February	10	8	22	65
March-April	8	16	20	137
May-June	5	22	22	296
July-August	20	21	20	270
September-October	9	7	26	107
November-December	8	7	26	49

Note: * One cycle completes in 38 days from one-day old chick to fully matured for meat.

** CV of broiler yield and net profit for each cycle is over different farms.

Conclusions

The above discussion clearly revealed that, contract farming in high-value food commodities is augmenting income, reducing transaction cost and assuring markets and prices. The study rejected the criticism against contract farming schemes for their bias against smallholders. It was found that the smallholders benefited more through contract farming. The study also noted that the speculation of monophonic behaviour by the firms did not exist. On the contrary, contract producers were enjoying benefits of assured procurement of their produce and higher prices. The fear that the contract farming would harm the interest of smallholders had no logic. It was rather noted that the contract farming models are encouraging smallholders to participate in sharing benefits from the emerging opportunities in high-value food commodities. It is expected that with the growth in contract farming models, the production portfolio of smallholders would change towards more commercial and remunerative activities. There is a need to replicate such initiatives by alleviating policy hurdles and developing appropriatc infrastructure by involving the private sector.

References

Asokan, S.R. and G. Singh (2003). "Role of Contract Farming in Agro-processing Industry", *Indian Journal of Agricultural Economics*, Vol. 58(3), pp.566-576.

Barghouti, S., S. Kane, and K. Sorby (2003). *Poverty and Agricultural Diversification in Developing Countries*, The World Bank, *Mimeo*.

Binswanger, H.P. (1980). "Attitudes Towards Risk: Experimental Measurements in Rural India", *American Journal of Agricultural Economics*, Vol. 62, pp.174-182.

Birthal, P.S., P.K. Joshi, Ashok Gulati (2004). "Vertical Coordination in High-value Food Commodities: Implications for Smallholders", *Discussion Paper*, MTID, International Food Policy Research Institute, Washington DC, USA.

Food and Agriculture Organization (2001). *Contract Farming: Partnership for Growth*, Food and Agriculture Organization of the United Nations, Rome, Italy.

Glover, D. (1987). "Increasing the Benefits of Smallholders from Contract Farming: Problems for Farmers' Organizations and Policy Makers", *World Development*, Vol. 15(3), pp.441-448.

Glover, D. and K. Kusterer (1990). *Small Farmers, Big Business: Contract Farming and Rural Development*, St. Martin's Press, New York.

Government of India (GoI) (2003). *Agricultural Statistics at a Glance*, Ministry of Agriculture, Government of India, New Delhi.

Haque, T. (2001). "Impact of Tenancy Reforms on Productivity Improvement and Socio-economic Status of Poor", *Policy Paper* 13, National Centre for Agricultural Economics and Policy Research, New Delhi, India, pp.114-143.

Hazell, P. (1982). "Application of Risk Preference Estimates in Farm-household and Agricultural Sector Models", *American Journal of Agricultural Economics*, Vol. 64, pp.384-390.

Hemme, T., O. Garcia, A. Saha (2003). "A Review of Milk Production in India with Particular Emphasis on Small-scale Producers", PPLPI *Working Paper* No. 2, Pro-Poor Livestock Policy Initiative, FAO, Rome, p.58.

Jha, D. (2001). "Agricultural Research and Small Farms", *Indian Journal of Agricultural Economics*, Vol. 56(1), pp.1-23.

Key, N. and D. Runsten (1999). "Contract Farming, Smallholders, and Rural Development in Latin America: The Organisation of Agro Processing Firms and Scale of Out Grower Production", *World Development*, Vol. 27(2), pp.381-401.

Little, P. and M. Watts (eds.) (1994). *Living Under Contract: Contract Farming and Agrarian Transformation in Sub-Saharan Africa*, University of Wisconsin Press, Madison.

Martinez, Steve R. (2002). "Vertical Coordination of Marketing Systems: Lessons from the Poultry, Egg and Pork Industry", United State Department for Agriculture, *Agricultural Economics Report* 807, USDA, Washington, DC, USA.

Narayanan, S. and A. Gulati (2002). "Globalisation and the Smallholders: A Review of Issues, Approaches, and Implications", MSSD *Discussion Paper* 50, IFPRI.

Rangi, P.S. and M.S. Sidhu (2000). "A Study on Contract Farming of Tomato in Punjab", *Agricultural Marketing*, Vol. 42(4), pp.15-23.

Ryan, J.G. and D.C. Spencer (2001). "Future Challenges and Opportunities for Agricultural R&D in the Semi-Arid Tropics", International Crops Research Institute for the Semi-Arid Tropics, Andhra Pradesh, India.

Saigal, Sushil, and Divya Kashyap (2002). *Company-farmer Partnership for the Supply of Raw Material to Wood-based Industry*, New Dehi, India and London, Eco-tech Services (India), and International Institute for Environment and Development, UK.

Singh, Gurdev and S.R. Asokan (2004). *Contract Farming in India*, Center for Management in Agriculture, Indian Institute of Management, Ahmedabad, *Mimeo*.

Singh, Sukhpal (2002). "Contracting Out Solutions: Political Economy of Contract Farming in the Indian Punjab", *World Development*, Vol. 30(9), pp.1621-1638.

Runsten, D. and N. Key (1996). *Contract Farming in Developing Countries: Theoretical Aspects and Analysis of Some Mexican Cases*, Report LC/L 989, Economic Commission for Latin America and the Caribbean, Santiago, Chile.

Ramaswami, B., P.S. Birthal and P.K. Joshi (2004). *Measuring Gains from Contract Farming: An Empirical Analysis of Poultry in Andhra Pradesh, India*, Draft report submitted to the International Food Policy Research Institute, Washington, DC, USA.

Warning, M. and N. Key (2000). "The Social Performance and Distributional Impact of Contract Farming: The Arachide de Bouche Program in Senegal", *Working Paper* 00-3, Department of Economics, University of Puget Sound.

Watts, M. (1994). "Life Under Contract: Contract Farming, Agrarian Restructuring, and Flexible Accumulation", in P. Little and M. Watts (eds.), *Living Under Contract: Contract Farming and Agrarian Transformation in Sub-Saharan Africa*, University of Wisconsin Press, Madison.

10

Agroprocessing Industry and Agricultural Development

New Vistas in Indian Agribusiness

SUKHPAL SINGH

Introduction

The experience of agricultural development in India has shown that the existing systems of delivery of agricultural inputs and purchase and use of agricultural output have not been efficient in reaching the benefits of better linkages between agriculture and agro-processing industry to the farmers or the agroindustry. The timely, quality and cost-effective delivery of adequate inputs still remains a dream despite the marketing attempts of the corporate sector and the developmental programmes of the state. The farmers are not able to sell their produce remuneratively. There is plenty of distress among farmers both in agriculturally developed as well as backward regions manifested in farmer suicides. Agricultural markets in India which are found to be both inefficient and imperfect, may not be able to ensure fair and reasonable returns to all the players. There are temporal and spatial variations in the markets and the producers' share in consumers' rupee has been quite low in general, except a few commodities. In fact, in some commodities like potato in some regions in India, producers end up making net losses at the same time when traders make substantial profits from the same commodity (Mitra and Sarkar, 2003). Though producers' relative share in the final price of a product will certainly go down with the increase in the number of value-adding stages in the coming years even in countries like India, and therefore, cannot be used as an indicator of a market's efficiency or inefficiency, the other aspects of the markets like absolute share of the producer in terms of remunerability, fluctuations in prices across seasons, large spatial price differences and lack of proper market outlets itself, are the issues which have become increasingly crucial in the present context. There are structural weaknesses of agricultural markets like unorganised suppliers as against organised buyers, real holding capacity of the producers and the perishable nature of the produce in the absence of any storage infrastructure. In the presence of these characteristics of the market, the rural producers cannot simply be left to fend for themselves so far as marketing of their produce is concerned. And if the marketing system does not assure good returns to producers, not much can be achieved in the field of product quality and delivery which are a must for processing and manufacturing sectors (Singh, 1995). In the environment of liberalisation and globalisation policies, the role of the state in agricultural marketing and input supply is being reduced, and an increasing space is being provided to the private sector to bring about better marketing efficiency in input and output markets. On the other hand, processors and/or marketers face problems in obtaining timely, cost-effective, and adequate supply of quality raw materials.

There has been large number of measures since the 1960s, to promote agroprocessing industries starting with the setting up of the agroindustries corporations at the state level and then even a separate ministry of food processing industries and specialised bodies like Agricultural and Processed Foods Export Development Authority (APEDA), and Marine Products Export Development Authority (MPEDA) in the 1980s when many large corporates and multinational companies (MNCs) also evinced keen interest in food processing sector, including the entry of Pepsico into India due to opening up of the sector for foreign investment and delicensing (Goyal, 1994). The recent policy steps for promoting growth of agroprocessing include temporary removal of licensing requirements for stocking and movement of various foodgrains and oilseeds by some state governments, removal of plant scale restrictions and licensing requirements for most of the food processing activities, removal of restrictions on futures trading in 54 commodities and setting up of new commodity exchanges, amendments to Agricultural Produce Market Committee (APMC) Act in some states to facilitate direct procurement from farmers by the agroprocessing entities (contract farming), and development of private markets (Landes and Gulati,

2004). The Ministry of Food Processing industries has been providing an incentive since the beginning of the Ninth Plan in the form of a reimbursement of 5 per cent of the value of raw materials procured through contract farming with farmers with a maximum ceiling of Rs. 10 lakh per year for a maximum of three years with the condition that any organisation (private/public/co-operative/non-government organisation (NGO)/joint venture/assisted) should work with at least 25 farmers under contract for at least three years (MFPI, 1998). Besides, many government agencies like National Bank for Agriculture and Rural Development (NABARD), National Horticulture Board (NHB) and Agricultural and Processed Foods Export Development Authority (APEDA) have been promoting agroprocessing units with various schemes for quite some time now. The 1990s has also seen major restructuring in the form of mergers, takeovers and consolidation of operations by the MNCs and domestic corporates, besides new investments in the Indian food industry (Banaji, 1996-1997). Therefore, it becomes imperative to explore the role of agro-processing sector in building linkages with farmers and bringing about agricultural development.

This chapter examines the role of agroprocessing sector in helping agricultural development in India. The role of agroprocessing industries is described in section II. It examines briefly their growth and status of agroindustry in section III. The competitiveness of Indian agribusiness chains, including cooperatives, and its implications are assessed in section IV. It then goes on to examine the extent of backward linkages as prevalent until recently and those emerging in the new context in terms of various contractual models in sections V and VI. It explores the relevance and implications of different modes of agricultural linkages (backward) for the Indian farmer by drawing on international, national and local experiences. The chapter concludes in section VII, by drawing lessons for policy and agribusiness strategy for it to play an effective role in agricultural development.

The Role of Agroprocessing Industries

The significance of agroindustries lies in the fact that they are supposed to create employment opportunities, mobilise investible resources from the rural sector, promote agricultural production, make use of local resources, add value to the farm product, improve product quality, achieve efficient marketing, combat rural-urban migration and promote industrialisation in an agricultural economy. According to a criterion laid down by the Indian Planning Commission and approved by the National Development Council, an agroindustry is one which (Venkaiah, 1987: 22):

a) encourages greater input into agriculture;

b) leads to better processing and conversion of agricultural commodities;

c) ensures high returns on processed goods; and/or

d) increases agricultural productivity.

There are two types of agroindustries processing and servicing—industries which utilise agricultural (including allied sectors) produce as inputs, and those which produce agricultural inputs and services. Since the present chapter deals only with the agroprocessing industries, it is important to look at the potential role of these industries in the development process. Agroprocessing industries are those, "which use not less than 50 per cent of the raw material from agriculture and where the value added as a result of the processing undertaken is not more than 50 per cent of the final value of output." (ACRC, 1990: 881).

Though the role of agroprocessing industries depends on the nature of the produce and the type of processing involved, they are expected to play, on *a priori* grounds, an important role in promoting agricultural development at least in those areas from where the raw materials are drawn. Viewed from this angle, an assessment of the feedback effects of processing industries on the business of farming in the hinterland, forms an important part of the role of processing industries in development. The second facet of their role is to bring about a greater integration in agricultural marketing. This integration may be vertical or horizontal. Whereas the former refers to the linking together of successive functions or operations in the production or marketing of a product under unified control, the latter means linking of different business units in the same stage of production or marketing under unified control. Whatever may be the form of integration, processing generally leads to the tying up of different on-farm and off-farm functions such as production, storage, transportation, wholesaling and distribution (Kahlon and George, 1966). In fact, the modern processing plants not only create form utilities, but their integrated structure, combining processing and distribution, has led to the adding of place and time utilities as well (Hill and Ingersent, 1982). Whereas form utility refers to value addition by way of processing or manufacturing which results in change in the form of produce, the time and place utilities are those types of value addition which take place when products are made available in specific places and at specific times. This value addition of time and place is performed by industries like processing units, and cold storage units.Value addition through agroprocessing and exports helps in generating further rounds of increases in employment from which the farmer would also benefit through better returns to his produce due to larger demand (Rao, 1994). Agroindustry in India is also found to be more labour intensive and capital saving than many other industries. In the organised sector, an investment of Rs. 1 lakh in agroindustry generates employment for 14 persons compared with only for 3 persons in other industries. Further, net value addition per unit of capital is higher in agroindustry (Gandhi *et al.*, 2001).

The growth of food processing industries not only reduces raw material losses and generates off-farm employment, but also encourages agricultural production through assured market and remunerative prices and adds value to the primary product in various ways. The processed foods can be promising items in the exports from the developing countries and thus, may help in saving and earning foreign exchange (Rao, 1986). The food processing industry can broadly be classified into two categories, primary and secondary. Primary processing industries process the agricultural output into a standard product with small costs, often relying on a byproduct for profitability. These industries are generally less capital intensive and less sophisticated, and perform an essential function even in developing economies. It includes preserving and simple processing like paddy milling, wheat milling, etc. On the other hand, secondary processing industries use the products of primary processing industries as inputs to produce identifiable, differentiated, packaged food, often marketed with branding, advertising and promotion and they make real or apparent product innovations. These industries include baking, vegetable oils, instant foods, etc. (Burns, 1983).

Most of the studies on agricultural marketing, agroprocessing, and agro-trade recommend setting up of agroprocessing facilities to reduce perishability, wastage, add value and to improve the quality of Indian products to gain competitiveness (Rao, 2003; Sidhu, 2002; Patnaik, 2003; Chengappa, 2004). The post-harvest losses ranged from 15-31 per cent across fruits and vegetables in Gujarat in 1996. A large part of it (50 per cent) was at farmer level and the remaining at the APMC (10 per cent), local trader (3 per cent), wholesaler (3 per cent), broker (7 per cent) and retailer (25 per cent) levels. In wheat and rice, it is estimated to be 10 per cent and 12 per cent at farm level, respectively and 13 per cent and 10 per cent at trader and FCI level in paddy alone (*The ET Knowledge Series–Rural Economy*, 2002-2003) compared with only two per cent in the USA (Chakraborty, 2003). The losses account for almost 20 per cent of total farm production and are valued at Rs. 50, 000 crore, annually. In fruits and vegetables, the wastage is of the order of 40 per cent of total value of production and estimated at Rs. 23,000 crore, annually. It is more than the value of annual fruit and vegetable consumption in the UK (CII and McKinsey & Co. Inc., 1997).

Some recent studies recommend promotion of agroprocessing activities, especially for cotton, vegetables and fruits so that farmer's share in consumer's rupee is raised (Bawa and Raikhy, 2000; Sidhu, 2002). But, very few examine the importance of agroprocessing in terms of the degree of value addition (Suryanarayana, 1994). A study of the food processing industry for the 1980s, found that the extent of value addition as percentage of input cost ranged from over 25 per cent for plantation crops like cashew and coffee to 5 to 6 per cent in traditional industries like grain milling and edible oils. The net value added as percentage of value of total inputs increased from 10 per cent in 1979 to 14 per cent in 1988 (Gandhi and Mani, 1994). But, value addition in agroprocessing should also take into account, besides the value added to main product due to processing, the value addition due to byproduct processing (Srivastava, 2000). Still, the value addition to food production in India is only 7 per cent compared to over 22 per cent in China, 45 per cent in Philippines and 88 per cent in the UK (Patnaik, 2003; Vaswani *et al.*, 2003; Chengappa, 2004). Further, only two per cent of the fruit and vegetable production is processed in India compared with 30 per cent in Thailand, 70 per cent in Brazil and the USA, 78 per cent in Philippines, and 83 per cent in Malaysia (Vaswani *et al.*, 2003). But, value addition possibilities in India are large and range from 14 per cent in green gram *dal* to 200 per cent in fruit products (Chengappa, 2004).

Empirical Evidence on the Role of Agroprocessing Industries

A study of primary food processing units (paddy milling and oilseeds milling) in Punjab in the early 1990s revealed that neither were they dependent on the local economy for employment nor for investible surpluses in a direct way (Singh, 1999). The industry was independent of local labourers to a large extent and dependent on migrant labourers who were willing to work at low wages for longer hours. As regards raw materials, the industry was more a consequence than a cause of the cropping pattern in the state. The role of food processing industry in changing cropping pattern has been nominal. The only important linkage promoted by these industries seemed to be the consumption linkage, which has its roots in the relatively high incomes in the state. Besides this, another very important backward linkage of these industries has been the growth of units manufacturing processing machinery, and the repair workshops within the state. This lack of backward linkages affected the state's primary sector, in that it today faces the problems of rural underemployment and unemployment, high cost of cultivation and unviable holdings. Another recent study also reveals the weak employment linkage of large and medium-scale agroindustries in the state, especially in terms of unskilled labour (Shergill and Singh, 2001).

But, on the other hand, the forward linkages of these industries were very strong. The growth of rice and oil mills led to the emergence and growth of a number of industries and activities such as solvent extraction industry, edible oil refining industry, *vanaspati* industry, cattle feed and poultry feed industry, soap industry, and activities like wholesale trading in rice, oil and oil cake, transport, packaging, and brokers' business. Further, rice husk has proved to be a cheap and easily available source of energy for steaming purposes in industries like oil milling, hosiery, dyestuff, etc. (Shergill and Singh, 2001; Singh, 1999) But, in overall linkage terms, paddy milling was found to be having weak linkages and no scope for further expansion. However, the secondary processing industries (baking) seem to have played an important role in both ways backward as well as forward linkages. Not only did they provide a market for the output of primary processing industries like wheat milling, but also promoted consumption linkage of the agricultural sector in the state by way of their output. For example, baking industry provided commercial market for the wheat flour produced by the flourmills and the *vanaspati* industry for the oil produced by the oil mills. But, with regard to employment, in this case also, the local workforce did not seem to have benefited (Singh, 2001). However, the overall linkages of this industry were found to be strong and it was perceived to have very good scope for expansion (Shergill and Singh, 2001). A study of growth linkage effects of agroindustrialisation in Tamil Nadu found that it contributed to non-farm non-industrial activity, and generated greater employment mainly, in agriculture, followed by trade, service, and other agroindustries (Sivakumar *et al.*, 1999). The multiplier for food processing was estimated to be 2.4 which was much higher than that for power or telecom industries (CII and McKinsey & Co, Inc., 1997). This means that the growth effects of food processing are much higher than that of many other industries. The above discussion reveals that food processing industries lead to greater agricultural stability through the price and market support, greater employment opportunities, and increased value addition to the primary product by way of creating time, place and form utilities.

Indian Agroindustry Growth and Competitiveness

The agroprocessing sector has grown appreciably during the last two decades. There are 35,000 modern rice mills besides 91,000 rice hullers, 4500 shellers and 8300 hullers-cum-shellers which together can process 2/3 of India's paddy production. There are 10, 000 pulse mills processing more than 75 per cent of the pulses produced in the country and 820 flour mills besides millions of *atta chakkis* (*The ET Knowledge Series–Rural Economy, 2002-2003;* Sekhon *et al.*, 2003; Chengappa, 2004). In the horticulture sector, there are 5198 units processing fruits and vegetables (Chengappa, 2004). The fruit and vegetable processing industry grew 2.5 times in its installed capacity between 1990-1996. This was also complimented by higher capacity utilisation (48 per cent) which was only 34 per cent in 1990. The exports grew more than five times during this period. However, this processing accounted for only 1.6 per cent of the total production of fruits and vegetables in India (Viswanathan and Satyasai, 1997). There are also more than 400 fish processing units in India (Scheuplein, 1999). In fact, in the Indian food market, processed food segment is only 10 per cent and semi-processed another 15 per cent. The food processing sector is dominated by unorganised sector units which account for 42 per cent of all units with small-scale sector taking another 33 per cent and the organised sector only 25 per cent of all food industry units (CII and McKinsey & Co. Inc., 1997). The organised sector comprises of 18000 units producing Rs. 9,000 crore worth of foods. The major sectors in food processing are meat and meat products, and oilseeds and vegetable oils, besides cereal products (Acharya, 1998). Besides, there are 3619 ginning and pressing units with 47194 gins and 810 presses. The value addition in agro-processing industry is estimated to be Rs. 25,00-3,000 billion with one third of it being in value-added food products alone (Chengappa, 2004).

In the rural sector, agroprocessing industries accounted for more than 70 per cent of number of total units and workers, and 43 per cent of total value added in the mid-1990s which was much higher than their share in the total for the country (65, 63 and 35 per cent, respectively) in the mid-1990s. In the organised (ASI) manufacturing sector, it accounted for 56 per cent of units, 61 per cent of workers and 34 per cent of the value added in rural areas against shares of 50, 54 and 28 per cent, respectively at the all-India level in 1999-2000. In the unorganised manufacturing sector (OAMEs, NDMEs, DMEs), agroprocessing industry accounted for 65 per cent of units and workers and 56 per cent of value added and in the rural sector alone, 70 per cent of units, workers, and value added each. In all, the unorganised sector of the agroprocessing industry accounted for almost all of the (99.7 per cent) rural agroprocessing industry units, and 93 per cent of workers therein and 43 per cent of value added. For all of the industry (rural and urban), the share of unorganised sector was again 99.4 per cent in number of units, 87 per cent in workers and 36 per cent in value added, Thus, agroprocessing in India is largely rural, and small scale i.e. either self-employing units or units with less than 20 workers without power or 10 workers with power. During 1994-95–2000-01, in the unorganised sector, textile products grew at the rate of 24 per cent in number of units and 15 per cent in employment which was the highest among agroprocessing industries in the unorganised sector followed by beverages (8.5 and 6.3 per cent, respectively). But, food processing at 5 and 3.5 per cent, respectively grew much slower than non-food processing (7.8 and 5.2 per cent, respectively) and total agroindustry sectors (6.7 and 4.6 per cent, respectively) in the unorganised sector. On the other hand, in the organised agroindustry sector (ASI category) which accounted for 46 per cent of all units (with 37 per cent of them producing food products), 43 per cent of employment and 22 per cent of value added in the industrial sector (Gandhi *et al.*, 2001), the picture was very different with textiles growing only at 3 and 6 per cent in units and employment and food products only at 1.6 and 0.9 per cent, respectively. The total food processing, non-food processing and agro-based sector witnessed almost an absolute decline in units and employment. For the entire agroprocessing sector, it was only textiles with very high growth rates (24 and 5 per cent, respectively) and beverages, paper and food products with very modest growth rates. The growth rates for food processing, non-food processing and all agro-based industries were 4.9 and 3 per cent, 7.8 and 4.6 per cent, and 6.7 and 4 per cent, respectively, for number of units and employment (Chadha and Sahu, 2003). But, the employment growth in agroprocessing industries during the early 1990s as against the 1980s, was higher in case of only fruit and vegetable processing, meat, fish, edible oils and cashew, and net value added growth rates higher than those in the latter half of 1980s (Gandhi *et al.*, 2001). During the post-1994-95 period, employment growth rates have been higher in case of fruits and vegetables, tea, starch, wines, textiles, and paper. The industry, especially small scale and rural based, suffers from low productivity, and lack of capital and market orientation (Mathur, 1994; Chadha and Sahu, 2003). Major problems of the agroprocessing industry are non-availability of quality raw materials in adequate quantity at reasonable cost and right time, besides financial and demand constraints (Gandhi *et al.*, 2001).

The cooperatives have been successful in processing of sugar, paddy, milk and cotton. Now, there are 273 sugar cooperatives which produce nearly 55 per cent of the total sugar production in India with the remaining being produced by private (153) and public sector mills. Similarly, more than 87,000 dairy cooperatives federated into 187 district-level cooperatives and 27 state-level federations working with 87 lakh milk producers have been important players in the milk business. There are 173 cooperative spinning mills accounting for 22 per cent of yarn and fabric production, and 431 ginning and pressing cooperatives accounting for 12 per cent of all units and 21 per cent and 18 per cent of all gins and presses. Besides, there are 13,000 fisheries cooperatives in India (*The ET Knowledge Series–Rural Economy 2002-2003*). The main reasons for the success of this segment of the processing sector have been focus on value addition and, therefore, high returns to producing members, functional vertical integration, high participation of members, and professional management and leadership (Dwivedi, 1996).

It is also well known now that Indian agro-chains are inefficient in processing and marketing stages, whereas the production part is quite efficient/competitive in terms of cost of production. A recent study of the competitiveness of Indian dairy sector under the WTO regime revealed that the milk price in India is one of the lowest in the world but the milk product prices are higher than the world prices. This means a taxing of the milk producers and a protection to the milk processors. The nominal protection coefficients (NPC) in 1998, were close to 2 in the case of butter and cheese and 1.4 in the case of skin milk powder (SMP). Even effective protection coefficient (EPC) was found to be 1.7 for cheese, 1.1 for butter and 0.9 for SMP. These coefficients show the lack of export competitiveness of Indian dairy products. The higher values of EPC for butter and cheese revealed that there is an incentive for their domestic production which is mainly due to low price of milk. The problem of export competitiveness is further complicated due to the quality aspects which have been reinforced by the sanitary and phytosanitary measures (SPSM) agreement of the WTO and anti-dumping actions against Indian product in export markets (Jha and Debroy, 2000; Singh, 2000b; Singh, 2003). A study of quality control and monitoring practices in two of the commodity sectors (fisheries and spices) found that there were serious problems of maintenance of hygiene and quality standards and processes at the primary production or procurement level. For example, the fishing boats did not have ice on their streams when they arrived at the pier. On the other hand, the processing centres were excellent at maintaining quality and hygiene standards and they had HACCP in place and in operation. But this may not be the case with all the 400 processing facilities in India. Most of the quality and hygiene problems at the primary produce level were due to lack of awareness and lack of infrastructure like portable water and landing facilities. Similarly, in spice production and processing, the major problems were in production which is carried out by small-scale farmers who lack knowledge of quality and hygiene and do not have an incentive to maintain them. Here too, the processing plants had all the quality systems in place. But, the contamination takes place at the farmer and the trader level (Scheuplein, 1999).

Building Linkages with Growers: Contract Farming

The entry of large businesses into agribusiness sector has led to a new arrangement in raw material production and procurement in India, known as contract farming. This is happening as good quality, timely, and cost-effective raw material is a prerequisite for any successful agribusiness firm, whether operating in the domestic or the international market. Given the Land Ceiling Act in India, agribusiness firms cannot own and cultivate land for their raw material requirements. Also, most of the times, it is not a viable option (Singh, 1998). Therefore, the only option for them to procure raw materials is to have contractual arrangements with the primary producers which is also suggested as an alternative to corporate farming or liberalisation of land ceiling laws (Vyas, 2001). Contract farming refers to the production and supply of agricultural produce under advance contracts, the essence of such contracts being a commitment to provide an agricultural commodity of a type, at a time and a price, and in the quantity required by a known buyer. It basically involves four things—pre-agreed price, quality, quantity or acreage (minimum/maximum) and time. The contracts could be of three types; (i) procurement contracts under which only sale and purchase conditions are specified; (ii) partial contracts wherein only some of the inputs are supplied by the contracting firm and produce is bought at pre-agreed prices; and (iii) total contracts under which the contracting firm supplies and manages all the inputs and the farmer becomes just a supplier of land and labour. The relevance and importance of each type varies across products and over time, and these are not mutually exclusive (Hill and Ingersent, 1982; Key and Runsten, 1999).

A contract reduces price risk for a farmer and can be terminated at reasonably short notice. Also, contractual arrangements are attractive to farmers seeking capital and new technology and other inputs and production services as generally new crops with modern technology or existing crops with new seeds and other inputs are promoted under such arrangements. On the other hand, food processors can minimise their overhead costs per unit of production by operating their plants at or near full capacity by obtaining assured, stable and quality raw material supplies from farms under contracts. For a processor, contracts are more flexible in the face of market uncertainty, make smaller demands on scarce capital resources and impose less of an additional burden on management. They also overcome land constraint for corporate firms, reduce production risk, and are politically more acceptable than corporate farming (Hill and Ingersent, 1982; Eaton and Shepherd, 2001). Contracting can give a positive image to the company as it may be perceived as progressive, especially if it works with small farmers, and can help it get access to state or donor funds (Baumann, 2000).

At more macroeconomic level, contracting can help to remove market imperfections in produce, capital, land and labour markets, remove intermediaries and therefore, make upstream value chain (agricultural marketing) more efficient, and can help in better co-ordination of local production activities as it often involves initial investment in processing, extension, etc. (Grosh, 1994; Gill, 2004). From an institutional economics perspective, contract farming could be looked upon as a way of creating positive externalities, created better by private sector instead of the state, which can result in overall rural development. Contracting can lead to more employment opportunities for farm and non-farm labour, as generally it deals with labour-intensive high-value crops requiring labour for harvesting, grading, and packaging at the farm level, and in processing, transportation, packaging and marketing at the post-farm stage, reducing the seasonality of employment and giving higher wages through competition in the labour market. There can also be larger developmental effects from the improvement in infrastructure and other amenities due to contracting and general expansion of demand due to higher incomes under contracting (Haque and Birthal, 1998). Therefore, contract farming figures as an institutional arrangement for agricultural development in the fields of inputs, product exchange, and product upgrading, the last referring to research and innovations (Christensen, 1992). Thus, state can play an important role in making contract farming meaningful for rural development by creating incentives and disincentives for agribusiness firms, in terms of allowing or not allowing captive farming, investing directly or through joint ventures for contracting, provision of infrastructure, and regulation and enforcement of contracts (Grosh, 1994).

However, given the failure of government mechanisms for support to agriculture, wide support for contract farming under the Structural Adjustment Programme (SAP) and liberalisation, and promotion of this mechanism by the international development agencies like the World Bank, the United States Agency for International Development (USAID), the International Finance Corporation (IFC) and the Commonwealth Development Corporation (CDC) (Little and Watts, 1994), it is inevitable that new forms of contracts will be tried by the agribusiness firms. This is the only way to ensure good quality and timely availability of raw material for processing, especially when, in India, captive farming is not allowed at present under the Land Ceilings Act. Besides, captive farming means, putting large resources in raw material production which may not be the best economic option for many agribusiness firms in India, especially small firms, or may not be a viable practice any more in competitive markets like in the case of tea plantations in South India (Hayami and Damodaran, 2004).

Corporate-led Contract Farming

Contract farming in India is currently being practised by multinational firms like Cadbury (cocoa), Pepsi (potato, chillies, groundnut), Unilever (tomato, chicory, tea, and milk), ITC Ltd. (tobacco, wood trees, and oilseeds), Cargill (seeds), domestic corporates like Ballarpur Industries Limited (BILT), JK Paper, and Wimco (in eucalyptus and poplar trees), Green Agro Pack (GAP) Ltd., VST Natural Products, Global Green, Interrgarden India, Kempscity Agro Exports, and Sterling Agro (all in gherkins), United Breweries

(UB) (barley), Nijjer Agro (tomato), Tarai Foods (vegetables), Indo-mint Agriproducts (a subsidiary of US based A M Todd, in mint), McDonalds (potato in Gujarat), (Singh, 2000a; Rangi and Sidhu 2000; Subrahmanyam, 2000; Dileep *et al.*, 2002; Saigal and Kashyap, 2002; Grewal, 2003), Namdhari Seeds (seeds), and various government and semi-government agencies, especially in seed production and perishables like vegetables and fruits, with varying degrees of success. There are many banks which provide finance for contract farming. These include NABARD, SBI, ICICI Bank and UTI Bank. Contract farming in India by the corporate sector has so far been more of a case of buy back, input supply and credit supply or linkage as depicted in Figure 10.1.

Figure 10.1

Tripartite Agribusiness Linkage Model

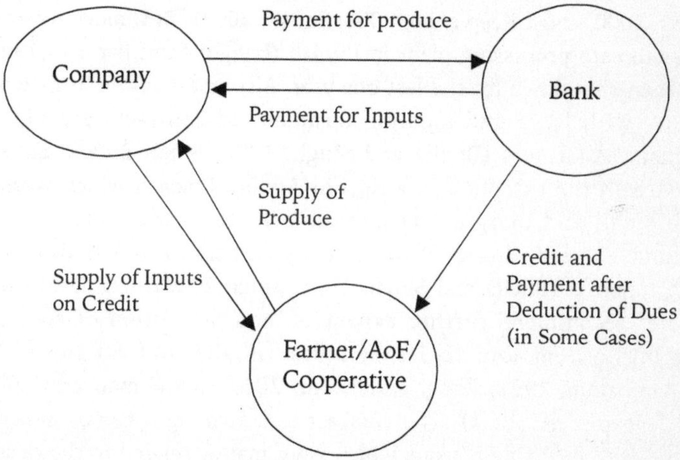

There have been some quick studies of the contract farming system in India recently. But, besides describing the contract system and operations of the companies, most of them look at the economics of the contract farming system in specific crops, compared with that of the non-contract situation and/or competing traditional crops of a given region, e.g. in gherkins (hybrid cucumber) in Tamil Nadu (Chidambaram, 1997), Karnataka (Subrahmanyam, 2000) and Andhra Pradesh (Haque, 1999) and in tomato in Punjab (Bhalla and Singh,

1996; Haque, 1999; Rangi and Sidhu, 2000), Karnataka (Subrahmanyam, 2000), and Haryana (Dileep *et al.*, 2002). It is found that contract production gave much higher (almost three times) gross returns compared with that from the traditional crops of wheat, paddy and potato in case of tomato (Bhalla and Singh, 1996; Rangi and Sidhu, 2000), and tomato and onion in the case of gherkin (Chidambaram, 1997) due to higher yield and assured price under contracts. The studies of tomato contract production in Punjab and Haryana (Haque, 1999; Dileep *et al.*, 2002) and of cucumber in Andhra Pradesh (Haque, 1999) also found the net returns from these crops under contracts being much higher than those under non-contract situations though production cost was higher under contract system (Dileep *et al.*, 2002). Contract growers in Punjab and Haryana faced many problems like undue quality cut on produce by firms, delayed deliveries at the factory, delayed payments, low price and pest attack on the crop (Bhalla and Singh, 1996; Singh, 2000a; Rangi and Sidhu, 2000; and Dileep *et al.*, 2002; Satish, 2003). But, more recently, HLL's tomato processing plant in Punjab (bought from Pepsi in 1995) has been shut down for the last one year. Also, most of the firms work mostly with large and medium farmers and contracts are biased against the farmers (Bhalla and Singh, 1996; Singh 2000a; Satish, 2003) with the exception of a firm in Andhra Pradesh which worked with small and marginal farmers due to the nature of the crop (cucumber) itself. Breach of contracts by farmers as well as firms has been reported (Bhalla and Singh, 1996; Singh 2000a). Some of these studies recommend further expansion and promotion of contract farming system due to its benefits (Bhalla and Singh, 1996; Chidambaram, 1997; Rangi and Sidhu, 2000; Subrahmanyam, 2000, and Dileep *et al.*, 2002). The contract tree farming schemes also did not do well for many reasons which were mainly related to the design of contract farming schemes and the management of the projects by the companies and their partner institutions (Siagal and Kashyap, 2002). Further, there are issues of monopsony of the processing/marketing firm and its disinterest in more backward areas where farmers need such interventions, besides the more crucial question of sharing of value-added surplus in processing and marketing which are at the centre of whether contract farming can contribute to more broad-based agricultural development (Gill, 2004). The above discussion suggests that it is not the contract *per se* which is harmful as a system but how it is practised in a given context. This involves questions of who is doing contract farming with whom, why, for what, and how. If there are enough mechanisms to monitor and use the contract for developmental purposes, it has the potential to lead to a betterment of all the parties involved, especially small and marginal farmers (Table 10.1).

Table 10.1

Relative Benefits of Alternative Marketing Structures for Small Farmers

Structure	*Sales Position of Small Farmers (SF) vis-à-vis Large Farmers (LF)*	*Sales Position of SF vis-à-vis Buyer*	*Input Facilities/ Technical Assistance*	*Government Support Required*
Private local firms (Nijjer in Punjab)	Can be against SFs due to bargaining power	Advantage of access to alternative outlets	May be available/ based on local experience	Provision of market infrastructure, information, ensuring competition, price stabilisation
MNCs/large firms (Pepsi, HLL)	Equitable prices through contract	Dependent but secure if supplies quality	Direct supply on credit/ direct and intensive	Should negotiate prices and participation for SFs
Cooperatives (Amul)	Equal if successful	Favourable if efficient co-op.	May arrange	Financial support
State boards/ bodies (PAFC/ HPMC)	Equal prices if can reach official buying position	May be exploited	Rare/left to other govt. agencies	Insist on reaching small farmers
Development agency (NDDB)	— do —	Protected if meets quality	Direct supply on credit	Financial support required

Source: Adapted from Abbott (1993).

Changing Dynamics of Contract Farming

The various types of contract system, as practiced by the corporate sector and other agencies, are discussed below.

Contract Farming with Groups/Cooperatives/AoFs

In Tamil Nadu, Appachi Cotton Company (ACC) has undertaken contract cotton farming with 8 farmer groups from 32 villages in Coimbatore district for bringing 1050 acres under cotton contract farming (Gurumurthy, 2002). The contract growers form an Association of Persons (AoP). The major features of the model adopted by ACC are: one village-one SHG, one village-one variety of cotton, cotton crop insurance, door delivery of inputs, crop loans at 12 per cent rate of interest, farm service centres, assured buyback from farmers though farmers are free to sell elsewhere if they find prices higher than contract price, contamination control from farm to factory and synchronised sowing of crop (ITCOT, 2004). Marico Industries has a tie-up with oilseed cooperatives in Maharashtra for safflower oilseeds wherein it provides working capital, infrastructural facilities, managerial inputs, and job work of crushing the oilseeds to these co-operatives. In turn, the cooperatives are responsible for getting contract produced for the company the oilseeds by their members (Bharadwaj and Palan, n.d.). The Cotton Corporation of India (CCI) has gone in for group contracts in Nagpur district of Maharashtra wherein an Association of Farmers (AoF) signs a MoU with the CCI, which promises improved yield and lower cost. It promotes single crop or a variety for a village, especially in cotton, to take care of the problem of admixture of different varieties. It is also popularising concepts like hand picked cotton to improve quality of produce. The farmer representatives will monitor cultivation of contracted cotton in the villages. In 2002, the CCI worked with 3500 cotton farmers in four states and achieved an average profitability of Rs. 25,000 per hectare in Baruch district of Gujarat and Rs. 10,000 per hectare in Andhra Pradesh. In Madhya Pradesh, it was only able to lower the cost by about Rs. 2,000 (Deshpande, 2003).

More recently, CCI has signed contracts with cotton growers for buyback of cotton in a non-cotton growing region, for example, in Bihar as its experiments there with cotton were found to be successful (Gupta, 2004). In tea, some small companies have undertaken contract farming under the Tea Board—United Planters Association of South India (UPASI) project where they work with Self-Help Groups (SHGs) of women who supply tea under contracts to the companies and the extension support is provided by the UPASI. One such company procures 90 per cent of its total tea leaves for processing into tea from 30 SHGs (Hayami and Damodaran, 2004). Ion Exchange Enviro Farms Ltd., a subsidiary of Ion Exchange India Ltd. undertakes contract farming with Community Grower Groups (CGG) having large acreage, on a profit-sharing basis. Prime Bio Products (India) Ltd., Coimbatore has a programme wherein 10-15 cotton farmers form a self-help group which has office bearers who work with company under contract and various other agencies like banks and monitor the performance of the group so far as contract is concerned. The National Dairy Development Board (NDDB, a development agency)'s Fruit and Vegetable project now under the Mother Dairy Fruits and Vegetables Limited ('Safal' brand) procures fresh produce directly from 75 growers' associations, with 15,000 plus growers in north Indian states and provides all inputs and information (Chopra, n.d.).

The Consortium Approach

Recently, several agribusiness companies have made forays into the farm service sector which is being seen as private sector participation in agricultural development. They are facilitators of contract farming systems most of the time. One such model is that of Mahindra ShubhLabh Services Limited (MSSL) which has an agreement with the Government of Punjab to facilitate contract farming of maize in one lakh acres for diversification for supply to AGS of Indonesia through PAFC. It plans to capture 16 per cent of the agri input market by 2005 and increase farmer profitability by 35-60 per cent by better and cost-effective input supply and better value realisation from farm produce by finding better markets. For this, it will leverage its tractor brand, strong customer base, dealer network and first-mover advantage. Its product portfolio includes seeds, pesticides, fertilisers, irrigation systems, equipment rentals, post-harvest services, information provision, and finance. For this purpose, various partners i.e. retail chains, NGOs, agri input companies, logistics companies, farm equipment companies, food companies, and agri finance corporations and banks, besides agricultural universities and research centres, are networked into the project. The company offers extension services to farmers for a fee but ensures a certain level of yield. If farmers get lower than the assured level of yield, then they need not pay the fee. This experiment of the company in Madurai in Tamil Nadu where farmers had to pay Rs. 500 per acre, achieved assured yield in 75 per cent of the cases in the first year which increased to 80 per cent in the second year, despite drought conditions. This ensures that the yield risks are low, and therefore, insurance scheme can be implemented (Naik, 2002). The MSSL plays the role of an integrated farming solutions provider. Other crops planned under the company's operations in the state are mustard, castor, pulses and vegetables. In *basmati* rice contract farming, Escorts Ltd., LT Overseas Ltd., United Rice Land Pvt. Ltd., and Pepsi, have MoUs with the PAIC (Grewal, 2003). LT Overseas Ltd. in collaboration with Rallis India Ltd. and ICICI Bank, have launched a programme for contract farming 30,000 acres of *basmati* rice in Punjab initially for three years with a possible extension for further two years, under the aegis of the PAIC. In Vidarbha region, CCI is collaborating with Bayer Crop Science for pesticides, Ankur and Nuziveedu for seeds and ICICI for a low interest credit for contract production of cotton. The cotton project by Prime Bio-Solutions in Coimbatore is again a multipartite arrangement involving bank (SBI), input companies (like Netafim for drip irrigation and Nuziveedu and Raasi for seed) and produce buying companies (textile mills) where PBS subsidiary (Prime Farm Solutions) co-ordinates the project.

This is similar to what has already been implemented by Rallis India in Madhya Pradesh, Maharashtra, Karnataka and Haryana. The company provides all the inputs, technical support and finance to the registered growers for a specific crop and facilitates the sale of produce at reasonable price. The company follows a consortium approach (Figure 10.2). It has tied up with banks like ICICI and SBI and with buyers of produce like HLL, Picric and Cargill. The system is run through a network of 10 Rallis Kissan Kendras (RKKs) across the country. For example, a farmer can avail of a loan up to Rs. 6,500 per acre for *basmati* cultivation in Panipat for a 6-month period at a rate of interest of 13 per cent per annum. In addition, every member farmer has accident insurance coverage of Rs. 1 lakh. The RKK has trained farmers to harvest *basmati* when moisture levels are at 16 per cent as harvesting at lower levels can lead to more broken *basmati* grains during milling. The farmers are paid prevailing market prices. The Rallis and the ICICI deduct the cost of inputs and the loan amount from the proceeds before paying the farmer on the spot

(Karunakaran, 2002). The bank has been able to get 10 per cent loan guarantee from the buying company in case of default by the company. Encouraged by this project, the company has set up new projects in fruits at Bangalore, and vegetables at Nasik. The ICICI collaborated with the company as they benefited from the rural penetration of Rallis, and the HLL gained as it could get good quality wheat for processing it into wheat flour (Subramaniam, 2002).

Figure 10.2

The Quadpartite Agribusiness Linkage Model

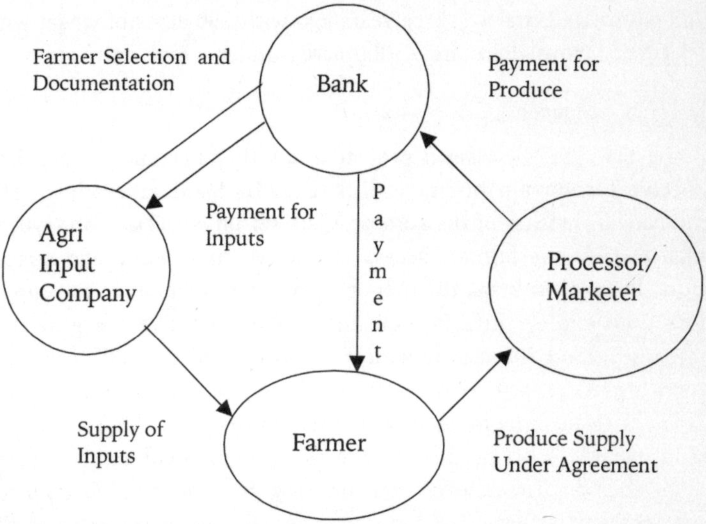

The ICICI Bank lays down preset criteria for farmer selection and informs input companies. The input companies/bank officials do the documentation, Input companies supply the inputs and send detailed accounts to the Bank which debits farmer account and credits input company account. At the time of harvest, the processing/marketing company collects produce and pays the bank its dues and rest to the farmer. The bank credits the farmer's account and the account is closed. An MoU among the bank, the input company and the output company is signed for the above arrangement. An undertaking from the farmer to supply produce under this scheme to the output company is taken by the bank. The ICICI Bank prefers four sector projects as against tripartite projects as it considers inputs service very crucial for cost reduction and quality enhancement leading to better value realisation for the farmer. The bank provided a total of Rs. 180 crore as loans for various contract farming projects during the year (2002-2003). The bank-funded project has a 'credit plus' approach which involves not only credit and input supply but also extension service and marketing support. The bank is now funding projects in *basmati* rice, chillies, potato and cotton besides wheat. It aims at raising prices of agriculture produce and lowering cost to make farming viable for the growers (Sabarinath, 2003). The Rallis' joint venture project with the Government of Madhya Pradesh, in which ICICI is involved, started three years ago with 250 acres of wheat with 50 farmers. Now, there are 15000 acres under wheat cultivation.

The ITC's e-choupal

The ITC Ltd.'s *e-choupal* project is another example of building effective farmer-agribusiness linkages. In Madhya Pradesh, the agribusiness division of the company has set-up *e-choupals* for soybean which provide the farmers access to market information and quality inputs. In order to break the monopoly of intermediaries in the supply chain who exploit information and make excessive margins, the company leased three soyabean processing and collection centres which were created in mid-1990s. Then, it started looking for *sanchalaks* (lead farmers/agents) to run *e-choupals*. In these *e-choupals*, the farmer takes his produce to the ITC procurement centre located at the block or district level after knowing price of the crop from the *sanchalak* in the village. He has the option to sell the produce to the company warehouse, factory, collection centre or the *sanchalak* (company agent who interacts with farmers for output and input transactions). The farmer takes only a sample of his produce to the local *sanchalak* and receives a spot price quote from the *sanchalak*. If the farmer accepts the price, he can deliver his produce directly to the company's collection centre and get paid within a few hours. The ITC offers Rs. 15-20 per quintal, higher price than the *mandi* price to the farmers for their produce. The *sanchalak* gets a commission of 0.5 per cent on the sales through him. The farmer produce is accepted by the company procurement centres only with a slip from the *sanchalak*. The farmers are reimbursed cost of transport if they deliver to the procurement or processing centre. The company has maintained a role for the traditional commission agents by making them *sanyojaks* (coordinators) in this project who manage physical flows in the supply chain and collect price information from local *mandis* and maintain records. Thus, the company has chosen to reintermediate, and not disintermediate (Sawhney, 2002).

The *sanchalak* is an interface between the computer terminal and the farmers. He provides information to the farmers about the company and the *mandi* prices of the produce, samples produce and even procures it sometimes, sells input of the company and other partner companies to farmers, and builds relationship with farmers. The *sanchalaks* are overseen by *sanyojaks* appointed by the company who coordinate groups of farmers, documents information at the procurement centre level, collect information about market prices, ensure transport of produce to the processing centre, supply inputs to the *sanchalak* and build relations with *sanchalaks* and farmers. The *sanyojak* identifies *sanchalaks* in the villages and recommends them to the company which finally appoints the *sanchalaks*. It is ensured that the *sanchalak* should be a medium farmer so that he is acceptable to other farmers and has interest in *e-choupal*. The *sanyojaks* are more often traditional commission agents in local *mandis* and the company leverages their strengths in trading and dealing with farmers. A *sanyojak* gets a commission of one per cent on the sales through him. In this backwards vertical e-coordination, the company provides and maintains the infrastructure and equipment for the *sanchalak* and trains him. Each *e-choupal* costs Rs. 40-60 thousand in terms of setup costs. The *sanchalak* bears all the operational costs. In some villages, where there is no computer made available, the information exchange is carried out through telephone. In some other places, there are computers without Internet connectivity (Gupta, 2003).

The company has tied up with Monsanto and MP Seed Corporation for seeds, NFCL for fertilisers, ICICI Bank for credit, and ICICI Prudential for insurance, for the supply of these inputs to farmers through its network system. It charges a commission of 10 per cent on the sales of these services of which 50 per cent goes to the *sanchalak* and the *sanyojak*. In the Madhya Pradesh project, the tie-up with input companies makes it possible for the *sanchalaks* to earn a commission of 2-3 per cent on sales, and for the *sanyojaks* who is distributor for the *sanchalak*, a commission of 1-3 per cent. The company collects between 2-3 per cent commission for itself for lending its network to input sellers (Assisi and Gupta, 2003). Figure 10.3 shows the linkages among various participants in the *e-choupal* project.

Figure 10.3

The ITC e-Choupal Network

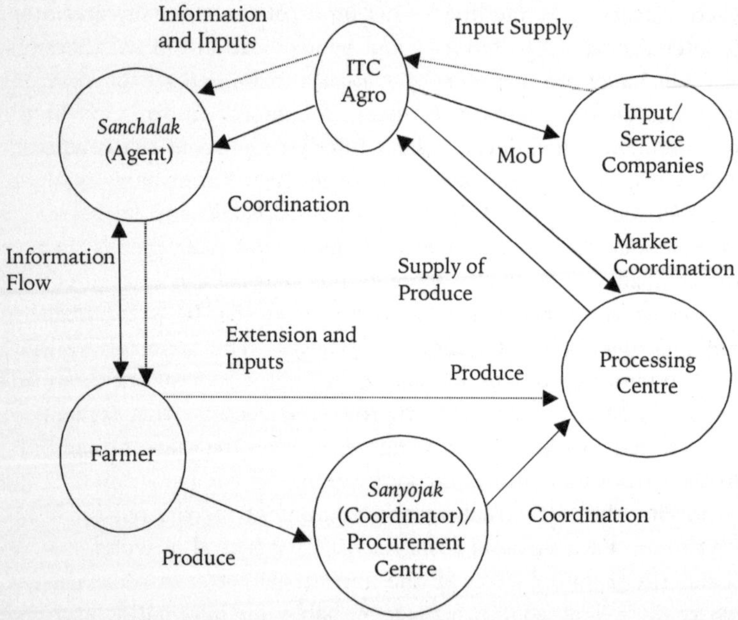

The farmer saves Rs. 25 per quintal on soyabean marketing as he no longer pays bagging, transporting, loading and unloading charges, and avoids wastage and wrong weighment at the *mandi*. On the other hand, the company saves about Rs. 20 per quintal even after paying for transport cost to the farmer (Shenoy, 2002). The farmers find that this system of ITC gives them better prices, reduces wastage of produce, ensures transparency and is faster and less costly compared with the market-based transactions. On the other hand, the company is able to procure its raw materials at lower cost with better quality of produce and less dependence on middlemen. In wheat, the company has managed to save Rs. 5-6 per quintal which is almost 10 per cent of the procurement cost. The traditional market players in soyabean have responded to this supply chain innovation of the company by adopting its practices like higher prices, credit facility, and fairer trade (Gupta, 2003).

The leveraging of information technology in this model takes place through: a) delivery of real time information and customised knowledge to the farmers to improve their decisionmaking ability for better alignment of produce to the market and better quality and productivity; b) aggregation of demand at the village level for accessing higher quality farm inputs and knowledge at lower costs; and c) setting up of direct marketing channel linked to the *mandi* system for price comparison and simultaneously, eliminating wasteful intermediation. This reduces transaction cost and makes logistics efficient (Paul, 2003). The project has already become the largest initiative among all Internet-based interventions in rural India reaching more than 10 lakh farmers in 11,000 villages through 1900 kiosks in four states i.e. Madhya Pradesh, Karnataka, Andhra Pradesh, and Uttar Pradesh in crops of soyabean, coffee, fish, and wheat, respectively. It is also planning to get into other crops such as *bajra*, *basmati* rice, sesame seeds and handpicked groundnut, besides spices and fruits and vegetables. These projects will be spread across 14 states over the next few years (Sanganeria, 2003).

State-led Contract Farming

The contract-farming programme launched by the Punjab government in October 2002 (for the *rabi* season) was aimed at taking away 10 lakh hectares from the wheat-paddy rotation over the next five years as part of the crop adjustment programme (read diversification) as recommended by the second (2002) Johl Committee. In 2002, a total of 29,000 acres had been proposed by the PAFC under the programme, implemented jointly by the Department of Agriculture, Punjab Agro Industries Corporation (PAIC through its subsidiary Punjab Agro Foodgrains Corporation (PAFC)) and the private companies. The PAFC not only provided seeds purchased from reputed seed companies like Adventa India Limited and Pro-Agro Limited and technical supervision and follow-up on agronomic practices to the contract growers, but also promised to buyback the entire produce at pre-agreed prices through a tripartite agreement involving PAFC, seed company through its dealer, and the farmer (Figure 10.4). The tripartite agreement specifies the fixed price and bonus to be paid by the PAF to farmer for the produce (bonus only if the PAFC is able to sell the produce at a higher price), type and quantity of seed to be supplied by the seed company at a given price for given acreage, farmer's responsibility of delivering the quality produce (produced by making use of recommended inputs bought from outlets prescribed by the PAFC) at a specified place, payment within two days after delivery and PAFC being the sole decider of weight of produce and the sole and only arbitrator in case of dishonouring of the contract by any of the parties. The contract is signed by the three parties in the presence of two witnesses for the farmer.

Figure 10.4

State-led Contract Farming System in Punjab (Tripartite Agreement Among Farmer, Seed Company/Dealer and PAFC)

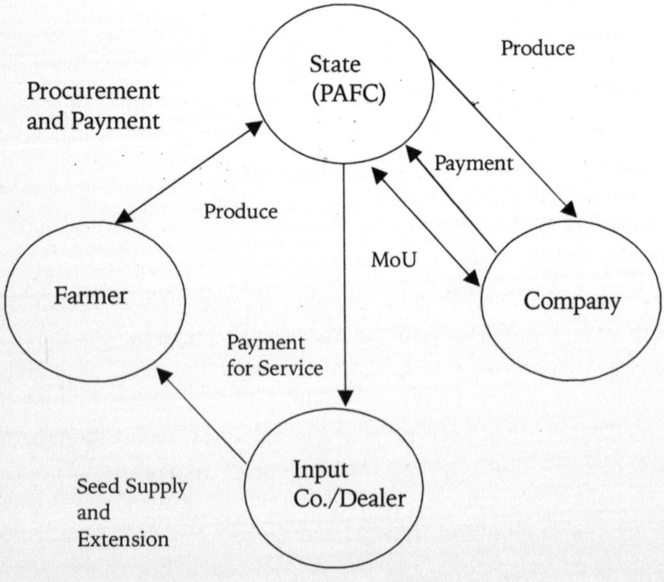

Towards the end of harvesting season for the contracted crops, the programme had run into rough weather. The contracted winter maize and hyola crops failed almost completely due to inclement weather and poor quality seeds (Grewal, 2003). In case of green peas, the contract growers were forced to dump their produce in open market, after being rejected by the PAIC on quality ground as per the contract specification, as there had been fungus infection due to inclement weather which was marked by heavy rains in winter season and then sudden rise in temperature. An area of 500 acres under contract production of green peas in Patiala and Fatehgarh Sahib districts had been affected. Some farmers found fault with the fungicide supplied by the contracted company in this regard. The dumping of contract-produced crop in open market led to fall in local market prices and it was being sold at Rs. 3 per kg. now as against a promised price of Rs. 5 per kg. by the PAIC (Singh, 2003; Rangi and Sidhu, 2003). In general, across crops and regions, the contract farming programme could not achieve the stated area goal. Not only it fell short as contracted area being less than stated by the agency, the farmers did not plant the contract crops in contracted area fully. The gap was much larger in latter case and even as high as 50 per cent in winter maize in Ludhiana and 20 per cent in hyola in both Ludhiana and Patiala. There was a different private seed company for each crop and they only provided seed and no other extension service. Finally, none of the companies procured the produce and advised the farmers to sell in open market either because open market prices were higher than contract price or quality was not as desired. Except the oilseed crops (hyola and sunflower), the net returns from contract crops were found to be lower than what farmers would have got from wheat crop. Most of the problems farmers faced related to production and quality (like quality of seed and extension) and not marketing of produce (except peas) as open market could take care of contract produce. Due to this experience, a large majority (60 per cent) were not willing to enter into contract farming arrangement again (Singh, *et al.*, 2003).

Conclusions

Though value addition is crucial for agricultural development, value addition gains may not be quick or automatic due to the lack of competitiveness of the Indian agroprocessing industries in technology as well as economic efficiency. While assessing the gains of the farmer from value addition and exports, it is necessary to take into account the adverse factor of price fluctuations in primary commodity markets. The farmer ends up being a price taker and the manufacturer a price fixer with the advantage being with the latter. It is only through group action (group marketing) that the farmer is able to achieve some parity with the buyer of his produce (Rao, 1994). Given the nature of modern farming involving tremendous amount of technological input and market orientation which require capital resources, it is but inevitable to involve private corporate business interests in agricultural development through contract farming system. What is required is marketing extension in terms of better product planning at the farmer level, provision of market information, securing/ accessing markets for farmers, provision of alternative markets and market orientation in terms of improved marketing practices at the farmer level (Patnaik, 2003).

The agribusiness facilitators are 'new banias' with knowledge and resources and strategy for sustained growth through partnership for sustainability. They will make money while helping others, including farmers, make money. Their strategies involve bundling of inputs and linking up of credit with input supply which is the agribusiness of the 21st century (Boehlje *et al.*, 1995). It is interlocking of factor markets coming back in another form. But, what is wrong with it if it can provide what state and cooperatives have not been able to provide for so long i.e. timely and cost-effective supply of quality inputs and finance and even tractors, and combine harvestors etc. on hire basis and assured market for produce? Theses agribusiness services focus on more efficient use of modern inputs with a two-pronged strategy i.e. yield increase or cost reduction through inputs and value addition (market improvement). This is a must for competitiveness whether domestic or international where quality and cost effectiveness are the driving forces. In fact, this is similar to what was proposed in 2001 by HLL Chairman M.S. Banga as a Farmer Service Centre (FSC) concept which can be a focal point for credit suppliers, crop insurers, agri-input suppliers, food processors for buy back from farmers, and farm equipment leasing and specialised grain transport and storage agencies to help the farmers with specialised services (Banga, 2001).

The Punjab government has also now resigned to a role of a facilitator of contract farming in the state. The Governments of Uttar Pradesh and Punjab have recently amended the APMC Act which did not permit farmer level (direct) procurement by companies. This legal reform process is being accelerated by the central government with the enactment of the Model Act for the state Agricultural Produce Marketing (Development and Regulation) Act, 2003 which deals with setting up of private markets, selling of produce by growers outside the APMCs (regulated markets), setting up of direct markets, specialised commodity specific markets, regulation and promotion of contract farming, provision for agencies and measures to promote quality, standards, and alternative markets, and public-private partnerships to facilitate more and better linkage between firms and farmers (GoI, 2004).

Contract farming as a mechanism is desirable if the crop is perishable, non-bulky, perennial in nature, and needs heavy processing and strict quality adherence (Goldsmith, 1985), credit market is in a state of failure or there is a need to encourage new crops. But, still there are other options which should be tried out i.e. state, co-operatives and NGOs for credit and other inputs, and if contracting is must, then, it should be regulated and monitored (Grosh, 1994). A case by case approach is necessary when allowing or encouraging contract farming as a lot depends on how and where it is practiced. As the crucial question for development under contracting is the division of value added between the agribusiness firms and farmers, it is important to examine carefully and design the pricing and other aspects of the contracts.

There is a role for the state agencies and the NGOs to intervene in contract situations as intermediaries to protect the farmer and broader local community interests. The NGOs can also play a role in information provision, and in monitoring and regulating the working of contracts. Better cooperation and coordination between companies and cooperatives for agricultural development also needs to be encouraged. Further, both companies and state should promote group contracts with the intermediation of local NGOs and other organisations and institutions so that contractual relationships are more durable, enforceable, and fair. An insurance component in farming interventions is must to protect the farmer interest and it is noted that some companies are already doing it. But, the most important thing is to ensure market for the farmer produce at better price under these agribusiness projects. Government should also play an enabling role by legal provisions and institutional mechanisms, like helping farmer cooperatives and groups, to facilitate smooth functioning of contract system.

The HLL experience showed that it is important to demonstrate continuously to initiate change. Also, building linkages requires time, commitment, patience and perseverance. The demonstration of new crop in nurseries or on the fields can be very effective. It is important to establish quality standards right from the beginning at every stage of the operation. The inputs should be provided across a wide range of crops and enterprises and not just for the contracted crop. It is important to ensure that the farmer benefits on a scale that motivate him to do better as he is generally a small landholder. This can be achieved through a combination of technology, service and networking. Whereas technology involves providing the best inputs and harvest and post-harvest facilities, service insures that resources are made available in time and the post-harvest off-take is efficient, and networking assures government support, infrastructure, banking facilities, and so on. In fact, earning the farmers' trust is very basic to success in building backward linkages. A number of small steps like prompt payments, being available on sight, sharing and updating best practices can help build trust. In fact, the best step is to increase demand for the produce by the company which improves farmer profitability (Datta, 1996). It is also important to realise that companies like the HLL had the first mover advantage when they undertook contract farming. But, in more competitive markets for contracts, these steps may be even more crucial for sustainability of the contract farming linkage.

The growing importance of corporate and contract farming systems has serious implications for the agribusiness co-operatives, which have been practising some form of contract procurement in the past simply because they are producer-owned organisations. They will have to now compete with these agribusiness organisations at the farmer/producer level in terms of providing competitive price and other incentives so that producer members do not turn away from the cooperative organisation. This will require more efficient functioning of the cooperatives. In Australia, the lack of financial support to co-operatives by the state and the competition from the MNCs and other local agribusiness firms under deregulated environment led to the closing of some cooperative processing plants or a change in the form of organisation in others (Burch and Pritchard, 1996). As a solution to this problem of the traditional cooperatives which performed poorly and were not member-focused, a new variant called New Generation Cooperatives (NGCs) have come up and evolved overtime in various parts of the world like USA, Canada, and India (Harris *et al.* 1996; Singh, 1997). A New Generation Cooperative is one which has restricted or limited membership, links product delivery rights to producer member equity, raises capital through tradable equity shares among membership, enforces contractual delivery of produce by members, distributes returns based on patronage, goes for value addition through processing or marketing, and makes use of information efficiently throughout the vertical system. However, it retains one member-one vote principle for major policy decisions. This kind of restructuring helps cooperatives to tackle problems; of free riding by membership, of horizon which is at the root of financial constraint, and that of opportunism, both of the members as well as of the cooperative. This arrangement by cooperatives has helped them become economically efficient, financially viable, and obtain member loyalty wherever it has been tried (Harris *et al.*, 1996). Additionally, non-member procurement and quantity or acreage contracts have been also used by cooperatives to tackle supply side problems (Hinman and Ricks, 1993). Some of the cooperatives like those dealing with sapota (*chickoo*) in south Gujarat have also attempted quality-based grading and pooling system, and contractual relations with members for procurement, along with market orientation strategies like multiple outlets, and efficient use of market information to achieve better business performance (Singh, 1997).

References

Abbott, J.C. (1993). "Marketing, The Rural Poor and Sustainability", in J.C. Abbott (ed.), *Agricultural and Food Marketing in Developing Countries–Selected Readings*, CAB International, Oxon, UK, pp.65-92.

Acharya, S.S. (1998). "Agricultural Marketing in India: Some Facts and Emerging Issues", *Indian Journal of Agricultural Economics*, Vol. 53(3), pp.311-332.

ACRC (Agricultural Credit Review Committee) (1990). (Chairman: A.M. Khusro): *A Review of the Agricultural Credit System in India*, Bombay, Reserve Bank of India.

Assisi, C. and I. Gupta (2003). "ITC's Rural Symphony", *Business World*, Vol. 22(34), January 14-20, pp.30-37.

Banaji, J. (1996-97). "Globalisation and Restructuring in the Indian Food Industry", *The Journal of Peasant Studies*, Vol. 24(1&2), Oct. 1996 and Jan. 1997, pp.191-210.

Banga, M.S. (2001). "Food Revolution—A Win-Win for Farmer and Consumer", (An abridged version of the HLL Chairman's speech), *Economic and Political Weekly*, Vol. 36(29), July 21, pp.2733-36.

Baumann, P. (2000). "Equity and Efficiency in Contract Farming Schemes: The Experience of Agricultural Tree Crops", *ODI Working Paper* No. 139, ODI, London, October.

Bawa, R.S. and P.S. Raikhy (eds.) (2000). "Editors' Note", in R.S. Bawa and P.S. Raikhy (eds.), *Punjab Economy—Emerging Issues*, Guru Nanak Dev University, Amritsar.

Bhalla, G.S. and Gurmail Singh (1996). *Impact of GATT on Punjab Agriculture*, Ajanta, Delhi.

Bharadwaj, M. and J.S. Palan (n.d.). "Cooperative Alignment with the Corporate—The New Direction", *Mimeo*, 4.

Boehlje, M, J. Akridge and D. Downey (1995). "Restructuring Agribusiness for the 21st Century", *Agribusiness*, Vol. 11(6), pp.493-500.

Burch, D. and B. Pritchard (1996). "The Uneasy Transition to Globalisation: Restructuring of the Australian Tomato Processing Industry", in D. Burch, R.E. Rickson and G. Lawrence (eds.), *Globalisation and Agri-Food Restructuring—Perspectives from the Australasia Region*, Avebury, Brookfield, USA, pp.107-126.

Burns, J. *et al.* (eds.) (1983). *The Food Industry-Economics and Policies*, Heinemann, London.

Chadha, G.K. and P.P. Sahu (2003). "Small Scale Agro Industry in India: Low Productivity is Its Achilles' Heel", *Indian Journal of Agricultural Economics*, Vol. 58(3), pp.518-543.

Chakraborty, D. (2003). "Corporate Participation in Marketing Activities: Scope and Challenges to Indian Agriculture", in Bibek Debroy and A.U. Khan (eds.), *Enabling Agricultural Markets for the Small Indian Farmer*, Bookwell, New Delhi, pp.185-234.

Chengappa, P.G. (2004). "Emerging Trends in Agro Processing in India", *Indian Journal of Agricultural Economics*, Vol. 59(1), pp.55-74.

Chidambaram, M. (1997). "A Study of Export Potentials for Gherkins (Hybrid Cucumber) in Tamil Nadu", Department of Agricultural Economics, Centre for Agriculture and Rural Development Studies, Tamil Nadu Agricultural University, Coimbatore (unpublished).

Chopra, A. (n.d.). "Mother Dairy Fruit & Vegetable Limited—Fruit & Vegetable Unit", a PPT presentation.

Christensen, S.R. (1992). "Between the Farmer and the State: Towards A Policy Analysis of the Role of Agribusiness in Thai Agriculture", Thailand Development Research Institute (TDRI) Background Report to the 1992 Conference on *Thailand's Economic Structure: Towards Balanced Development?*, Chon Buri, Thailand.

CII and McKinsey & Co. Inc. (1997). *Food and Agriculture Integrated Development Action (FAIDA)—Modernising the Indian Food Chain*, Confederation of Indian Industry (CII) and McKinsey & Co. Inc.

Datta, S.M. (1996). "Linkages with Agriculture—The Experience of the Food Processing Industry", *The Economic Times*, June 27, Ahmedabad. (text of the speech delivered at the AGM of BBLIL held in Calcutta on June 26).

Deshpande, V. (2003). "Cottoning on to Contracts", *The Indian Express*, April 4, Ahmedabad p.11.

Dileep, B.K., R.K. Grover and K.N. Rai (2002). "Contract Farming in Tomato: An Economic Analysis", *Indian Journal of Agricultural Economics*, Vol. 57(2), pp.197-210.

Dwivedi, R.C. (1996). "Role of Cooperatives in Rural Economy", *Indian Journal of Agricultural Economics*, Vol. 51(4), pp.713-727.

Eaton, C. and A.W. Shepherd (2001). *Contract Farming—Partnerships for Growth*, FAO, Rome.

Gandhi, V. and G. Mani (1994). "Agroprocessing for Development and Exports: the Importance and Pattern of Value Addition from Food Processing", paper for the 54th Annual Conference of the ISAE, Kolhapur, November 26-28 (summary published in IJAE, Conference Number, Vol. 49(3), p.444).

Gandhi, V., G. Kumar and R. Marsh (2001). "Agroindustry for Rural and Small Farmer Development: Issues and Lessons from India", *International Food and Agribusiness Management Review*, Vol. 2(3/4), pp.331-344.

Gill, S.S. (2004). "Small Farmers and Markets", (a book review), *Economic and Political Weekly*, Vol. 39(23), June 5, pp.2356-2358.

GoI (Govt. of India) (2004). *Economic Survey 2003-04*, Ministry of Finance, GoI, New Delhi.

Goldsmith, A. (1985). "The Private Sector and Rural Development: Can Agribusiness Help the Small Farmer?", *World Development*, Vol. 13(10-11), pp.1125-1138.

Goyal, S.K. (1994). "Policies towards Development of Agro-industries in India", in G.S. Bhalla (ed.), *Economic Liberalisation and Indian Agriculture*, ISID, New Delhi, Chapter 7, pp.241-280.

Grewal, M. (2003). "Cropped by Corporates", *The Indian Express*, Ahmedabad, April 27, *The Sunday Express*, Section, III.

Grosh, B. (1994). "Contract Farming in Africa: an Application of the New Institutional Economics", *Journal of African Economies*, Vol. 3(2), October, pp.231-261.

Gupta, A. (2004). "Cotton Plays Ball in Lalooland", *The Indian Express*, Ahmedabad, May 1, p.12.

Gupta, R.K. (2003). "E-choupal So Far and Ahead", A Case Study in a Village in M.P., *Theme Paper*, Fieldwork Segment, PRM 2002-2004, IRMA, February.

Gurumurthy, G. (2002). "Eight Farmer Groups Signs up for TN Integrated Contract Cotton Scheme", *The Hindu Business Line*, June 3, p.7 (Agribusiness page), Chennai.

Haque, T. (1999). "Contract Farming in India", National Centre for Agricultural Economics and Policy Research, New Delhi (unpublished).

Haque, T. and P.S. Birthal (1998). "Prospects of Contract Farming in India", in K.T. Chandy and O.S. Tyagi (eds.), *Future of Farming in India: Contract or Co-operative Farming*, Indian Social Institute, New Delhi.

Harris, A., B. Stefanson and M. Fulton (1996). "New Generation Co-operatives and Co-operative Theory", *Journal of Cooperatives*, Volume II, pp.15-28.

Hayami, Y. and A. Damodaran (2004). "Towards an Alternative Agrarian Reform—Tea Plantations in South India", *Economic and Political Weekly*, Vol. 39(36), September 4-10, pp.3992-3997.

Hinman, L.D. and D.J. Ricks (1993). "Co-operatives, Marketing Orders and the Coordination of Supply and Demand for Perennial Crops in the US", in Csaba Csaki and Yoan Kislev (eds.), *Agricultural Co-operatives in Transition*, Westview Press, Boulder, USA.

Hill, B.E. and K.A. Ingersent (1982). *An Economic Analysis of Agriculture*, Heinemann, London.

ITCOT (2004). *Report on Contract Farming, Industrial and Technical Consultancy Organisation of Tamil Nadu*, (ITCOT) Chennai.

Jha, B. and B. Debroy (2000). "Towards Globalising Indian Dairy Sector", *Asian Economic Review*,

Vol. 42(2), August.

Kahlon, A.S. and M.V. George (1966). "The Role of Processing Industries in Agricultural Marketing Integration", *Indian Journal of Agricultural Economics*, Vol. 21(4).

Karunakaran, N. (2002). "Money Grows on Trees...", *Intelligent Investor*, August 31, *ISAP@yahoogroups.com*.

Key, N. and D. Runsten (1999). "Contract Farming, Smallholders, and Rural Development in Latin America: The Organisation of Agroprocessing Firms and the Scale of Outgrower Production", *World Development*, Vol. 27(2), pp.381-401.

Landes, R. and A. Gulati (2004). "Farm Sector Performance and Reform Agenda", *Economic and Political Weekly*, Vol. 39(32), August 7-13, pp.3611-3619.

Little, P.D. and M.J. Watts (eds.) (1994). *Living Under Contract—Contract Farming and Agrarian Transformation in Sub-Saharan Africa*, University of Wisconsin Press, Madison.

Mathur, A. (1994). "Discussant's Comments" on S.K. Goyal "Policies Towards Development of Agro-industries in India", in G.S. Bhalla (ed.), *Economic Liberalisation and Indian Agriculture*, ISID, New Delhi, pp.283-286.

MFPI (1998). *Food Processing Industries*, outline of assistance under schemes of the Ninth Plan 1997-2002, Ministry of Food Processing Industries (MFPI), Govt. of India, November.

Mitra, S. and A. Sarkar (2003). "Relative Profitability from Production and Trade—A Study of Selected Potato Markets in West Bengal", *Economic and Political Weekly*, Vol. 38(44), November 1, pp.4694-4699.

Naik, G. (2002). "Enhancing Food Security through Market Reforms", *Productivity*, Vol. 43 (1), pp.60-66.

Patnaik, G. (2003). "Marketing, Storage, and Extension Services: State of Agriculture in India", in Bibek Debroy and A.U. Khan (eds.), *Enabling Agricultural Markets for the Small Indian Farmer*, Bookwell, New Delhi, pp.81-120.

Paul, P. (2003). "The Mandi is now on the Net", *Deccan Herald*, January 6, *wwwitcportal.com*.

Rangi, P. S. and M.S. Sidhu (2000). "A Study on Contract Farming of Tomato in Punjab", *Agricultural Marketing*, 42(4), pp.15-23.

———. (2003). "Contract Farming in Punjab", *Productivity*, Vol. 44(3), pp.484-491.

Rao, C.H.H. (2003). "Reform Agenda for Agriculture", *Economic and Political Weekly*, Vol. 38(7), Feb. 13, pp.615-620.

Rao, V.K.R.V. (1986). "Balance between Agriculture and Industry in Economic Development", *The Indian Economic Journal*, Vol. 34(2).

Rao, V.M. (1994). "Farmers in Market Economy: Wood Farmers' Gain through Liberalisation?", *Indian Journal of Agricultural Economics*, Vol. 49(3), pp.393-402.

Sabarinath, M. (2003). "Corp India Gets Agro as States Sign Up Exec Farmers", *The Economic Times*, Ahmedabad, April 14, 1.

Saigal, S. and D. Kashyap (2002). *Review of Company-farmer Partnerships for the Supply of Raw Material to Wood-based Industry*, India Country Sub-study published by Eco-tech Services (India) Pvt. Ltd., New Delhi and International Institute for Environment and Development (IIED), London.

Sanganeria, S. (2003). "ITC e-chaupal in UP Wheat Buying Spree", *Business Standard*, February 13.

Satish, P. (2003). "Contract Farming as a Backward Linkage for Agro Processing—Experiences from Punjab", *Indian Journal of Agricultural Economics*, Vol. 58(3), p.603 (abstract).

Sawhney, M. (2002). "Fields of Online Dreams", *The CIO Magazine*, October 15, *www.itcportal.com*.

Scheuplein, R.J. (1999). "An Analysis of the Safety of Indian Food Exports—the Quest for International Safety Equivalence", *Indian Food Industry*, Vol. 18(6), pp.364-381.

Sekhon, M.K., P.S. Rangi and M. Kaur (2003). "Rice Processing Industry in Punjab: Problems and their Remedies", *Indian Journal of Agricultural Economics*, Vol. 58(3), pp.544-553.

Shenoy, M. (2002). "Transforming Agribusiness the e-way", *Business India*, No. 634, June 24-July 7, pp.102-104.

Shergill, H.S. and G. Singh (2001). *Alternatives in Agriculture—Punjab*, Ajanta, Delhi.

Sidhu, H.S. (2002). "Crisis in Agrarian Economy in Punjab—Some Urgent Steps", *Economic and Political Weekly*, Vol. 37(30), July 27, Review of Agriculture, pp.3132-3138.

Singh, J. (2003). "Contracted Green Peas Dumped in Open Market", *The Tribune*, Chandigarh, March 28, p.15.

Singh, J. *et al.* (2003). Evaluation of Contact Farming Scheme in the Punjab State, Department of Economics, PAU, Ludhiana.

Singh, S. (1995). "Agricultural Marketing in the New Economic Environment: Search for Strategies", *The Bihar Journal of Agricultural Marketing*, Vol. 3(4), pp.406-409.

———. (1997). "Managing Marketing: Co-operatives in Horticultural Business in South Gujarat", *Indian Journal of Agricultural Marketing*, Vol. 11(1&2).

———. (1998). "Should Indian Farming Go Corporate?" *Business India*, Aug. 24-Sept. 6.

———. (1999). "Green Revolution and Agro Industrialisation: A Case Study of Primary Food Processing Industries in the Indian Punjab", *International Journal of Punjab Studies*, Vol. 6(1), pp.55-83.

———. (2000a). "Contract Farming for Agricultural Diversification in the Indian Punjab: A Study of Performance and Problems", *Indian Journal of Agricultural Economics*, Vol. 56(3), pp.283-294.

———. (2000b). "New Barriers to Trade under WTO: Implications of TBT and SPS Measures Agreements for the Indian Agro-Food Industry and Agro-Exports", in G.K. Chadha (ed.), *WTO and the Indian Economy*, Deep and Deep, New Delhi.

———. (2001). "Employment, Efficiency and Entrepreneurship in Small Industry: A Study of Baking Industry in Punjab, India", *The Journal of Entrepreneurship*, Vol. 10(1), pp.71-88.

———. (2003). "The WTO Agreement on Anti-Dumping Measures: Scope, Practice and Problems", in Y.K. Alagh (ed.), *Globalisation and Agricultural Crisis in India*, Deep & Deep, New Delhi.

Sivakumar, S.D., R. Balasubramaniam, and N. Srinivasan (1999). "Growth Linkage Effects of Agro Industrialisation", *Indian Journal of Agricultural Economics*, Vol. 54(3), pp.412-419.

Srivastava, U.K. (2000). "Modernising the Indian Food Chain: A Critique of the CII-McKinsey & Co. Report", *Indian Journal of Agricultural Marketing*, Vol. 14(2), pp.1-9.

Subramaniam, A. (2002). "Field Day in Store for Farmers", in *http://www.tata.com/rallis_india/articles /2002060_ farming. htm.*

Subrahmanyam, K.V. (2000). "Linkages Between Farm and Non-Farm Sector: Role of Processing of Horticultural Products", *NABARD Occasional Paper* No. 16, National Bank for Agriculture and Rural Development (NABARD), Mumbai.

Suryanarayana, M.H. (1994). "Rapporteurs' Report on Prices, Marketing including Agroprocessing, and International Trade", *Indian Journal of Agricultural Economics*, Vol. 49(3), pp.532-536.

Vaswani, L.K., V. Venkatakrishnan, R. Upadhyay and J. Talati (2003). *Agriculture-Market Linkages: Evaluating and Evolving a Conceptual Framework in Indian Context*, DEAR, NABARD *Occasional Paper* No. 28, NABARD, Mumbai.

Venkaiah, V. (1987). *Impact of Agro-based Industries on Rural Economy—A Case Study*, Himalaya, Delhi.

Viswanathan, K.U. and K.J.S. Satyasai (1997). "Fruits and Vegetables: Production Trends and Role of Linkages", *Indian Journal of Agricultural Economics*, Vol. 52(3), pp.574-583.

Vyas, V.S. (2001). "Agriculture: Second Round of Economic Reforms", *Economic and Political Weekly*, Vol. 36(10), March 10, pp.829-836.

11

Cooperatives in Maharashtra

Challenges of Stagnation and Decline

B.S. BAVISKAR

Introduction

Maharashtra is recognised as one of the leading states in India in the field of cooperation. The period of two decades (1960-1980) is often considered to be the golden age of cooperative movement in the state. During this period, cooperatives were prospering and expanding in all spheres. Moreover, several bold and innovative experiments were being conducted all over the state. However, cooperatives in Maharashtra are currently facing challenges of stagnation and decline.

Cooperative Ethos in Maharashtra

The Marathi speaking state called Maharashtra was created on 01 May 1960. The people of Maharashtra welcomed the new state with great enthusiasm. The state government was led by a popular, strong and competent leader, Y. B. Chavan. He declared that his government was committed to bring about democratic socialism through cooperatives and *panchayati raj*. At the national level, the Congress Party ruled under the leadership of Jawaharlal Nehru, and the same party dominated under the leadership of Y. B. Chavan in Maharashtra. After the Chinese aggression in 1962, Chavan was called to Delhi as the Defence Minister. He was succeeded by Dadasaheb Kannamwar for a while, followed by Vasantrao Naik for over 11 years. However, Chavan continued to dominate the politics of Maharashtra from Delhi for several years.

During this period, there was all-round development of cooperatives in Maharashtra, particularly the emergence of cooperative sugar factories attracted the attention of people from all over the country. The first sugar cooperative was set up in India in 1951-52 in Ahmednagar district with the initiative of V.E. Vikhe-Patil and D.R. Gadgil. Four years later, the second cooperative sugar factory came up with the efforts of Ganpatrao Autade at Kolpewadi near Kopargaon in the same district. With the success of these two ventures about a dozen factories came up in 1959-60. In a short period, a large number of such factories emerged all over the state. By 1980, their number crossed 100. And by 1988, Maharashtra overtook Uttar Pradesh as the largest sugar producing state in the country.

During the same period, with the help of agricultural scientists in sugar cooperatives, the farmers in Maharashtra increased the average per acre output of sugarcane. At the same time, they maintained the top position in sugar recovery in the country. The sugar cooperatives in Maharashtra surpassed private, cooperative and state-owned sugar factories in other parts of the country in productivity and efficiency.

Thanks to the success of sugar cooperatives, the people in rural areas and activists in the cooperative field acquired new enthusiasm and confidence. They seemed to have absorbed and mastered the new 'mantra' of cooperation. As a result, a vast network of cooperatives emerged in the vicinity of sugar cooperatives. A large number of cooperative spinning mills, cooperative poultries, cooperative dairies, other agricultural processing cooperatives, cooperative sale and purchase unions, and several other cooperative industries emerged. Thanks to these industries, cooperative credit societies and cooperative banks flourished.

The emergence and growth of sugar factories and other processing cooperatives created economic prosperity in the rural areas which proved useful for the all-round development of the region. As a result, a large number of schools, colleges and hostels were set up in the rural areas. Health services became available for the first time. With the construction of roads, transport and communication facilities improved. The farmers in rural areas were now seen going on motorcycles and in jeeps. This was all a result of prosperity achieved through cooperatives.

New Centres of Power and the Congress Party

Along with the expansion of the cooperative field, the new *panchayati raj* experiment was being pursued vigorously. Beginning from 1962, the state introduced the innovative pattern of three-tier structure of democratic decentralisation. It gave a share in power to a large number of people in rural areas. Right from the bottom—from the village—to *taluka* and district levels, large number of political workers and leaders emerged. With the creation of many new centres of power in *panchayati raj* and cooperatives great many people who were deprived of power all these years acquired at least some share in it.

In that period, the Congress was the only statewide dominant party. It was ruling in Maharashtra and most of the other states. Being part of the freedom movement, the Congress Party had reached down to the village level. It was also active at the *taluka,* district and state levels. This gave a scope to a large number of people to enjoy power and prestige. Who should occupy positions of power in the legislative assembly, Lok Sabha, *zilla parishads,* district central cooperative banks, cooperative sugar factories and similar other organisations was decided by the senior Congress Party leaders.

This means in the Maharashtra politics of those days, there were three important centres of power. Those active in politics had to work either through panchayati raj institutions, or cooperative organisations or the Congress party organisation. Those aspiring to be MLAs, MPs or ministers had also to work through this route only. These three centres had certain special characteristics. The Congress being a dominant party and the Congressmen being dominant in all power structures from village *panchayat* to State Assembly, and from rural credit society to sugar factories and district banks, the struggle for power was mostly confined to Congressmen. As a result, there used to be at least two rival factions among Congressmen at every level. The factions competed with each other to acquire control over *panchayat* bodies, and cooperative organisations or to grab the positions of MLA or MP. Since the other parties were weak, the internal rivalry among Congressmen did not cause any serious damage to the party. In fact, the Congress high command cleverly used the existing factionalism to manage the power struggle within the party.

These three centres of power were closely related and intertwined with each other. For example, Shankarrao Kale of Kopargaon was the *zilla parishad* President of Ahmednagar and also, the Chairman of the Kopargaon cooperative sugar factory. The local Congress MLA,

K.B Rohmare was also the Chairman of the Ahmednagar District Central Cooperative Bank and Godavari Pravara Sale and Purchase Union. These are the examples of interlocking positions of power. There were many such examples all over Maharashtra. Some leaders simultaneously occupied 5 to 6 positions as office bearers and also directorships of 20-25 cooperative, and other organisations. If a leader lost control over a cooperative, he faced the danger of losing his grip over the *zilla parishad*. Or if he lost power over the *zilla parishad*, then he faced the prospect of losing his claim over the party ticket for the Assembly.

Most of the people in power in these structures belonged to the Maratha caste. They occupied the important positions. The Marathas dominated the *panchayats*, cooperatives, party organisation and the state legislature. They were the largest single caste group in the population of the state. Even though only 35-40 per cent of the population, that strength fetched them more than 70 per cent positions of power. The minority castes such as the Malis, Dhangars and Vanjaris, could enjoy a limited scope in acquiring positions of power. As a consolation, they were offered a vice-chairmanship of a sugar factory or a secondary position in *zilla parishad*. Most of the highly coveted posts of MLAs, MPs and ministers were monopolised by the Marathas. The minority caste leaders resented this, but had to suffer the humiliation in silence.

Y.B. Chavan had a grip over Maharashtra politics which strengthened his position in the corridors of power in Delhi. And his influence in Delhi ensured his dominance in Maharashtra. In those days Maharashtra was considered to be a modern and progressive state.

The Golden Age of Cooperation (1960-1980)

During this period the cooperative movement spread throughout the state. The all-round progress of this period was often called the golden age of cooperation. Outstanding leaders, such as V.E. Vikhe Patil, D.R. Gadgil, Tahyasaheb Kore, Ratnappa Kumbhar, Vasantdada Patil, Annasaheb Shinde, Yashwantrao Mohite, Shankarrao Mohite-Patil, Shankarrao Kale and Shankarrao Kolhe emerged in the cooperative field in the state. They were dynamic, innovative and popular in their respective fields of activity. They made cooperatives in their areas self-reliant, economically strong and shining examples of successful enterprises.

Pravaranagar and Kopargaon sugar cooperatives in Ahmednagar district repaid 12-year block capital loans within 8 years and returned the state government's share capital, thus making the farmer members full owners of the enterprises. They brought about all-round development of their areas and transformed the region into a prosperous tract. There was similar progress in several other districts. What is important to note is that there was remarkable development in agriculture, education, health and industrial fields through co-operation in Pravaranagar, Warananagar, Karad, Kopargaon, Sangli and other areas. This golden age of cooperation continued from 1960 to 1980.

Decline of the Golden Age

When did the golden age come to an end and why? What were the causes of its decline? It is difficult to provide definite answers to these questions. The process of decline of cooperatives is on for the last two decades. There are many reasons for this. Some are internal and some are external to the cooperative field. All the reasons are mixed with one another which makes it difficult to identify specific cause/s or effect/s. It is not easy to determine if the Congress Party lost its grip over cooperatives because it became weaker as a party or did it become weaker as a party because it lost control over cooperatives? It is not at all easy to answer this question with confidence.

Jawaharlal Nehru died in 1964. He was succeeded as the Prime Minister by Lal Bahadur Shastri for a short period. Then, Indira Gandhi ruled as Prime Minister for 11 years from 1966 to 1977. The Congress Party suffered a serious setback in 1967, when it lost power for the first time in eight states. However, the Congress remained firmly in power in Maharashtra. The party returned to power in Maharashtra in 1972 too. In Nehru's time, the party organisation enjoyed a great deal of importance and autonomy. Indira Gandhi started dismantling the well-established party structure itself in order to concentrate power in her own hands. She converted the party into her personal instrument of power. Indiraji did not relish the dominance of cooperative sugar barons in Maharashtra and Y.B. Chavan's hold over them. She started encouraging another

Maratha (Shankarrao Chavan) against Y.B. Chavan. Her dual objective was to reduce the power of sugar barons and their leader Y.B. Chavan. During the period of Sanjay Gandhi's ascendancy, leaders without any mass base such as Babasaheb Bhosale and A. R. Antulay were made State Chief Ministers, thus sidelining the once powerful cooperative lobby.

The Cancer of Corruption

In my opinion two events in this period led to the decline of cooperatives. In the general elections of 1977, Indira Gandhi and her Congress Party were defeated and the Janata Party government under the leadership of Morarji Desai was installed at the Centre. The new government decided in favour of total decontrol of sugar which brought about a dramatic fall in prices. Sugar sold as cheap as Rs. 2.5 per kg. The collapse of sugar market adversely affected sowing of cane and sugar production, resulting in severe shortage of the commodity in the following year. The central government imposed ceiling on sugar prices to control inflation. With the scarcity of sugar in the market, and demand far exceeding the supply, the traders started offering 'on money' to sugar factory owners. 'On money' was the amount paid to the manufacturer over and above the price fixed by the government. Whoever paid the highest amount as 'on money' could buy the available supply of sugar from the factories. Thus, a kind of black market emerged in the sugar industry.

At first the sugar barons were confused and did not know, how to handle the sudden pouring in of 'on money' in their coffers. Some leaders decided to adopt a transparent policy to avoid allegations of corruption. A large number of sugar cooperatives called meetings of their Boards of Directors to discuss the issue of 'on money'. Some went to the extent of discussing the matter in the General Body meetings. Resolutions were passed to keep the 'on money' separately and use it for the development of surrounding area. As a lot of money is spent on the frequently held elections in the area, some leaders decided to utilise the sudden windfall of 'on money' for various election campaigns. In the end, the skeptics proved to be right. All such money was pocketed by the leaders. Nobody openly offered any account of 'on money' they had collected. Since all such transactions were illegal, there were no receipts, accounts, and audit of the vast funds collected. Whoever collected the money pocketed it. This paved the way for the leaders to openly indulge in corruption.

It is nobody's case that there was no corruption in cooperatives in earlier days. But it was restricted and not so open. Most of the leaders used cooperative's vehicles, guest house and other resources for private and political purposes. Such behaviour was criticised as acts of corruption by the rival leaders. But such protests were not taken seriously since it was believed that whoever came to power will indulge in such practices. The arrival of 'on money' changed the character of corruption. Now corruption emerged as big money and it was accepted as legitimate reward for controlling the sugar cooperatives. Around the same time, the sugar factories manufacturing liquor from molasses also started receiving 'on money'. The government had imposed a ceiling on prices of liquor also. But the scarcity of the commodity generated its own 'on money' paid by needy traders to greedy leaders. They had, by now, learnt how to pocket the 'on money' for themselves.

The second event of this period involved open encouragement to corruption at the government level by the Chief Minister, A.R. Antulay. Antulay was appointed Chief Minister of Maharashtra in 1980, on the recommendations of Sanjay Gandhi. The main aim of this move was to sideline the powerful Maratha leaders of cooperatives. Antulay had nothing to do with cooperatives nor did he have a popular support base among the masses. In order to please Indiraji by proclaiming his loyalty and devotion to her, he set up Indira Gandhi Pratibha Pratishthan (Indira Gandhi Talent Foundation). He pressurised sugar factories and other cooperatives to contribute donations for the foundation. In fact, he assigned a quota for donation for all the big cooperatives. He also compelled the traders in controlled commodities such as steel and cement to donate generously for the foundation. With Indira Gandhi's name and Chief Minister's pressure and insistence for contributions, corruption acquired official approval.

Cooperative leaders of Maharashtra learnt an important lesson from Antulay through this episode. Following his example, they set up educational trusts and foundations in their own areas and compelled the sugar factory members to donate for them. However, they cleverly kept these trusts legally separate from the cooperatives. They appointed themselves and their family members as life-long trustees. Thus, they ensured that the trust remained under their control even if they lost control over the sugar cooperative or similar organisations. In this way, trusts controlling crores of rupees came up all over Maharashtra. Corruption in this manner became an open and integral feature of cooperatives in Maharashtra with the silent approval of all concerned.

With the money collected from ordinary members of cooperatives, the leaders set up big educational enterprises. They charged heavy capitation fees for admission to their engineering, medical, computer and management colleges. Thus, yesterday's cooperative bosses (*Sahakar Maharshis*) transformed themselves into education lords (*Shikshan Maharshis*). They soon realised that their new trusts were like hens laying golden eggs. Through them they collected crores of rupees. In the cooperatives there was at least some check against misappropriation of funds. The government audit and supervision exercised some control on corruption. But under the new dispensation, all transactions being under the table without any receipts and audit, there being no record of receipt of capitation fee as in the case of 'on money', the leaders could freely grab the funds without any fear or risk of being caught. Cooperation and education had never acquired such a disgraceful reputation in the past.

Rise of Dynasties

Along with corruption, sugar factories and other prominent cooperatives in Maharashtra were afflicted by the disease of dynastic rule. Nobody wants to give up power. That is human nature. The sugar barons and other leaders of cooperatives managed to install their sons, nephews and grandsons as their successors in the positions of power in the cooperatives under their control. Democratic management is known to be the speciality of cooperatives. In fact, democratic control is regarded as one of the basic principles of co-operation all over the world. In certain areas of Maharashtra, some leaders have established a monopolistic control over power and perverted the very principle of democracy in cooperation. Most of the senior leaders have succumbed to the temptation of dynastic rule. In the pioneering sugar factory at Pravaranagar admired as a pilgrim centre of ideal cooperation, the founder V.E. Vikhe Patil was succeeded by his son Balasaheb who in turn, installed his son Radhakrishna as the chairman of this 'model' sugar cooperative, thus retaining the cooperative under family control continuously for three generations.

The same history was repeated at Warananagar in Kolhapur district, another hallowed place for co-operators in Maharashtra. After the founder Tatyasaheb Kore died, his son took over as chairman, and now the grandson Vinay is occupying the throne. Whether it is Vasantdada sugar factory at Sangli or Rajarambapu sugar factory at Walva, at both the places sons of founders, Prakashbapu and Jayantrao respectively, are in power. At Kopargaon and Sanjivani in Ahmednagar district powerful leaders Shankarrao Kale and Shankarrao Kolhe have taken care to install their sons in chairman's seats of these prominent sugar factories. The long-standing political rivalry between Kale and Kolhe continues with both the sons contesting against each other in the October 2004, Assembly elections, in Kopargaon constituency. The loser, Bipin Kolhe was the official candidate of Nationalist Congress Party (NCP) while the winner Ashok Kale was in the Shiv Sena camp. In Karad, another big cooperative complex in Satara district, two brothers, Yashwantrao Mohite and Jayantrao Bhosale, have been fighting for power against each other for the last two decades, thus restricting the power struggle within one family. There are many such examples of dynastic rule in cooperatives all over Maharashtra.

It is often argued that a dynastic rule helps in smooth functioning of cooperatives. Moreover, it is also justified on the ground that the leaders are elected through democratic procedure. Is it their fault if they belong to a particular family? Leaving aside such spacious arguments, it must be admitted that the leaders have failed in inculcating genuine democratic spirit in the management of cooperatives. This is the real implication of dynastic rule.

The Stagnating Situation

There is one marked difference between the old leaders and the new leaders of cooperatives. The old leaders acquired political power to strengthen the cooperatives under their control. The new leaders capture cooperatives to acquire political power.

With the advent of globalisation, cooperatives are facing new challenges. The trends of privatisation have adversely affected the cooperatives. How many cooperative leaders are fully aware of these changes? They still seem to be living in the past. If that were not the case, they would not have continued with old and ineffective management practices. Even today, there is no evidence of modernisation in the day-to-day administration of sugar factories and other cooperatives. There is so much competition all over the world forcing the industries to curtail costs and effect economies in the production process. The leaders of cooperatives seem to be unaware about this and are indulging in employing excess workforce and wasteful expenditure. Corruption has reached new heights. If such practices continued unhindered cooperation will lead us to disaster instead of development. The leaders are under the illusion that whenever they are in trouble, the government will come to their rescue with financial help. They seem to forget that the government itself is facing bankruptcy, how can it help the cooperatives?

Decline of Cooperation: Some Disturbing Figures

What do we mean when we say cooperatives declined in Maharashtra? What has been the extent of damage? It is not possible to give a comprehensive picture in a brief chapter like this. I will give a few examples as a sample.

According to a report, there were in all, 30 District Central Cooperative Banks in Maharashtra in 2000. One for each district. Only 15 of these banks were in profit. The rest of the 15 were in loss. The total profit was Rs. 88.19 crore only, while the total loss was Rs. 386.79 crore.[1] Really speaking, normally a bank should not incur any losses. Uncontrolled corruption is the main cause of losses suffered by these banks. Sixty-four directors of Nagpur, Wardha and Osmanabad district central cooperative banks and 65 directors of 4 urban cooperatives banks together misappropriated government bonds worth Rs. 250 crore. The Maharashtra government has confiscated property worth Rs. 22.89 crore of these 129 directors.[2] One reads about several such scams in newspapers. For the moment, this example should be enough.

---

1. *Sahakari Maharashtra* (2000). p.79, November.
2. *The Link* (2002). Vol. 8(5), p.2, September-October.

A large number of Maharashtra's cooperative sugar factories are sick. The then Chief Minister Sushil Kumar Shinde announced that 52 of the 110 working factories in Maharashtra were sick in the year 2004. He also declared that no permission for a new cooperative sugar factory will be given unless there is improvement in the financial condition of the state.[3] Seventeen sugar cooperatives in the state had not paid their dues (with interest) to the extent of Rs. 157.95 crore as on 31 March 2000.[4] In spite of such pitiable condition, the outgoing Chief Minister gave a parting gift of Rs. 1,500 crore to these sick factories hoping that it will improve their health.

There are many other cooperatives in Maharashtra which are seriously sick because of heavy debt burden. Among the agricultural processing cooperatives, 6 units owed debts (with interest) amounting to Rs. 153.50 core on 31 March 2000.[5] Similarly, 25 cooperative spinning mills in the state had outstanding debts of Rs. 295.31 crore on the same date.[6]

In Ahmednagar district alone, 200 cooperative credit societies, out of the total of 2,000, have been proclaimed bankrupt.[7] Many cooperatives in Maharashtra suffer from huge losses in their economic activities, misappropriation of funds, and scams of various kinds. But what happened in Terna sugar cooperative in Marathwada is indeed shameful and shocking beyond imagination. This sugar factory is chaired by Padmasinh Patil, Maharashtra's Irrigation Minister and Sharad Pawar's close relative and trusted lieutenant. During 1999-2001, Patil mobilised shareholder-farmers of Terna and other donors in Osmanabad district to donate for various deserving causes such as Rs. 10.60 lakh for Assam Relief Fund, Rs. 15.05 lakh for Kargil War heroes and their families, Rs. 10.30 lakh for Gujarat Earthquake Fund, and Rs. 16.01 lakh for Sugar Complex Fund. In all, Rs. 51.96 lakh were collected through donations. But not a single rupee was used for the purpose for which it was collected. All this money was diverted to salvage Patil's sinking cooperative, using most of it for working

3. *Cooperative Sugar Press News* (2003). Vol. 34(6), p.3, March 13.

4. *Sahakari Maharashtra* (2000). p.80, November.

5. *Ibid* (2000). p.79.

6. *Ibid* (2000). p.80.

7. *Ibid* (2000). p.109.

expenses. At the last count, outstanding dues of the cooperative to various financial institutions amounted to nearly Rs. 200 crore. Besides, permanent factory workers have not been paid regular salaries, shareholder-farmers have not received dividends, and retired workers are still awaiting their dues that run into lakhs. Patil also admitted that Rs. 1.3 crore meant to be grant for shareholder-farmers to improve sugarcane yields were diverted to daily expenses.[8] All in all, it shows that financially Maharashtra's cooperatives are in dire and pitiable condition.

Rays of Hope

Is there no remedy for the depressing state of the cooperative field in Maharashtra? Is it possible to come out of this difficult situation and revive the old period of glory? What should be done for that? Are there any rays of hope in the widespread darkness? I don't think the situation has gone totally out of control. There are still certain positive elements in Maharashtra cooperatives which could be used to regenerate a new life in them.

In 1999-2000 in India as a whole, there were 504,000 cooperative societies having 20 crore 91 lakh members.[9] Maharashtra alone had 152,619 of these societies with 4 crore 14 lakh members. It means Maharashtra alone has India's 30 per cent of cooperative societies with 20 per cent members. Thus, Maharashtra is at the top both in the number of cooperative societies and their membership strength. This is a big asset. During the same year, the share capital of cooperatives in Maharashtra amounted to Rs. 4,560 crore, deposits accounted for Rs. 35,311 crore, and the working capital was Rs. 70,501 crore.[10] In all the above respects, Maharashtra occupies the top position among states. Cooperatives in no other state have such a financial strength. This is undoubtedly the plus point in favour of Maharashtra co-ops.

India is the largest producer of sugar in the world since 1988. And within the country, Maharashtra is the largest sugar producing state continuously for the last several years. In 2001-02, India produced 18.52 million tonnes of sugar. In this, Maharashtra alone contributed

8. *Outlook*, 21 June 2004, p.31.
9. *Maharashtra Cooperative Quarterly*, Vol. LXXXV(1).
10. *Sahakari Maharashtra* (1999). p.19, November.

5.56 million tonnes. Moreover, all this sugar was produced in cooperative sugar factories. This is something to be proud of for sugarcane farmers in Maharashtra[11]. Hutatma Ahir sugar cooperative in Walva is recognised as the model sugar factory in India. It has occupied the first position in India in respect of highest sugar recovery. It has often surpassed its own earlier records. It has acquired an all-India fame for corruption-free transparent administration and highest productivity.

As in sugar, India is the largest producer of milk in the world. In 1998, India produced 74 million tonnes of milk, thus reaching the world's top position as a milk producer. It has retained that position since then.[12] Dairy cooperatives in Gujarat are leading in this field. However, milk cooperatives in Maharashtra occupy the next or second position in the country which is not a small achievement.

There are over 1,500 urban cooperative banks in India. Maharashtra alone has more than 600 or 40 per cent of them. Urban cooperative banks in the country together have total deposits of Rs. 40,700 crore. Again, Maharashtra urban cooperative banks alone have Rs. 23,000 crore of deposits (56 per cent of the total).[13]

Another example of successful co-operation in Maharashtra is Warana cooperative bazar located in the well-known Warana cooperative agro-industrial complex in Kolhapur district. The consumer cooperative's area of operation covers 78 villages in the Warana valley. Its annual turnover is over Rs. 40 crore. It is among the top five consumer cooperatives in the country in terms of annual turnover. But it is the only one of its kind in a rural area in India. What is noteworthy is that, the cooperative is headed by a woman as chairperson and there are 9 women among the 17 directors on the board. The cooperative has 131 women as employees in its various departments. This is an impressive example of women's empowerment.[14]

Maharashtra enjoys certain special characteristics in its cooperative field. It is worth noting how cooperation has penetrated in the

---

11. *Cooperative Sugar Press News* (2003). Vol. 34(6), p.10, March 13.
12. *Sahakari Maharashtra* (1999). p.19, November.
13. *Sahakari Maharashtra* (2000). p.131, November.
14. *Maharashtra Cooperative Quarterly* (2001). Vol. LXXXIV(3), p.33, January-March.

different spheres of state's social and economic life. In Maharashtra, there are 147 potters' cooperatives, 82 leather workers' cooperatives, 16 cooperative hospitals, a large number of cooperatives organised by washermen, auto rickshaw-drivers, student hostels, and cooperative educational societies. These are peculiar to Maharashtra and rarely found in other states.[15] It is the reflection of how deeply and widely the cooperative spirit and thinking have penetrated in the state. It shows how social and economic life of people in different strata is permeated by the ideology of cooperation. That is why, even today one finds a network of vibrant cooperatives in the rural areas of Kopargaon, Pravaranagar, Warananagar, Karad, Sangli, Baramati and Akluj in Maharashtra.

Concluding Observations

The winds of liberalisation, privatisation and globalisation are blowing all over the world. Nobody can stop these trends. They are irreversible. However, this should not lead one to conclude that the cooperative era has ended and there is no scope for co-operation now. It would be a wrong conclusion to draw. On the contrary, in today's changing situation, there is a greater need for cooperation. There is cut-throat competition in trade and industry. It is going to intensify further as time goes. Those sections of people who are economically strong and able, would survive in this competition and may go ahead. The poor and weaker sections will not be able to survive. Co-operation is the only way for them to stay alive. They will survive only if they organise themselves on cooperative basis. Small farmers, agricultural labourers, small artisans and producers would survive and prosper only if they come together through cooperatives.

Fortunately the circumstances are still favourable to go ahead through cooperation in Maharashtra. The state has enough social and material resources. If they are used judiciously it should be possible to arrest the decline of cooperatives and march ahead. Maharashtra's history and long experience of working through cooperatives would be useful for the recovery. There is no scarcity of activists in the state. The need is to motivate and lead them on the right path.

---

15. *Sahakari Maharashtra* (2000). p.193, November.

If the leaders work sincerely, it is still possible to recreate the golden age of cooperation. However, it will require determination and harsh policy decisions. The main thing is to emphasise quality in place of quantity. Enough of cooperative sugar factories. There are too many of them compared to availability of cane. No more addition to them at any cost. A genuine cooperative movement must help a small producer and make him stronger. It should also reduce poverty and control inequality. That should be the ultimate test of success or failure of cooperation.

The cooperatives must be made free, autonomous and self-reliant by suitably amending the cooperative laws. It is essential to liberate cooperatives from the clutches of bureaucracy and power hungry selfish politicians. That will need the determination to reject government grants and subsidies. The temptation to grab government grants and loans and slogans of autonomy cannot go together. If inefficient cooperatives are making losses, let them die their natural death. It is harmful to keep them alive with the artificial life support of government help. If we enable the emergence of selfless workers with social conscience to operate cooperatives, it should be possible to recreate the golden age of cooperation.

12

Indian Agribusiness Institutions for Small Farmers

Role, Issues and Challenges

G. SRIDHAR and VISHWA BALLABH

Introduction

India is one of the very few countries in the world, endowed with rich and diverse agroclimatic zones, vast land resources for cultivation (about 160 million hectares), huge chunk of human resources in agriculture (nearly two-thirds of the population), wide variety of crops grown, and strong R&D facilities. Indian agriculture has performed at the most satisfactorily (Deshpande and Indira, 2004) and have comparative advantage in much farm production but does not enjoy competitive advantage (Bhalla, 2005). However, its share in world trade is insignificant though it has 20 per cent of world's irrigable land under foodgrains, is second largest grower of vegetables, and produces nearly 17 per cent of world's cotton (Firodia, 2006). Many paradoxes still exist, for instance, inspite of good surplus of food-grains there are millions of poor dying of hunger, many farmers are poor and in debt in spite of having reasonable marketable surplus, despite good R&D facilities, farmers still practice subsistence agriculture.

One of the underlying reasons for such paradoxes is the existence of a large number of small farmers.[1] Through successive family generations and the resulting fragmentation of land, small farmers in India are poor, undernourished, poverty stricken, depend on monsoons

1. India has more than 100 million small farmers with an average farm size of less than 1.2 hectares. The share of the small farmers (1 to 4 hectares of land) in the total number of holdings increased from 70 per cent in 1971 to 80 per cent in 1998 and is expected to reach 83 per cent by 2010 (GoI, 2003; Jha, 2001).

and practice subsistence agriculture. As their risk-taking abilities are low, productivity declines. Poor market orientation and low value addition capacity, gives them low margins leading to low risk-taking abilities. Thus, small farmers enter a vicious circle and find it difficult to break. Little bargaining power and heavy dependence on their farm produce for basic needs, add to their woes and they end up becoming victims to the exploitative market intermediaries who deny them a fair share of the consumer rupee.

Small farmers in India in a bid to hedge their miseries embraced diversification of agriculture. During the past two decades, there has been a perceptible increase of incomes from livestock, fisheries and forestry. Food crops have been replaced by cash crops in many areas (Joshi, 2005). However, the experience of agricultural development in India has shown that benefits will not accrue to the small farmers unless they are integrated into the markets as recognisable players through innovative institutional arrangements. Institutions, especially cooperative and corporate, have attempted to integrate small farmers into the market by removing bottlenecks in marketing of agricultural produce and regulating the market in favour of small farmers. A few institutional arrangements have claimed to have reduced the transaction costs by steadily transforming from manpower driven to technology driven, from disintegrated supply chains to integrated supply chains, from finance as a source of control to information as a source of control.

Two institutional arrangements, namely, Anand pattern of cooperatives and *e-choupal* have received wide attention for the benefits they claim to have passed on to the small farmers. There have been various studies conducted to evaluate and verify such claims, but most of the studies evaluated these two institutions exclusively. Hardly any study has been conducted comparing and contrasting both. In this chapter, we attempt to do the job. The purpose of comparison is to bring out the salient features embedded into the arrangements that benefit small farmers and look for the institutional arrangement that offers better services to the small farmers. The outcome of the analysis would be helpful for policy makers to take appropriate initiatives.

In analysing the institutional arrangements we first look at how these institutional arrangements have reduced transaction costs in terms of opportunism, information asymmetry and asset specificity at various levels. Our premise is that institutional arrangement that has been able to reduce transaction costs for the small farmers and for itself should be preferred. Our premise also configures design of the institution as a key determinant of transaction costs. Thus, in our analysis we go beyond organisational structure, physical layout of facilities and consider creative process of problem solving of the small farmers, services offered and procedures and policies of the institutions that expand the opportunities for the small farmers (Shah, 1996). The chapter is based on an exploratory study and does not empirically measure transaction costs or design elements but analyses theoretically. Our analysis is based on the available literature and field visits to a few select villages where the institutions are in operation.

Cooperative Institutions

Voluntary and democratic in nature, participatory in approach, commitment towards ethical standards, socially responsive, are some of the distinguishing and differentiating features of cooperatives (Vaswani *et al.*, 2003). Unlike corporates which have profit as major motive, cooperatives attempt to reduce income disparities, improve the social conditions, combat exploitation and strive for a better society through sustainable developmental activities.

Cooperatives offer a good alternative for small farmers when there are wider market imperfections. Cooperatives can procure supplies at lower transaction cost through suitable backward linkages and aggregate them appropriately to harness the benefits of economies of scale. They can be helpful to small farmers in providing credit, inputs and extension services. More often they are also involved in the processing of the produce so that a higher value can be generated. Noted among the agribusiness cooperatives in India and world across is the Anand pattern of cooperatives.

Anand Pattern of Cooperatives (Amul Model)—Gujarat

Anand pattern of cooperatives (APC) famously known as Amul model was initiated in 1946, by Sri Tribhuvandas Patel with 247 litres of milk in two villages. Later on, when Dr. V. Kurien took over the reins it turned into a mighty cooperative movement.

Two reasons provided the trigger for the establishment of APC in Gujarat. Firstly, as milk is extremely perishable, harvested daily by a large number of small producers on a subsistence basis in India, value addition becomes extremely difficult and a costly proposition at individual level. Secondly, milk markets were highly unorganised and exploited by middlemen.

APCs are organised on a three-tier system, at the village level are primary cooperatives, cooperative union at the district level, and cooperative federation at the state level (Figure 12.1). Let us take a look at each of the levels in some detail.

Figure 12.1

Anand Pattern of Cooperatives in Gujarat

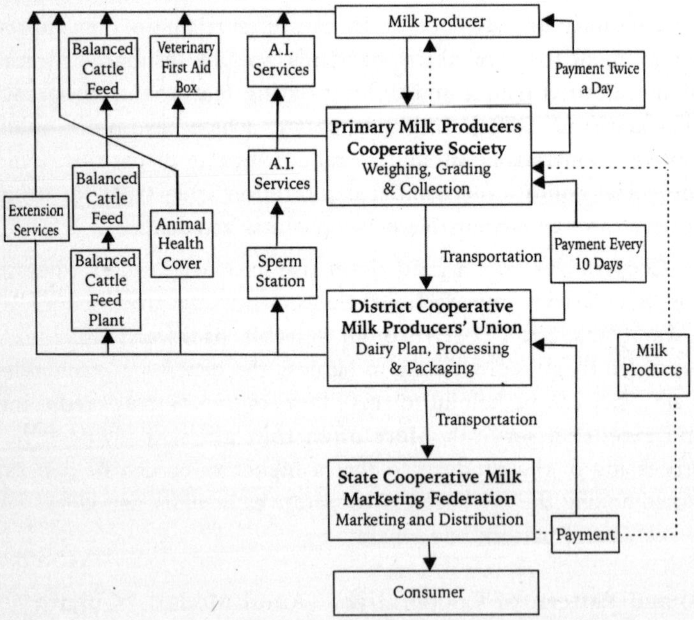

Note: A.I – Artificial Insemination.
Source: Adapted from Rao (1989).

At the village level, a dairy cooperative society is formed with primary milk producers. A milk producer becomes a member by paying an entrance fee and buying a share of the society. A farmer producer becomes eligible to get a voting right in the society if s/he is a member and supplies at least 700 litres of milk per year and 180 days of supply in a year. The allocation of voting rights is one member-one vote and there is no reservation of seats on the basis of social class, caste or gender. Members of the society elect a managing committee as per the by-laws and the committee elects its chairman. Committee members are honorary and their role is restricted to policy formulation and overseeing the programme. The society has a few critical functions like collecting milk (twice a day), making regular payments to milk supplier members and providing cattle feed, fodder and animal breeding and health care services to members at their doorstep. Member producers bring milk to the collection centre in the village every morning and evening. Initially, union provides each collection centre with a fat testing machine free of cost. The cost of repairs or replacement of the machine is borne by the society. Once the quality (i.e. fat content) and quantity is assessed, cash payable to each producer is worked out. When the producer comes to the centre in the evening, s/he is paid for morning delivery and for the milk delivered in the evening; money is paid the next morning. Apart from the daily cash income, members also get bonus and a difference in price at the end of the year. Amount of bonus is *pro rata* to the value of milk supplied by the producers at the society. The society also makes profit on the milk it sold to the union and gets difference in price. However, the entire profit of the society is not distributed to member producers. A part is allotted for the developmental activities within the village and maintenance of the society. Societies also act as dissemination modes for various activities of the union programmes like member education, production enhancement and so on. The staff at the societies is trained to undertake the veterinary first aid and artificial insemination.

A cooperative union is the representative of all the village societies located at the district level which is governed by the Board of Directors having representatives from village societies, financial institutions, state cooperative department, dairy experts, federation, government nominees, individual shareholding members and the managing director of the union. Allocation of voting rights is one society-one vote and there is no reservation for specific class of members. Zones are formed to coincide with *talukas* or equal number of primaries. The Board elects a Chairman and Vice Chairman and appoints a Managing Director who in turn appoints supporting staff. The Board is responsible for policy formulation and the staff is responsible for looking after the day to day operations. One-third of the village representatives in the Board retire every year and the vacancy is filled by election. Chairman is elected every year. Procuring, processing and managing macro-level inputs like veterinary health clinics, semen banks and cattle-feed distribution to village dairy cooperative societies are the tasks of the district milk unions. Given the perishable nature of milk, it was imperative for the cooperative to devise ways and means of transporting the milk procured from distant villages in the shortest possible time, and under refrigerated conditions to the processing units. Hence, milk routes are designed by the dairy unions in order to organise transportation routes in a manner that all villages are covered in the shortest possible time and in a cost-effective manner. Bulk cooling units and chilling centres are set up along these milk routes. Milk is lifted by unions from villages twice a day with the help of private transport vehicles on a contractual basis. At the dairy, milk is graded into two categories: good and sour. Good milk from the society is measured for its quantity and quality (Fats and SNFs i.e. Solids-Not-Fats). Each village-level society is paid by the union for the fat and SNF received in its milk. Low-grade milk gets low price. Payments to the societies are made for every 10 days. Cooperative unions provide extension services to its farmer members in addition to the supply of feed and credit. Unions run semen product centres, train the society staff in artificial insemination (AI), have veterinary dispensaries and conduct various programmes for increasing the productivity of milk.

Till 1974, milk and milk products were produced and marketed by unions all over the state. Later on, all the unions were federated in the state of Gujarat under Gujarat Cooperative Milk Marketing Federation (GCMMF). Since then, it is the sole marketing agency for the products produced by different cooperative unions of Gujarat under the brand names 'Amul' and 'Sagar'. The GCMMF plans what products would sell and arranges to manufacture for each year and how much. The key objectives of GCMMF are to market dairy and agricultural products of cooperatives through common branding, centralised marketing, centralised quality control, centralised purchases and pooling of milk efficiently (Kurien, 2003). With a dealer network of over 3,500 dealers and 5,00,000 outlets, the GCMMF provides quality products at the best price for the consumers (Subramanyam, 2004). At present, the GCMMF markets milk and milk products like ice cream, chocolates, cheese, bread spread worth above Rs. 3000 crores. It has a low-cost advantage over its competitors, the advantage acquired due to elimination of middle men, lean organisation and lower overheads. Its strong brand name "AMUL" stands for purity and quality and its scale and scope of operations are its assets. Ownership/control and operational management are well demarked in GCMMF. Farmer producers exercise control over the management of GCMMF and business operations are handled by qualified professionals.[2] The performance of the professionals is reviewed and audited by the farmers through the elected representatives in the Board.

Thus, APC represents a methodology of building and sustaining an economic enterprise and has ensured high levels of patronage cohesiveness, governance and operational effectiveness (Shah, 1996). APC has made an enormous difference in the lives of millions of farmers by offering steady income in regions where agriculture is still rainfed. By providing benefits of contemporary dairy technology–an access that would otherwise be effectively denied to farmers (Rao, 1990), APC has been able to modernise Indian agricultural commodity markets and transformed rural structures by bringing economic and social justice in a fair, efficient and sustainable manner.

The Corporate Sector

With an eye on the significant improvements in agricultural sector, the corporate sector started venturing into the arena. They have invested in R&D to bring new varieties of crops, cropping patterns (Pal and Jha, 2004), generated employment and income opportunities

---

2. Federation is highly professionalised, for example, it has 225 management graduates, 59 CAs/ICWAs, 37 dairy technologists, 76 post graduates, 25 computer graduates, 54 master degree holders, 229 degree holders 49 undergraduates out of total 759 employees (Kurien, 2003).

and lessened the burden of marketing of produce from the farmer who can better concentrate on their production. Through backward linkages and aggregation,the corporate organisations have been able to reduce transaction costs. Leveraging the information technology (IT), they have brought about innovative business models to integrate farmers into the markets. One such widely recognised corporate initiative is ITC's *e-choupal*.

e-Choupal

Indian Tobacco Company's (ITC) pioneering agribusiness initiative 'e-choupal' is unique in many ways. The *e-choupal*:

i. is a complete end-to-end solution as it delivers real-time information and customised knowledge to improve farmers' decisionmaking ability to align farm output with market demands, and to improve productivity;

ii. aggregates demand like a virtual producers' cooperative and provides access to high-quality farm inputs at lower cost;

iii. acts as a direct marketing channel with more efficient price discovery and lower transaction costs in output marketing;

iv. is scalable as it is built on market principles;

v. is replicable across different crops and geography in India because of its conceptual strength; and

vi. integrates farmers to the market place and simultaneously, meets the needs and challenges of consumers at the bottom of the economic pyramid (Prahalad, 2005).

Currently, there are 5,500 *choupals* in 26,000 villages covering 2.6 million farmers spread across six states of India (personal communication, 2006). *E-choupal*, in addition to forward integrating farmers into the markets, sells agricultural inputs and other products of the organisations through backward supply chain movements. The extension services offered by *e-choupal* at the village level include e-governance, health and education services. A second layer of infrastructural facility 'choupal sagar' is also offered with facilities like warehousing, weighment of farmers' produce, soil-testing laboratory, training centre for farmers, life and general insurance, supermarket, e-health facility, pharmacy, diesel station and so on. In the next seven years, *e-choupal* intends to be present in 15 states, one lakh villages, and deal with wider range of commodities like grains, oilseeds, coffee, spices, cotton, horticulture and aquaculture.

At present, there are four types of *choupals* tailored specifically for four different commodities, *viz.*, soybean, wheat, coffee, and shrimps. We discuss the soy-*choupal* model for two reasons; firstly soya in India is grown largely by small farmers and secondly, it is the first commodity for the model becoming the benchmark for other *choupal* models.

Internet-enabled multimedia computers with solar power backup and VSAT connectivity is set up at company's cost for every 5 or 6 villages. This set up is called *e-choupal* and it is installed in a selected farmer's place called *sanchalak* who is chosen on the basis of high social status, entrepreneurial and development orientation. *Sanchalaks* once chosen, take an oath in public to serve the village and are given training by ITC on basics of computers and internet, design of e-choupal and the role they need to play in villages. They receive 0.5 per cent of commission on the procured crop and bear the operational costs of the installed equipment.

The company has reintermediated rather than disintermediating the role of the traditional commission agents by making them *sanyojaks* (coordinators) in the network (Sawhney, 2002). They are the source of liquidity as they manage the physical flows of the soya, collect price information from the local *mandis* and maintain records. For these services, they are paid a commission of one per cent on the total procurement of soya by the *e-choupal*.

e-choupal *design works as follows;*

i. *E-choupal* offers daily price quotes of ITC for soya (generally prices are Rs. 15–20 per quintal more than *mandi*) on its website which can be accessed by farmers through the internet kiosk. Farmers get the ITC quote either by personally visiting *Sanchalak*'s place or by calling him over phone. Information on price quotes of soya in various *mandis* and international markets, latest agricultural practices of various crops, weather, and news are also posted on the website to aid farmers' decision to sell the soya.

ii. If the quote is not up to the farmers' expectation, he is left to take a decision to sell the produce elsewhere. And, if the farmer is satisfied by the quote he can sell the produce to ITC by taking a sample of produce to local *choupal* and receive a spot quote from the *sanchalak*.

iii. Depending on the fair average quality (FAQ) and quantity, farmers are paid immediately for selling their produce to ITC at hubs or *sagars*. Sometimes, if the farmer is located in some remote location he can sell his produce to *sanchalak*. Small farmers would prefer such an arrangement because of various transaction costs they are likely to incur. Payment is done at the *e-choupal* hub or *sagar* facilitated by the *samyojak*. *E-choupal* ensures material handling, weighbridges and transportation at the *e-choupal* hub/*sagar*.

iv. Procured soya is sent to the processing unit which in turn, is sent to the *e-choupal* division. The processed soya is then marketed by ITC to various customers. Some of the processed produce like soya oil and *atta* are sent back to the hubs/*sagar* for selling it to farmers and other consumers.

v. ITC also sells products of other organisations at it hubs like farm inputs, insurance, and various consumer products.

vi. *E-choupal* also facilitates services for other organisations through its network like e-governance, education and health services and helps various NGOs in their work. The e-choupal charges these organisations for using its platform and network (see also chapter 10).

E-choupal has been successful in providing an alternative platform for the farmers and increases the competition in market to procure. Substantial commitment of financial and human resources from *e-choupal* has made possible its rapid expansion and acceptance from various segments of farming community. In a visit to villages in Sehore mandal of Madhya Pradesh, we found that farmers rate *e-choupal* 60 per cent over and above the services and benefits of *mandis*. Through its design, farmers were offered good financial returns, freedom of choice to sell and reduce wastage.

Figure 12.2

Soy–Choupal Model

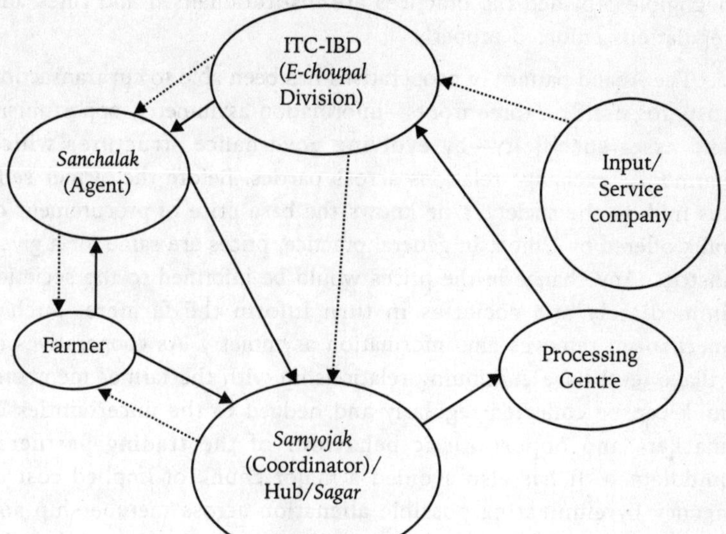

Comparing Transaction Costs

In transaction cost analysis, the extent of information available between the parties of exchange, opportunistic behaviour of the members in the exchange and the level of asset specificity to the transaction outline the cost (Williamson, 1975). Further, as exchange relations are not always cooperative in nature, the perspective of the implications would differ from the sellers to buyers (Håkansson, 1993 cited from Loader, 1997). While comparing the transaction costs of two institutional arrangements discussed above, we consider these aspects. As mentioned earlier, the evaluation of institutions' performance and the choice of better institution emerging thereof is based on their ability to reduce transaction costs on various fronts and especially, for the small farmers.

Farmers have been able to reduce their transaction costs considerably, after becoming members of the cooperative society. As cooperatives did not act as any typical middlemen who hide market information, the costs associated with information asymmetry were minimised to a great extent. As each member has equal voting rights, the opportunistic tendencies within the cooperative society are negligible provided the practices are institutionalised and rules and regulations enforced properly.

The Anand pattern of cooperatives has been able to cut transaction costs for itself on three fronts—information asymmetry, opportunism and asset specificity—by evolving governance structures which harmonise exchange relations across parties. Before the farmer sells his milk to the society, s/he knows the base price of procurement of milk offered by Union. In general practice, prices are same for a given district. Any change in the prices would be informed to the societies immediately and societies in turn inform the farmers. Such a mechanism removes any information asymmetry. As cooperatives at village level have continuing relationship with the farmer members, milk can be collected regularly and hedged to the uncertainties of markets and opportunistic behaviour of the trading partners/ middlemen. It has also avoided a major chunk of implied cost of agency by eliminating possible alienation across membership and conflict with management among the members. By training the society staff on specialised skills like artificial insemination and animal health care, it has reduced transaction costs considerably. Staff members of the cooperatives, including chairman are equal share holders in the society. They are equally benefited as any poor or low caste member of the society. Such an arrangement would also ensure little opportunity for transaction costs to arise due to opportunistic behaviour. Further, as membership of the cooperatives is long term, asset specificity-related transaction costs also are reduced to a considerable extent. Most importantly, if the cooperative society has been able to reduce transaction costs substantially, the benefits would be trickled down to each of its members. This kind of savings is unique to cooperative system which unfortunately is not possible in any other institutional arrangement, more so in a corporate.

By generating enough economies of scale, in terms of collection of milk and by routing appropriately so that maximum milk is collected within minimum distance of transportation, the union has been able to reduce transaction costs to a good extent. Costs in the way of asset specificity have been reduced for the union through outsourcing the transportation activities. Supply of inputs and cattle feed is done through the same transport arrangement further reducing transaction costs. The arrangement of APC is such that all unions do not produce same milk products, thus nullifying costs arising out of conflict of interests and competition among unions. With ERP packages, federations have been able to network through the dealers and able to reduce transaction costs on all three aspects, *viz.*, information asymmetry, opportunism and asset specificity in the forward supply chain.

E-choupal has also been able to reduce transaction costs for the farmers and in its own operations. Farmers have saved transaction costs approximating to Rs. 270 per MT which would have been incurred in *mandi* (trolley freight to *mandi* = 100, filling & weighing labour = 70, labour *Khadi Karai* = 50, Handling Loss = 50), (as given to us in presentation by the company officials). Another study stated that *e-choupal* has enabled the organisation to reduce transaction costs of procuring soya from 8 to 2 per cent. About half of these savings are shared by the farmers (Singh, 2004). As an institution, *e-choupal* has been able to considerably reduce transaction costs in terms of information asymmetry and asset specificity. However, we suspect that the transaction costs which might arise out of opportunism still need to be reduced. For example, one of the choice criteria for considering a farmer as *sanchalak* is his entrepreneurial aptitude. An entrepreneur in any system would always attempt to maximise his returns. This attitude would most likely make him more opportunistic, thus raising the scope for increase in the transaction costs. Therefore there is need to improve the accountability of *Sanchalaks*.

Comparing Design

Broadly, both the institutional arrangements have been successful in reducing transaction costs to a considerable extent and increase financial returns to the small farmers. However, Anand pattern of cooperatives' design scores as a better alternative compared to *e-choupal* in terms of the producers, control over the agribusiness, consistency in the share of consumer rupee, response to the farmer's needs, removal of intermediaries, transparency of operations from the small farmers' perspective and purchase guarantees (Table 12.1). *E-choupal* fares equal to Amul design on fronts like inputs and technical assistance, and response to farmer requirements and fares better on response to market requirements.

Table 12.1

Comparative Analysis of Amul and E-Choupal Models

Criteria	*AMUL (Cooperative)*	*E-choupal (Corporate)*
Motive to establish	Better value and increased returns for farmer members	Improve market standing, top and bottom line
Response to market requirements	Medium	Fast
Response to farmer requirements	Fast	Medium
Removal of intermediaries	Disintermediation	Reintermediation
Transparency of operations (from small farmers' perspective)	High	Moderate
Cost of maintaining relationships with small farmers	Low	High
Discriminating small farmers *versus* big farmers in procurement	No possibility	Possible
Impact on social structures of village	High and wide-spread	Moderate
Purchase guarantees	Yes	No
Inputs and technical assistance	Yes, at subsidised price	Yes, at prevailing market price
Propagating sustainable agricultural practices	High	Moderate, but not a concern
Bargaining power of small farmers	Very high	Moderate to low
Farmers' share in consumer rupee	High, consistent	Medium-high, varying
Farmers' control on agribusiness	Very high and independent	None and dependent

Some of the other design issues which can be compared between APC and *e-choupal* are:

a. *Sanchalak versus* Society Head: APC has successfully removed intermediaries but e-choupal has reintermediated. These middlemen might act as a key source of discomfort once they start bargaining for more facilities and control over the supply chain. In fact, ITC is presently facing this problem. In some cases, election of *sanchalak*s by the farmers might unnecessarily lead to a spurt in the political activities in villages and might favour the strong against the week small farmers. This is not possible in case of Amul model as each member has one vote, irrespective of the size of their landholding and social status.

b. Area of Operations and Market Expansion: *E-choupal* has initiated its operations only in the areas endowed with rich agricultural practices and established markets of the commodity unlike Anand pattern which has been responsible in creating the market where there was no substantial milk market.

c. Risk: In providing information to the farmers, *e-choupal* might have reduced the transaction costs due to information asymmetry, but risk of taking decisions regarding prices is still with the farmer. Much of the price risk is absorbed by the Union and Federation in vertically linked cooperative organisation. Farmers are paid the difference of price every year in case of Anand pattern which is not in case of *e-choupal*.

d. Peoples' Institution: Anand pattern is a testimony to what farmers can achieve when they exercise control over the resources they create. The Anand experience has established that agricultural development is not just a matter of technology but is a matter of building people's institutions (Singh, 1992). However, this is not the case in *e-choupal* which emphasises much on the information technology rather than building people.

e. Legal Issues: In few villages where we visited, *sanchalak*s who sell products like pesticides act as outlets for *e-choupal*. However, for offering such services to villages, they are not authorised legally to sell these products neither by *e-choupal* nor by any statutory body which might lead to complications. This does not happen in Anand pattern because inputs are sold through societies which are authorised legally.

Conclusion

Challenges before any agribusiness institution is to integrate small farmers into the market and benefit them in an efficient, equitable, sustainable and transparent manner. Unless they are in control of the business, they will be in control of the business. Cooperatives have been successful in benefiting small farmers for a long time as they are owned and controlled by the farmers. Corporate on the other hand, is known for its shrewd profit motives and poor social concern. Their inclination towards sustainable agricultural practices is obviously less as they are neither owned nor controlled by the farmers. These arguments have received support from our analysis of the two institutional arrangements; Anand pattern of cooperatives and *e-choupal*. In most of the criteria for evaluation of the institutional offers to the benefit of the small farmers, Anand pattern of cooperatives stand out. A World Bank report on Anand pattern of cooperatives and its replication across India has concluded "...there should be no further lending to the dairy sector in states which have not yet adopted the full Anand Pattern of cooperatives or which do not treat these cooperatives equally with private cooperatives" (Candler and Kumar, 1998). In another recent development, World Bank is attempting to replicate Anand pattern of cooperatives in South Africa (Singh, 2006). In a statement, World Bank states,

> The World Bank agrees that the model used in Operation Flood is a viable business model for farmers as it provides high returns. World Bank will now identify the African countries where Operation Flood could be replicated so that the poor farmers there could become self-sufficient.

These statements are the testimony of the success of Anand pattern. Hence, we strongly feel that policy formulators should encourage relatively more of cooperative form, more so, Anand pattern of institutions than that of corporate institutions.

However, we do not insist that the role of corporate institutions should be undermined and not encouraged. The comparison that we have done here is in the present context and only relative in nature, not in absolute terms of benefits offered. Further, Anand pattern of cooperatives is more than half a century old which has withstood the test of time and has evolved over years. *E-choupal* is a recent emerging institutional arrangement and might take some time to settle down and benefit the small farmers. Whether or not small farmers would benefit in same manner as the large farmers though *e-choupal* of ITC, would largely depend upon benevolence of top management and concern for small farmers. There is no inbuilt mechanism in *e-choupal* to ensure that the small farm households would not be ignored once their initial euphoria of social concern dies down and efficiency aspects begin to count more than equity and equal participation of all farm households.

References

Bhalla, G.S. (2005). "Globalisation and Indian Agriculture", *State of the Indian Farmer: A Millennium Study,* Volume 19, Academic Foundation, New Delhi, and Department of Agriculture, Government of India.

Candler, Wilfred and Nalini Kumar (1998). *India: The Dairy Revolution*, The World Bank, Washington DC.

Deshpande, R.S. and M. Indira (2004). "Globalisation and Indian Agriculture: Performance Under A New Paradigm", Presented at Silver Jubilee Symposium on *Governance in Development, Issues, Challenges and Strategies,* December 14–19, Institute of Rural Management, Anand.

Firodia, Arun (2006). "Back to Roots", *Times of India*, January 04.

GoI (2003). *Agricultural Statistics at a Glance*, Government of India, New Delhi.

Håkansson, H., J. Johansson (1993). "The Network as Governance Structure: Interfirm Cooperation Beyond Markets and Hierarchies", G. Grabher (ed.), *The Embedded Firm: On the Socioeconomics of Industrial Networks*, Routledge, London. Cited from Rupert Loader (1997). "Assessing Transaction Costs to Describe Supply Chain Relationships in Agri-food Systems," *Supply Chain Management*, Vol. 2(1), pp.23-35.

Jha, D. (2001). "Agricultural Research and Small Farms", *Indian Journal of Agricultural Economics*, Vol. 56(1), pp.1–23.

Joshi, P. K. (2005). "Crop Diversification in India: Nature, Pattern and Drivers", Paper presented at National Centre for Agricultural Economics and Policy Research (NCAP) Policy Retreat and Seminar on *Agriculture, Food Security and Rural Development*, Vol. 3, pp.1–34, November.

Kurien, V. (2003). "Successful Cooperatisation: The Amul Story", Speech delivered at the Madras Management Association, Chennai, December 11.

Pal, Suresh and Dayanatha Jha (2004). "Public–Private Partnership in Agricultural R&D: Challenges and Prospects", Presented at Silver Jubilee Symposium on Governance in Development, Issues, Challenges and Strategies, December 14–19.

Prahalad, C.K. (2005). *The Fortune at the Bottom of the Pyramid*, Wharton School Publishing.

Rao, V. Madhav (1989). "The Anand Pattern–A Model for Dairy Development in India", Paper presented in *Dairying as an Instrument of Progress: The Indian Experience* organised by National Dairy Development Board, India at Anand from January 16–21.

———. (1990). "Modern Dairy Technology: Anand Pattern of Cooperatives", Moving Technology, October 3–6.

Sawhney, M. (2002). "Fields of Online Dreams", *The CIO Magazine*, October 15, *www.itcportal.com*.

Shah, Tushaar (1996). *Catalysing Cooperation*, Sage Publications, New Delhi.

Singh, S.N. (1992). "Anand Pattern Cooperatives—The Indian Experience: A Cooperative Model for Asia", Paper presented at *XXX ICA Congress, International Research Forum Meeting*, Tokyo, October 23–25.

Singh, Namrata (2006). "Taste of Africa: Amul Eyes New Operation Flood", *Times of India*, January.

Singh, Nirvikar (2004). "Information Technology and Rural Development in India," in Bibek Debroy and Amir Ullah Khan (eds.) *Integrating the Rural Poor into Markets*, Academic Foundation, pp.99–121.

Subramanyam, N. (2004). "An Integrated Approach for Effective Supply Chain Management: A Case Study of Amul", *Paradigm*, Vol. 8(1), January–June, pp.7–14.

Vaswani, L.K., V. Venkatakrishnan, Ravindra Upadhyay, Jayesh Talati (2003). "Agriculture–Market Linkages: Evaluating and Evolving A Conceptual Framework in Indian Context", *Occasional Paper 28*, Department of Economic Analysis and Research, NABARD.

Williamson, Oliver E. (1975). *Markets and Hierarchies: Analysis and Antitrust Implications*, Free Press.

Index

D

H

I

T

U

V

W

Y